Priceless Gifts

Using What God's Given You to Bless Others

by

Barbara A. Glanz, CSP, CPAE

TELEMACHUS PRESS

M&M's® is a registered trademark of Mars, Incorporated
CARE® is a registered trademark of CARE
Band-Aid® is a registered trademark of Johnson & Johnson Consumer Companies, Inc.
Pass It On® is a registered trademark of Argus Communications

Cover designed by Telemachus Press, LLC

Cover art:
Copyright © iStockPhoto/16975754/Creativeye99

Interior images:
Copyright © iStockPhoto/21903448/Gift Box/FrankRamspott
Other images reprinted with permission

Published by Telemachus Press, LLC
http://www.telemachuspress.com

Visit the author website:
http://www.barbaraglanz.com

ISBN: 978-1-939927-03-3 (eBook)
ISBN: 978-1-939927-04-0 (Paperback)

Version 2013.07.31

Printed in the United States of America

10 9 8 7 6 5 4 3 2 1

Praise for *Priceless Gifts: Using What God's Given You to Bless Others*:

"My friend, Barbara Glanz, could have called this book, 'The Ultimate Guide for Givers.' Not only does she help motivate you to reach out to others, she provides practical guidance along the way and great stories to illustrate her points. Barbara shows us that if you truly want to do something good for yourself, do something good for someone else. It is the very heart of Christian love."

~Edward Grinnan, Editor-in-Chief, *Guideposts* magazine

"This is a warm, cheerful uplifting book that shows you how to put more joy in your life by putting more joy into the lives of others."

~Brian Tracy, Author of *The American Spirit*

"I'm a big fan of Barbara Glanz and also of giving. What a combination! Barbara is one of the most giving people I know and the perfect person to write this wonderful little book. As you read it, remember: In giving, we receive, and in receiving, we give."

~ Ken Blanchard, Coauthor of *The One Minute Manager*®
and *The Simple Truths of Service*

"Wow! I challenge you to read this book. You'll be inspired, encouraged and motivated to give more of yourself to others and to be the person God always intended. The stories are bound to stir your soul. Please read this book."

~Debbie Macomber, #1 NYT bestselling author

"Like a burst of morning sunlight—and the magic of a glorious sunset—Barbara Glanz has, once again, managed to convert a 'valley moment in life' to become a celebration of 'the mountain top.' Her insights will help you appreciate what is truly precious and what genuinely matters."

~Bob Danzig, Former CEO of Hearst Newspapers

"Made me feel warm inside after reading. Oh, the sweet memories of gifts given and special gifts received! Barbara Glanz's book *Priceless Gifts* will help you learn bountiful ways to give many kinds of low cost or no cost 'gifts' that lift the spirits and hearts of those around you."

~Roy Saunderson, Chief Learning Officer, Rideau Recognition Institute and the author of *Giving the Real Recognition Way*

"Barbara Glanz's *Priceless Gifts* teaches us that we can change the world, one gift and one person at a time."

~Tommy Spaulding, Author of *It's Not Just Who You Know*

"*Priceless Gifts* is a powerful, purposeful, precious reading which compels us to realize all God's blessings that are not 'material' gifts, but gifts to extend joy, peace, harmony, love and gratitude to a hurting world. In the scriptures it says eloquently, 'Give as it has been given to you, pressed down, shaken together, and overflowing the cup.' May this book help us be 'shakers and sharers' who are wealthy in return by the overflow of gifts given and received."

~Naomi Rhode, CSP, CPAE Speaker Hall of Fame

"Inspiring and heartwarming. Glanz has turned a grateful heart into a gracious gift for readers everywhere. Both poignant and practical stories that point to one clear message: Make memories for those you love!"

~Dianna Booher, author of *Creating Personal Presence* and
Communicate with Confidence

"If you live by the Golden Rule, if you are more personally satisfied by psychic satisfaction than by monetary or special recognitions, and if you want to make a positive difference in the world, then Barbara's "Priceless Gifts – Using What God's Given You to Bless Others"is a 'must read' book for you. As a 'giver,' Barbara Glanz has blessed the world many times over with her priceless gifts, and I think this book truly hits it out of the ballpark."

~Colleeen C. Barrett, President Emeritus, Southwest Airlines Co.

"This book could easily be titled 'Chicken Soup for the Giving Soul.' It is a treasure of beautiful reminders to take time to share our love, our joy, and our time with the people in our lives. Open the book, read it, and then open your heart and share it. I promise you that you will be glad you did."

~Jack Canfield, Co-creator of the #1 New York Times
best selling *Chicken Soup for the Soul* series

Dedication

- To our Heavenly Father who has blessed us all with the gift of His unfailing love,

- To all the precious people who have, throughout my life, generously and lovingly and sometimes unknowingly given me their special gifts of love and caring,

- To all the contributors to this book who have been willing to share the joyful and unique ways they have used their gifts to bless others,

- To all of you readers who will continue to make this world a better place by your unselfish and joyful giving, and

- Most of all, to my dear husband Charlie who is now with the Lord. This book is for him.

Author's Note:

I originally wrote this book when my precious husband, Charlie, was dying of lung cancer. One day as we were driving to our little vacation home in Florida to give him some rest time after going through two bouts of radiation, he said to me, "You know, I think you should write a book on 'Giving.' You love to share ideas with others in your books, and so many people have given special gifts to us during this time that would help and encourage others. Why don't you write about that?"

Although almost all my other books at the time had been business books, his words started me thinking about how many things we can give to others that cost little or no money and how seldom we think of those things as being important. Yet they can encourage and sustain others at times in their lives when their emotional bank accounts are completely overdrawn. And not only do we encourage others, but, by giving, our own emotional bank accounts get a deposit.

Over those last months of his life I began collecting ideas of all kinds of things people can give to one another, and this book became something positive and loving that we shared together as his life on earth was slowly ebbing away. I remember every day sitting at my desk across the room from Charlie while he watched sports on TV and I wrote. Then every hour or so, I would read to him what I had written, and he would add his thoughts and ideas. Little did I know at the time that this book would be his memorial. Writing it gave us both a purpose and a mission to make those last weeks of his life focused not on the pain of our loss but rather on helping others—OUR giving back to the world!

After his death, I gave this book to several agents, but at the time I was so well known for my business books that publishers were only interested in more of that work. So the book has been sitting on my computer for over ten years. Each time I have gone back to read some of the manuscript, my heart has been deeply touched with the love and caring and simplicity in these stories, yet an extremely successful career as a business speaker has kept me from taking the time to get this book published.

Finally this year, as I continue to watch how the economy worldwide has impacted so many lives and the desperate need we all have for hope, I realized the time was right to share this heartfelt, practical book with others. We all need to find ways to share our gifts with others—we just sometimes need to be reminded that gifts do NOT have to cost money! I hope the book will help you realize some of your own special gifts, whether they be of time, of talent, of spirit, or of the many other ideas shared in the book, and that you will be encouraged to do whatever you can to make this hurting world a better place. That will be Charlie's final legacy!

Preface

It is more blessed to give than to receive. Acts 20:35

This book is about giving. It's about moments when a gift—sometimes tangible, sometimes intangible—changes a life. It's about individuals whose lives were touched by the caring and generosity of others. Sometimes the gifts were large and expensive; most often they were small and ordinary. Many of the gifts were special because of the timing—they came when the receiver needed them the most. Yet others were a complete surprise. Some came from friends, some were anonymous, others came from complete strangers. Each gift, regardless of the giver, the timing, even the item itself, was a precious act of joyful caring.

Many of you may have seen the touching MasterCard "Priceless" commercials that have played for years on TV. They share precious stories about someone doing something special for someone else. I love the one about the elephant whose keeper has a bad cold. The elephant goes to the store and buys: Hot soup $4, Cold medicine $11, Tissues $1, and a blanket $24. Then he brings it all back to his sick keeper. The final tagline is, "Making it all better = PRICELESS." That is what the gifts shared in this book are—priceless.

Much of my earlier writing on Customer Service and Employee Engagement has used the simple, internationally understood metaphor of CARE packages, those special gifts most of us have either given or received at some time in our lives that let us know someone is thinking specially about us.

During my writing, I thought a lot about the original CARE packages of food and clothing we sent from this country to the victims of the war in Europe during World War II and how those gifts became a means of survival for many of the recipients. I believe that as we give and receive metaphorical CARE packages in our lives today, these gifts, too, become a means of survival for lonely, hurting people. In this often cynical, self-centered, materialistic world, these gifts, whether physical things or simple gestures of love, demonstrate that someone CARES!

People began telling me their own care packages stories, stories of gifts they had given or received, stories filled with deep joy and extraordinary caring. As I began to collect these stories, I realized the beautiful lessons we can learn from them and the ideas they can give us for new ways to CARE for others in our lives. The stories contain lessons of thoughtfulness, self-sacrifice, gentleness, creativity, surprise, fun, and the ability to see a gift in the smallest things of everyday life.

I hope the stories in this book will "whack" the thinking of every reader to do two things:

1. To become more deeply committed to sending metaphorical CARE packages to others on a daily basis (GIVING).

2. To become more aware of all the metaphorical CARE packages we each receive every single day of our lives (RECEIVING).

It is amazing to know that in the giving, we receive, and in the receiving, we give!

Recently as I was waiting to get on a delayed flight at O'Hare Airport, I observed the giving and receiving of these gifts: Two lovely women, Ann and Katrina, spontaneously invited me to join them for "dinner" when the airline gave us a food voucher during the delay.

A person near us offered to watch another lady's bags while she went to the restroom. And during a conversation with a teenage brother and sister who were going to visit their grandparents, I said to them, "One day you'll probably be best friends." The young man answered, "We kind of already are." How precious it is to see these metaphorical CARE packages being given all around us!

One of my favorite quotations is from William Winter: "As much of Heaven is visible as we have eyes to see." I share these stories with love and with the prayer that we'll each begin to look more closely with our heavenly eyes for those small, precious gifts we both give and receive daily. May your life and work always be filled with CARE.

Warmly,

Barbara

Barbara A. Glanz
6140 Midnight Pass Road, #802
Sarasota, FL 34242
Email: bglanz@barbaraglanz.com
Website: www.barbaraglanz.com

Acknowledgments

I owe a very special debt of gratitude to my late dear husband of nearly 34 years, Charlie Glanz, who had the inspiration for this book as we were listening to a set of tapes on a drive to our vacation home in Sarasota, Florida. He read and reread the manuscript as well as giving his very honest input which sometimes I did not value until after the fact! Honey, even though you will never see the finished manuscript in person, thank you for your constant affirmation and support over all the years of my many intense projects of the spirit. I could never have written this book, or any other, without you.

A special gift I received as I was writing this book was from Andrew Grossman. He asked if he could write an original poem for the beginning of each chapter of the book. Thank you, Andrew, for the gift to us all of your beautiful spirit.

And a special thank you to all the special people who contributed ideas for the book—I celebrate the difference you are making in this world. Your stories will touch hearts and give our readers new and wonderful ideas of ways to give to others.

Table of Contents

PRICELESSS GIFTS

Using What God's Given You to Bless Others

Introduction:

"The Joy of Giving"

A Gift of Love

It seems so very strange to me …
Just what folks think a gift should be.
They fret o'er things that money buys;
   See not the beauty of the skies.

Those fancy gifts, I know it's true
   Can stir some joy in me or you.
   But soon their value tends to fade
Like many things that man has made.

The beauty that the skies behold
   Will still be there as we grow old.
   And when we give a gift of love,
It comes through us from God above.

©Robert Bruce, 1999
Howie-in-the-Hills, Florida

i

THINK ABOUT THE very best gift you have ever received. Now think about the best gift you have ever given to someone. Which brought you more joy?

For many of us, giving has been a learned response depending upon our culture and our immediate environment. Young children go through stages of selfishness (two year olds who do not want to share their toys) as well as times of pure generosity when they are willing to give away anything to anybody. How those around us, usually our parents, respond to these behaviors help us to form patterns of either sharing or hoarding what we have.

I was very blessed to be born to a mother who was a natural giver, so from the time I was very young, I had a role model of someone who loved to do things for others. However, many people have grown up in an environment which stresses "accumulating" and "looking out for number one." For them, giving must be learned in other ways. Often we learn to give through our religion. Nearly all forms of belief in a higher power teach that our possessions, skills, and talents are all gifts so we have a responsibility to share those gifts with others. Other times we learn through a positive role model later in life—a spouse, a friend, even a child. And sometimes we learn to give through deep pain such as experiencing a loss and realizing what is really important in life. Certainly not things!

What I have found interesting as I have been exploring the art of giving over the past two years is that no matter what our life situation is, we ALWAYS have something we can give. Even those who have few or no material possessions can give of their time, their skills, their ideas, their prayers, their love. And these are often the best gifts of all!

Just as I was finishing this book, my husband of nearly thirty-four years, Charlie Glanz, to whom this book is dedicated, died of lung cancer. We were struggling with this disease the entire time I was writing most of this book. I cannot complete a book about giving without sharing some of the many precious gifts I received from others during that time:

* Rita Emmett, a fellow professional speaker and dear friend, took full responsibility for sending out emails to all my friends in Professional Speakers of Illinois, constantly updating them on Charlie's condition and our specific needs for prayer. The prayer chain of the National Speaker's Association constantly held him in their hearts, and we were deeply touched by hundreds of cards, notes, and emails from people we had never even met! **(Gifts of Friendship, Love, and Support)**

* Mike Wynne, the president of Professional Speakers of Illinois at the time, had the courage to ask this secular professional group to stand and unite in prayer for Charlie and me at each meeting they had throughout the year. **(Gifts of the Spirit)**

* John Blumberg, a dear friend and deeply spiritual young man who had recently left a prestigious executive position to begin his own speaking career, gave a special presentation to a large corporate group in Charlie's honor and as a prayer for his healing. Since he is the sole support of a family of five, it was even more significant that he returned the check he had received from them as his legacy to Charlie. **(Memorial Gifts)**

* Louanne Service, a former client from the State of Michigan and newly retired, knew how Charlie always used to drive me to Michigan when I was doing sessions during my five year contract with the State. She also knew how difficult it was for me to drive long distances myself. I go to sleep in the car! So three times during the time Charlie was sick and could not drive me, she offered to pick me up in Lansing and drive me to the small towns where I would be presenting. One of those trips was a seven hour drive in a snowstorm! **(Practical Gifts)**

* While we were in Florida in February and March, Charlie had to be hospitalized at Moffit Cancer Clinic in Tampa. We did not know anyone there, so I was completely alone. When our church family in Illinois heard about that, our pastor called to tell me that a new family in the church who did not even know us called and offered to purchase two round trip airline tickets so that someone from the church could be with us. **(Anonymous Gifts)**

* George Winkler, a neighbor and friend from church, came over when Charlie had just gotten home from the hospital for the fifth time. He installed a handheld shower in our downstairs bathroom and brought over a plastic shower chair since Charlie was too weak to stand up to take a shower. **(Labors of Love)**

* Sondra Brunsting helped plan a shower for our daughter who was married during the last days of Charlie's life, something I could never have done under the circumstances. She also gave me a card as I was caring for Charlie that I will never forget. It said, "You are giving the 'Ultimate Gift' … you are giving yourself!" What a blessing that thought was! After Charlie died, she gave me a beautiful photo album with the following quotation in the front:

"You have been given the Gift of a very special love … a Gift that was never intended to be 'forever' … but one that will lifelong be <u>unforgettable!</u> Treasure the joy, the memories, the moving reality that you have shared life and death in all of its tumultuous fullness with one of God's finest!"

The first page contained the following poem by George Eliot:

What greater thing is there for two human souls
Than to feel that they are joined for life,
To strengthen each other in all labour,
To rest on each other in all sorrow,
To minister to each other in all pain,
To be one with each other in silent unspeakable memories
At the moment of the last parting?

She said to fill it with all my favorite pictures of Charlie and take it with me whenever I travel. **(Practical Gifts, The Gift of Words** and **Romantic Gifts)**

* Carol Jo DeFore, a dear friend from college days, wrote a beautiful card which said that because she was so far away and could not be there to help me physically, she wanted to do something to show me how much she cared. She enclosed an overwhelmingly generous check, saying that she wanted me to use it to do something special just for myself. I used that precious money to have 400 copies of a memory booklet for Charlie designed and printed in the two days after his death. That booklet has already touched many, many lives. **(Sharing our Wealth and Resources with Others)**

* Jim Feldman, a member of Professional Speakers of Illinois who had lost his wife from cancer several years before, generously offered his help even though we barely knew one another. With just one day's notice Jim did a presentation in my place in Toronto, Canada, and then insisted that I keep the money from the client. That presentation occurred on the very day Charlie died! **(Gifts of your Talents)**

* Scott and Melanie Gross, other dear speaker friends, offered me a free airline ticket. We used that ticket to bring my newly married daughter, Gretchen, home from Portland, Oregon, to see her Dad. We had no idea Charlie was so close to dying, so it was a miracle (a gift from Scott, Melanie and the Lord) that she was there on the very day he died. **(Life-changing Gifts)**

* On the morning of Charlie's death, we had decided to bring him home from the hospital and begin hospice, thinking that we had several weeks at least. Dr. Christine Winter, his oncologist, asked to meet at 9:00 am with my three children and me. She expressed concern about taking Charlie in an ambulance from the hospital to our home because of his weakened condition. She knew, however, that one of my promises to him was that he would die at home. I will never forget her loving words that day. She said, "Barbara, I know you promised Charlie that he would die at home. However, according to everything of yours I have read, 'home' is not a place. 'Home' is where your loved ones are. So Charlie IS home!" **(The Gift of Words)**

* Suzanne Aiken, a new friend whose husband had died four years earlier, flew in from Boston to stay the weekend with our family for Charlie's wake and service. Her presence meant a great deal to all of us. **(Gifts of Friendship, Love, and Support)**

* During Charlie's illness, Kay DuPont, whose mother had died just months before, offered to come at any time to help me care for Charlie, even though we had just become friends a short time before. After his death, she and her husband, Jeff Dissend, invited me to spend a long weekend with them in Atlanta. They made me feel loved and cared for, and I enjoyed myself for the first time in many months. Because of my experience, Kay realized how long her mother, a widow for many years, had been alone, and she wanted to help someone else even though it was too late to help her mother. **(Pass It Along Gifts)**

* David Roth, who is a magnificently talented and famous singer and song-writer, became a special friend when we were both speaking at the International Conference on Humor and Creativity a number of years ago. Over the years he has sent me his newest CDs and even wrote a song about my story of "Johnny the Bagger®" titled "A Little Something More." (You can hear his work at www.maythelightmusic.com.) Charlie loved his music, and when he was going through his chemotherapy treatments, the only thing he listened to on his CD player were David's CDs.

The day after Charlie died, I talked with David, and he offered to fly from Cape Cod to sing at his funeral. On the flight he wrote a song just for Charlie which he sang at the service. His presence and song would have pleased Charlie beyond measure, and it was one of the most precious gifts I have ever received! **(Gifts of your Talents)**.

* Rosita Perez gave me a special gift she called "Flowers for Charlie." Instead of sending flowers for his service, she decided to invite me to spend a long weekend with her at her beach house on Anna Maria Island. She would not let me pay for anything and made it a weekend filled with nurturing, love, and peace. **(Gifts of Friendship, Love, and Support)**

* Bud Verdi, a longtime friend from Indiana, came with his wife Mary, my best friend from high school, after Charlie had died. He spent the afternoon taking me around the house, showing me where to turn off the gas, the water, the toilets, and demonstrated things like how to change my furnace and air cleaner filters. **(Practical Gifts)** His wife, Mary, knew that June 25 was our 34th wedding anniversary, so she came to stay for the weekend with me so I wouldn't be alone. **(Gifts of Friendship, Love, and Support)**.

* On my birthday, two weeks after Charlie died, Shannon Johnston, one of my oldest friends, overnighted a homemade chocolate birthday cake, complete with candles, smiley face paper plates and napkins. I have not had a homemade birthday cake for years and years! **(Little Things mean a Lot)** When I came back to our home in Sarasota, Florida, for the first time, she not only picked me up at the airport and stayed the first night with me, but she also gave me a huge, soft stuffed dog to keep me company and to hug when the nights were lonely. **(Treasure Gifts— Keepsakes)**

We received many other gifts during that time—flowers, cards, visits, plants, telephone calls, beautiful meals from our church family and neighbors, and most of all prayers. However, the best gift of all occurred on the day of my birthday—and it was from Charlie! Several days after he died, I was having a very difficult time. Within six weeks of his death I was having to face Mother's Day, Father's Day, my birthday, and our 34th anniversary. One night when I was desperately lonely, I called out to God for a sign that Charlie was all right. After that anguished cry of pain, I was finally able to sleep a little, and the next day I wondered if God would ever answer my request. Although I knew in my heart that Charlie was in a better place, my head wanted some proof!

The only thing my husband did outside of our family was to go to a golf outing once a year with twenty men from the *Chicago Tribune*. It was the first week of June every year, and they called it the "Peacock." All year long they talked about those four days, planning, reminiscing, and joking about funny things that had happened. About ten years ago Charlie began writing humorous newsletters several times a year about this outing, so they called him "The Voice of the Cock!" These letters were "for cocker eyes only," so I had seen only one or two of them. After his death when I was going through his things, I found a file folder in which he'd saved a copy of each of the newsletters he had written to his "Peacock" friends. I immediately had a copy made of the letters for each of our children and his four best golfing buddies.

Exactly two weeks after his death it was my birthday. Mary Schulz, a friend for over thirty years, came to take me to lunch and then to the cemetery for the first time since Charlie's service. As I was finishing getting ready, she was thumbing through all the Peacock letters and laughing at Charlie's witty writing, remembering how he loved this event.

She took me to a nearby Chinese restaurant where they sat us back in a far corner. Interestingly, we were about the only ones there at the time. We talked a lot about Charlie at lunch, and I shared with her my anguished cry for a sign. Just as we were finishing eating, Mary's eyes suddenly got bigger and bigger, and she said in a whisper, "Barbara, you're not going to believe this. Look behind you ..." Directly behind me was a huge, at least 4 feet by 4 feet, plaque—of a PEACOCK! We both had goose bumps—AND the assurance that Charlie was just fine. That is what I call in this book an **Angel Gift**!

A postscript for those of you more cynical readers: Two weeks later I was speaking in Atlanta, and I met a good friend whom I had not seen for months in the Atlanta airport. We went into a little bar near my gate to have a glass of wine while we visited. On the way to the gate I had shared the "Peacock" gift with her. While she went to get the wine, I stood back against a wall on one side of the bar. As she returned with the glasses, she got an amazed expression on her face, and she exclaimed, "Barbara, look behind you ..." There on the wall, directly behind where I stood, was a large black and white photo—of the PEACOCK THEATRE! Gifts occur in our lives every single day if we are just looking for them.

This book contains stories about giving from all walks of life, from the very rich and from the very poor, from countries all over the world, and from all ages, men as well as women. You will be challenged, touched, amazed, and humbled by their actions. My hope is that you will find many ideas in the book that will stimulate your own giving spirit and that will encourage you to make a difference in many other people's lives. These will be priceless gifts! Please let me hear your stories. You will find instructions at the end of this book.

Give to the world the best that you have and the best will come back to you.
Madeline Bridges

Chapter One:

"Angel Gifts"

Angel Gifts

morning fog
winter blanket
brown bare

flash of color
blue jay at the feeder
a reason for joy

©Andrew Grossman, 1999
Newton, CT

Give what you have.
To someone, it may be better
Than you dare think.
Henry Wadsworth Longfellow

MOST PEOPLE TODAY, research has shown, believe in angels, those heavenly beings that watch over us and guide us as we often stumble through life. They appear out of nowhere, usually in the form of another person; however, they always surprise and amaze us by coming at just the right time. They are the ultimate givers!

I also believe there are earthly angels, those special folks who are thoughtful and compassionate and who seem to be drawn to caring for others. Think of those situations in which you have received completely unexpected and desperately needed gifts that have touched your very heart and soul.

Now think of special ways you can give to others that will surprise and delight them. These gifts are especially meaningful when they are given for no special reason except to show that you care. I call these "angel gifts" because they always seem to come at a time when you need them most, and they bring you the deepest kind of joy in knowing that someone else truly understood your need.

Two of the most special "angel gifts" I have ever received both came when I desperately needed encouragement and love. When our third child Erin was born, Garrett was seven and Gretchen was two and a half. Just six weeks after Erin's birth, Charlie hurt his back and was completely immobilized, leaving the full responsibility of caring for him, the house, and the children to me.

During the first week he was in bed, I (Super Mom in action!) was boiling water very late one night to make Easter eggs for the children to color the next day since it was Easter weekend and I had not been able to get to it before. At the same time I was talking with a friend whom I'd been too busy to call back earlier in the day. Cradling the phone between my ear and my chin, I carried the pot of eggs and boiling water over to the sink. While pouring the hot water out and trying to carry on a conversation at the same time, I accidentally dumped the boiling water all over my forearm and wrist, causing second and third degree burns all up and down my arm. Because it was very late and Charlie was unable to move, I had to drive myself to the emergency room!

Can you imagine what my life was like trying to take care of a new baby, an injured husband, and two other young children—with a badly burned arm? Since my mother was unable to come to help, I had a neighbor who came in each day to bathe the baby and another friend who came over to change my bandages twice a day. In the midst of all this, the doctors decided that Charlie needed surgery, so he was taken to the hospital for a laminectomy. Now I was not only trying to care for a house and three young children, but also to be at the hospital to support Charlie, and still breastfeed a seven and a half week old baby! On top of everything else, this was a difficult time for us financially because I had chosen to postpone my career and stay home with the children, and Charlie's was our only income.

In those days a good mother only used cotton diapers which she bleached and washed herself several times a week. It was an extremely time-consuming and unpleasant task! (Young people today probably don't even remember cotton diapers.) Several days after Charlie's surgery, as I returned home from the hospital very late one night, completely exhausted and nearly in tears, on the front porch step sat a huge round plastic hamper, three dozen sparkling white diapers tied in a large plastic bag, and a note which read: "The Edward Burkeen family has given you the gift of diaper service for one month. Please put the soiled diapers in this hamper, and we will pick it up and bring you a new supply of fresh diapers twice a week for the next four weeks. We hope this will help make your life a bit easier." At that moment I truly felt that I did have a guardian angel. Never ever will I forget the compassion and encouragement those dear, practical friends gave me in one of the most difficult times of my life.

My other most memorable "angel gift" came from my younger brother Brian. He was living in Kansas City at the time, serving as Executive Director of the National Child Abuse Foundation. I was a stay-at-home Mom with three young children, we were on a limited budget, and rarely was there ever time or money for me to do something "just for me."

Brian was coming to Chicago for meetings and called to say that he was going to stay an extra day or two, and he had a surprise planned for his "big Sis." He said I was to call a baby-sitter to come for the whole day, I was to dress up in my best outfit, and take the train downtown and meet him for lunch. Then Charlie was to join us after work for a special dinner—all on him!

At lunch Brian announced that "we were going to go shopping to find me a wonderful new dress." I will never forget my absolute delight in going to all the "best" downtown stores and trying on beautiful dresses and then coming out for Brian's approval. Since Charlie doesn't like to shop, I have rarely had the experience of having a man come along shopping and the fun of watching all the sales ladies give you extra attention because they think you'll spend more money. I really felt just like a princess!

We finally found a bright red dress (my favorite color) that was simply made for me—and much more expensive than I ever could have afforded. Years later, even though it is nearly worn out, I cannot bear to throw that dress away because of the precious memories of Brian's "angel gift." What amazes me the most is that he was a very young, single man at the time; yet he somehow knew what could touch a young mother's heart and spirit in an unforgettable way. Thank you, Brian, for making me feel so special at a time when I needed it the most!

Let's look at some angel gifts that you will never forget. Some will remind you of things you can do to surprise others at a time when they need it most, and others will make you stop and think about incidents in your lives that the world may call "coincidences," but that you will know are your "angel gifts!"

The Books

By Lynn Gibson
Columbus, Ohio

If you want to know the value of an individual, ask not for the sum of all that he owns, but look instead to the total of all that he has given.

Douglas K. Freeman

MY SENIOR YEAR in high school, my grandfather, George Angel, passed away after an unexpected struggle with heart bypass surgery.

My grandfather was the most wonderful man and I was so blessed to have had him in my life for as long as I did. Despite the fact that he and my grandmother (also a wonderful person) lived in Ohio and my family lived in New Jersey, they never missed a single birthday or holiday with my family. My grandpa was always my entertainer, my game inventor, amusement park riding partner, advice giver ... oh, I could go on and on. Never have I found someone so deserving of a name as "Grandpa Angel!" He was, and I believe still is, my dear angel.

When I was little, I would always set up a lawn chair in the front yard hours before Grandma and Grandpa were due to arrive. I would anxiously watch each and every car as it would drive by, waiting for the one that would bring my grandparents. I understand that many people feel very fondly about their grandparents, but I want to make clear how dear my grandpa was to me and what a void I felt with his passing.

The night before his funeral, I lay in bed at my grandparents' house, the same house that was now devoid of his hugs, smiles, and calm ways, just crying and crying, questioning why, and going through all the natural responses to losing someone you love.

At his funeral, I don't remember much at all except going through a box of pink tissues at the funeral home. The other memory I have was a kind and wonderful man from Bowling Green, Ohio, coming up to me and saying that he knew my grandpa and knew why I felt he was such a great person. He asked me a few other questions and said that I would be okay in time.

A few months later, I received a package in the mail. I barely recognized the name on the return address, but inside there were three books and a note. The books in the box were: Og Mandino's *The Greatest Miracle in the World*, *The Greatest Salesman in the World* and a book by Leo Buscaglia entitled *Love*. The note said that he hoped I had a smile on my face and that he just wanted me to know that he was thinking of me and my grandpa. It was from the man at the funeral home with whom I had spoken.

I don't know if that man will ever know how much that gesture meant to me, but that day, whether or not there was a smile on my face prior to receiving that package, there most certainly was as I read that note. And that smile has not yet faded! I keep those books in my nightstand by my bed. Ten years later when I see those books, I don't particularly remember the words on the pages within. I remember the random act of kindness of the man who cared enough about a girl he didn't even know to make a difference in her life.

I regret that I cannot find the name of that man who touched my life. But if he is still out there, I would want to say, thank you from the bottom of my heart for a care package that brings memories of my grandpa close to my heart each time I open my night stand. Thank you, too, for the reminder that there are people who make a big difference with the little things they do.

THOUGHT TO PONDER:
Have you ever sent something to a person in need, even though you may have just met them? And even though there is nothing in it for you? That is an angel gift!

My Angel Gifts
By Amy Hanssen,
Batavia, Illinois

For what is it that angels do? They bring us good news. They open our eyes to moments of wonder ... We can do that for each other. Angels minister to us. They sit silently with us as we mourn ... We can do that for each other.

Joan Wester Anderson

WHEN I WAS in college and living in an apartment, I didn't have a lot of money or resources to purchase pictures/paintings for the empty walls. One day my good friend, who was also my high school chemistry teacher, came to visit me. She brought me seven framed affirmations (positive encouraging statements) to fill my empty walls. What a difference they made in my life!

When I was finishing college and planning my wedding, I was pretty stressed out. My Mom, who realized I was extremely stressed, flew up to Michigan for an engagement party and brought me a stuffed puppy dog (my favorite—a golden retriever). Ever since that day, just seeing my stuffed puppy brings me peace and happiness and good memories. He has traveled with me to four apartments and a house!

THOUGHT TO PONDER:
What "comfort" gift may you give to someone in special need of love and affirmation? We can never realize how those angel gifts may impact another's life.

The Miracle of Giving
By Betty Unterberger
Manhattan, Kansas

To become the perpetrator of random acts of kindness, then, is to become in some sense an angel.

Daphne Rose Kingma

THE EARLY 80'S were lean times for us. We made ends meet, but it was a balancing act. My husband, Ken, and I shared our one vehicle, and we had just driven home from work and had pulled up to our rural mailbox. Ken was reaching for the lid when we saw our neighbor's old station wagon coming up the road in a cloud of dust. Times might have been "lean" for us, but they were a real struggle for Bill and Bonnie with a family of seven children. They were poor, hardworking, and proud. We admired them because they were a happy family and one where there was always enough love to more than offset the material wants.

"Something's wrong," my husband, Ken, was quick to note, and he swiftly got out of our car and stood next to the road. Indeed, something WAS wrong! Their grown daughter, Candy, was driving, and as she stopped the car, she was obviously sobbing. Ken, in his usual caring, controlled, manner, got her calmed down long enough to find out that her dad had suffered a massive heart attack and had died earlier in the day. Bill had been a wonderful neighbor and friend, and we were stunned. Candy explained that her family had begun to gather at her parent's house, and her mother was sending her into town to bring back food for their evening meal. Ken said, "Candy, now, don't you worry about supper. Betty and I will take care of feeding your family this evening. You go home and take care of your mother. We'll be back within the hour with everything you need." With that, Candy turned the car around and headed for home.

Ken hopped back in the car, and as we headed back to town, he explained the situation and told me his plan. He was going to provide fried chicken, potato salad, baked beans, rolls and dessert for about 20 people. He had promised to deliver it all within an hour. It was a noble thought, and while I was proud of him for taking control of the situation, I knew that even if we had plenty of time to prepare a meal, our meager budget would not handle my writing any "good" checks to pay for *this* deed. On the way to town, we prayed together for Bill and his family. I secretly prayed that God would forgive me for writing "hot" checks in this, the face of this emergency.

Ken dropped me off at the supermarket where I was to buy a fruit basket, paper plates, cups, napkins and Kleenex. He then sped over to the restaurant, where the manager, after hearing the story, quickly went into action and packaged up a huge pan of fried chicken and big containers of potato

salad, baked beans, and hot rolls from their evening buffet steam tables—
and at a very nominal price. I was waiting in the grocery store parking lot
when Ken returned, and within minutes, we were back at Bill's house delivering on Ken's promise to a very surprised and grateful family.

We went back home and sat down at the kitchen table to add up the
charges: $55.67. Tomorrow, we would somehow work out the details for
covering our checks. Tonight, we knew we had done the right thing.

After supper, Ken returned to the mailbox to finally get our mail and
brought it back to the kitchen. "I wonder what the IRS wants?" he said,
holding an official-looking envelope. My heart sank as I watched while he
opened the envelope. He just kept looking at the document and slowly
handed it over to me. There, in my hand, was a check for $55.75 made out
to us for "overpayment of income taxes."

THOUGHT TO PONDER:
In ending her story, Betty said, "Some might say this is merely coincidence,
but we believers know better." Another angel gift!

Divine Encounter on San Andres

By Ron Metzger,
Colombia

*An angel doesn't have to have wings and a halo. An angel can take on a
variety of forms: it can be a smiling child, a stranger who gives directions, or a
gas attendant.*

Heather Down, *Angel-grams*

WHEN OUR SON, Eric, was approaching graduation from Lomalinda High School and anticipating leaving Colombia, perhaps for the last time, to attend LeTourneau University, Lois and I began thinking about a special graduation gift for him. During all our years in Colombia, our only family vacation time away from our tribal home and the Center was spent in Bogota. We wanted Eric to have at least one trip to another part of Colombia. Both a trip to Quito, Ecuador, and San Andres Island interested us. (Our colleagues, the Smothermons, had given us a report on the former, and we had often heard about Betty and Birdie West's trip to the latter).

Lois and I did not really have adequate funds for either experience. However, we began praying about it, dreaming, and sharing these dreams with some of our Center prayer partners. One evening several weeks later one of these friends came charging up the winding cement walkway to our house on his mega motorcycle. He came to the door, said the familiar, "Knock, knock," and, after entering, told me that he wanted to speak to me privately. At first I thought, "Oh no, what have my kids done now? Which one is in trouble?"

My friend had not come to critique any of my kids, but rather bless them! He told me that both he and his wife had been praying about our request, felt that Eric, Miriam, Kurt and Peter needed this experience, and wanted to help. And help they did! They gave us their whole income tax refund which was nearly the exact amount we would need to supplement our funds to make this trip a reality.

So, after Eric was graduated from our Center High School, we all made our way to San Andres (after a side trip to Cartegena). Upon arriving on the island, we donned swimming gear and headed for the incredibly beautiful, cobalt blue waters of the Caribbean. Our trip included swimming, snorkeling and an absolutely fantastic scuba diving trip on the leeward side of the island that we talk about to this day. We also enjoyed a neat cross cultural experience Sunday in the old, but majestic, evangelical church sitting atop the highest hill on San Andres.

Each day, upon leaving our hotel, we passed an Ecuadorian Otovalo Indian family, dressed in their bright native garb, making a living by selling tourist items. It seemed so strange to me that they were so far from "home." One might expect to see them in Bogota, but on a hot, humid Caribbean Island? I was bold enough to strike up a conversation with the father and over the days got to know them fairly well. I learned that they were believers, but pretty lonely for fellowshlp with their Christian family back home.

On the day that we left San Andres, the Olivers, Southern Baptist missionaries on the island, whom we had known previously, invited us all for lunch. It was neat being in their home talking about their work among the native population and about ours among the Carapana on the mainland. Just before we left, Mrs. Oliver told us about some of their friends in the States who had just sent them four New Testaments, each in a different native American indigenous language. These friends, they told us, were thoughtful, but really had not understood their work very well. The Olivers never had contact with anyone other then those who spoke Spanish. She asked if Lois and I could either use the New Testaments or pass them on to another linguist who could. We said we would try.

On the way back to our hotel to get our baggage, I looked more carefully at the translations and discovered that they were Quichuan languages. The thought occurred to me that maybe the Otovalos outside our hotel might better know how these new Testaments might find a "home." Obviously, we were in a bit of a hurry at this stage, but I took the time to show each book to the mom of the family, who was currently manning their kiosk. She had both of her teens, a boy and a girl, working beside her. I showed her the first, and she said, "Yes, I know about that language. It is spoken by a group of people at ..." Then, I showed her the second, and her eyes got really big, almost exploding out of her sockets. "That's my language! That's my language!" she cried in disbelief. Then, the kids got into it. They both wanted to see it at the same time, trying to wrestle the copy away from mom.

By that time, our baggage was in the Oliver's car, and they were waiting for me. As we were just beginning to drive off to the airport, one of the teens ran up behind us and stuck one of the San Andres tourist shirts they were selling into the window of the car as a "thank you." We turned to see Mom Otovalo wave happily in the distance as she flashed a golden smile.

Tell me now, did the Oliver's friends know what they were doing or not? Maybe not, but God, who wanted to do something very special for some of his Indigenous family far removed from home and fellowship, certainly did.

We will always remember this divine encounter and our very special Lomalinda family who blessed our family with their thoughtfulness and, through us, another of God's family.

Is our God great, or is He great!

THOUGHT TO PONDER:
Have you ever had a Divine Encounter? My guess is that these "small miracles" happen every day in our lives, but we are often too busy or too skeptical to see them. Remember to keep your heavenly eyes open!

Look for the Blue Jays
By Suzanne Aiken
Arlington, Massachusetts

You don't have to go to the gates of heaven to see an angel, just open your eyes and look around.

Heather Down, *Angel-grams*

"DEAR GOD, SHOW me the way. I cannot survive this without your leading my every step. I don't know what to do without David, I'm afraid and I just don't understand why this is happening. Take my hand because I can't do this alone." That is what I prayed the day my husband died from surgical complications.

Suddenly and totally unexpectedly, my entire world came crashing to a halt. David was dead! I had two daughters, Nicole, age six, and Amanda, age four, and a baby due for delivery by cesarean section in thirteen days. Somehow I had to keep my head clear to make important decisions. I needed the courage and strength to tell my daughters that the father they adored was dead. I had to be healthy for our child yet to be born. I felt utterly alone and exposed.

Yet the prayer that I prayed had come naturally to me. I knew that God had always been a source of goodness for me. I knew He would take my burden and help me to continue forward, though the pain and shock were extreme. And I was not disappointed. Divine guidance flowed throughout my entire ordeal. I managed to find the loving words to share with my children. I was able to make important business decisions.

I even asked for guidance on where to bury David. He was only 38, and we had not purchased cemetery plots. I asked God for a site like the pastures described in Psalm 23 as beautiful, peaceful and green. I wanted a spot that the children would love to visit. In his goodness, God directed me to a plot at Mount Auburn Cemetery in Cambridge, Massachusetts. David was buried on a grassy knoll overlooking gardens and a willow pond. There is a bench beside his headstone where I can sit and reflect on all the beauty of nature. Despite the magnificent location, however, I found it very difficult to go there at first and decided that I would return when it felt right for me. Meanwhile, I knew that David was present with us from heaven.

I gave birth to our son, David, Jr., on June 28, 1996, thirteen days after David died. David, Jr., was a great source of joy at a very tragic time. Still I struggled with the loneliness and pain that accompanied the loss of David, Sr. Doing everything without him, making all the decisions for our family, recreating our family structure, and helping my children heal was a daunting task. I knew that God and even David, Sr.,were helping me, but I still longed to see David just once to reassure myself that I was headed in the right direction. Many times I was completely overwhelmed by all the changes.

I finally went to the grave for the first time on a cold January day. Six months had passed, yet so much pain was still there. I sat on the bench and cried and cried, longing to see David one more time or at least a sign that he was there. I needed something to show me I was on the right track. There had been many miracles along the way, but I still wanted more. I felt very selfish asking for divine proof that David was still with me, but being alone was such a struggle and we had been partners for so long that I had become used to his encouragement. Finally, I got back in my truck where David, Jr., was sleeping. Just then he woke up and gave me a huge smile that melted my heart and made me realize that a part of David, Sr., WAS still with me. What I saw in little David's eyes was the sign I needed at that moment.

I did not return to the grave for several weeks. It was now Valentine's Day, and I felt especially alone. David had died eight months ago. I was having a particularly tough day and was struggling to remain positive and focused. So much had changed in our lives. "Was I making the right decisions? How could I be better as a mother? Was I doing enough to move my career forward?" These questions and worries tumbled around in my mind, and I felt I needed to be close to him. Since David was a chocoholic, I took a chocolate candy heart and laid it on his grave, tearfully delivering my valentine and again missing him desperately and praying for a sign of his presence.

As I pulled up to the house upon my return, I noticed a blue jay perched on the front stairs of our home. I had always loved these birds. They are so glorious, their colors so vibrant and blue! Seeing them in the wintertime when everything else was bare and stark had always delighted me. They provided hope that the winter would soon end. I sat still for several minutes as the blue jay hopped up one stair and down the other. Finally he flew away. I could not help thinking that this small bird was a sign from David since it had brought me such joy. It seemed to say, "You are doing fine. Keep going. There is still so much beauty ahead."

From that day on, I always saw blue jays on special days. They appeared at times when I especially needed reinforcement. Each one would stay around just long enough for me to point it out to the children. I came to view these blue jay sightings as a sign of encouragement to move forward, to know that God and David, Sr., were with me every step of the way.

I planned a vacation trip with my girls in May and left David, Jr., with my sister for a week. I had never left any of my children as babies, and I was feeling very uncertain about leaving David, Jr., behind. In fact, I was on the verge of foregoing the entire trip. Just as I went to go to the car for his clothes, a blue jay flew into a tree in the yard. It seemed to say, "I will be watching over him; go ahead."

I visited David's grave on the one-year anniversary of his death. I brought David, Jr., along and decided to take him to the willow pond for a short walk. As we walked down to the water, a gorgeous blue jay landed not six feet from us on the branch of a small tree. He looked at us for some time, and despite our movements toward him, he did not move from his perch. I thanked God for the reassurance I experienced. It knew it was a message, an "I love you" from David, Sr.

On a recent trip to Ireland with my children, while touring the Yeats Castle, I spotted a plaque of a bird on the gift shop wall of the Castle. Struck by the symbol that has meant so much to me, I picked it up and read the description of the work on the back. It was a representation from the Celtic Bible. It was believed that birds are the messengers between heaven and earth, so that was the inspiration for the plaque. What I already knew to be true had been recorded in the Celtic Bible from centuries past! It was yet another reassurance that David was present and watching over us like a guardian angel on our trip.

I have shared my blue jay story with many friends, family, and especially with my children. I tell them that when they need encouragement at tough times, God and David, Sr. will send them a blue jay. I tell them that this is a sign to them that they are not alone! I have received many calls from surprised friends who have seen a blue jay within hours or days of hearing my story. My children have seen them at special moments as well. God is so good. He sends us a message of love in a way we can understand as encouragement for us to go on in a very difficult world. We have only to open ourselves to His love and it will always come when we need it most. Do I need to see blue jays to know that God is with me? No. But I needed a gift from the heart, and it was given to me. I am grateful.

THOUGHT TO PONDER from Suzanne:
Today is June 15. It is the anniversary of David, Sr.'s death. As I began to write this, a blue jay landed on a branch just outside my office window. It reminded me that the past three years have been filled with much sadness, many adjustments, and a great deal of learning. They have also been filled with laughter, love, forgiveness, and joy. I look forward to my new life, I look to God for my guidance and I appreciate all the blessings He has given me. I will always have David, Sr., with me, and my heart will cherish the gift of the blue jay. My heart's wish for you is that you will recognize your own "blue jay" and know that God is always with you to love, encourage and guide you as you move forward on your journey!

A note from Barbara: Guess what I saw out my window in Illinois on the day I received Suzanne's story—a blue jay!

The Gift of an Angel
By Shannon R. Johnston,
Oceanside, California

Sometimes angels whisper softly in your ear, other times it may be necessary for them to scream at the top of their lungs.

Heather Down, *Angel-grams*

RAIN WAS POURING down as a forlorn, skinny cat—mostly black, with white chest and paws—sat on our stoop peering through the front-door, glass side-panels at our home in Tampa. I didn't think much about it, but when it was still there at the end of the day, curled up on the stoop, I took another look. It was clear that it was underfed—skinny as a cat could be. It suddenly was also clear that "she" had just had kittens. I wondered where they were.

We had no cat food, so I put out a can of tuna into a small bowl, with some water and stood back. She buried her head in the bowl and didn't come up for air until it was gone. She looked at me as if to say "Is that all?" I thought about it and then put out some dry dog food (we had a dog), in a little milk. When that, too was gone, she sat down on her emaciated haunches and began to lick her paws and clean her face.

I hated to think she would spend the night out in the still-raining weather, so I put a big white towel on the steps for her, under an overhang. The next morning she was still there. Now what to do … My soft-hearted husband Ken headed to the store to get some "real" cat food, which she seemed to appreciate by cleaning her plate each time it was set out. Another day went by, and she was clearly attracted to what now was a steady food source.

We decided the best thing we could do was to take her to the vet to be neutered. At least she would have some chance in the wild if she didn't have to care for more kittens. Our vet said she was probably just a year and a half old, almost still a kitten herself, and that she weighed probably half of what her full weight should have been—six pounds instead of twelve. She wouldn't have had much longer to live at that rate. Even though it's a cat's nature to hunt, we concluded that she must have been pretty inept at it, to have been so starved.

Initially we had no interest in adding another animal to our care; however, this small, sick kitty ingratiated herself day by day, hugging Ken's lap for warmth, and continuing to eat as if it were her last meal. The day she started to purr sealed the deal! She was ours, and we would have to give her a name.

We thought about the name "Angel," because she had arrived the day two people put a bid on our house, which had been for sale for several months with no bids. Suddenly, we had two families, both willing to pay our full price. Our caring for her must have triggered our luck. But, Angel is a pretty heavy name for a cat to live up to on a daily basis, so we chose "Krikit." Her voice was squeaky, and she also chirped with a sound that reminded me of a cricket.

Krikit may not be a real angel, but she certainly was a gift to us, and I assume we were a nice present for her as well. Today she is sleek, healthy, and a little fat. Sometimes when she comes up for air from her food bowl, I think I hear a small "thanks" for the rescue. No more hunting. No more hunger. Just love, a warm bed, and plenty of food.

THOUGHT TO PONDER:
What angels do you have in your life?

God's Faithfulness
By Marty and Heidi Zaworski
Minnesota

Some people don't believe in angels, but remember, some people used to believe the world was flat!

Heather Down, *Angel-grams*

I REMEMBER THE call from the emergency room at the hospital. Marty had fallen and hurt his arm. They said. "Please come immediately." I remember leaving the house half numb, thinking to myself, "Well, I know this won't be anything serious. It couldn't be. We have already been through enough for one year."

After arriving at the hospital and learning Marty would need several hours of surgery, I wondered how I could call our parents to tell them. "Here we go again!" During the hours and days following the surgery we learned this could be a very long haul, possibly months before Marty could return to work. I remember so clearly thinking, "We can do this. Jesus is with us. He promised he would take care of us. Everything is going to turn out fine."

I had no idea what was ahead for us. I truly had no idea! I was a wee little bit nervous as all the answers were not scripted out for me to clearly see at that time. But I knew what I needed to do was not to take my eyes off of the Lord. I knew we had lots and lots of people praying for us, and I know God answers prayer, especially when two or more gather in His name. I had read it myself!

The first gift came in monetary form. I remember saying to this person, "Oh we are O.K. We aren't hurting yet." They insisted I take the gift, and before I could open my mouth again to argue, God said to me, "I am sending my children to help you. Please don't deny me." It was still very difficult for me to look up and thank this person for their generosity. I wanted to do the giving—it was hard for me to accept help. However, the gifts continued to come in. We had just incredible meals delivered to our home. People brought us groceries. Miraculously, we had monetary gifts weekly equal to Marty's salary!

We even received a Sony Play Station complete with several fabulous games for the kids for Christmas. One of my kids looked at me after opening the play station and said to me, "Mom this is the coolest gift we ever got!" I remember feeling really stung by that. I knew the small gifts we had given them this year were not as fabulous as other years. But I had already explained to them that Christmas was going to be about the giver this year, not the size of the gift but the love the person sent with the gift. The gift was just a symbol of the love.

Before I could open my mouth to set my child straight about her selfishness, however, God said to me, "What about your selfishness and pride? Why does your gift have to be the best present for her? Why can't the gift I gave her be the coolest? You know I sent that gift. My gifts are always going to be the coolest!" I took a deep breath, smiled, and looked at her and said, "God's gifts are the coolest! Please remember to thank him in your prayers."

Another miracle was that Marty was given permission to return to work, something we never believed could happen. We were told that the majority of the time when employees were not hurt on the job and were not completely healed, they couldn't return to work for legal reasons. But Praise God, Marty will be returning to work on Monday without the use of his left arm whatsoever for about 4 to 6 months.

We have received many wonderful gifts. Some are material; some came in the form of Prayer. All are so very precious to us! Please continue to keep us in your prayers as our battle is not quite over. But now when we say, "I know God will take care of us," we are a living testimony to his faithfulness!

THOUGHT TO PONDER:
How has God taken care of you in difficult times?

The Angel Priest

By Kathleen Ellertson,
Moore, Oklahoma

One angelic act can hide a hundred mortal flaws.
Heather Down, *Angel-grams*

I BEGAN WALKING away from my idea of who God was at age 26. It wasn't a conscious decision of "I don't want or NEED you anymore, God", but rather, I just got busy with the business of living and making a life for myself. And over the course of time I forgot ... forgot to go to church, forgot to pray, forgot to talk to God ... FORGOT WHO I WAS.

It was like my heart just started getting smaller and harder and colder ... like it went from being THIS BIG to this big ... and I didn't feel like "ME" anymore. The "ME" I remembered loved to laugh and sing and play and liked EVERYONE ... and the person I saw in the mirror didn't laugh or sing at all ... and didn't like ANYONE much ... including herself. I knew something was wrong. I knew I was sick inside. I just didn't know how sick.

BUT GOD DID.

At 36 I was diagnosed with metastatic breast cancer and told I had a 25% chance of survival. I was scared. I was unhappy, I was LOST—and the only thing I knew to do was cry out to a God I hoped existed ... so I did. And He answered. He answered in quite a remarkable way, in a way I could not miss or misunderstand.

I was staying at a friend's house on the ocean, and as I hung up from talking to the doctor, I went over to the balcony overlooking the ocean to pray. It had been such a long time since God had heard from me, I figured my prayer would never make it through a ceiling. I'd better be able to see sky! So I prayed. I prayed that God would allow me to beat the odds, that this would become a "beginning" for me rather than an end ... and as I prayed, across the clear blue sky, out of nowhere came a double rainbow! I felt a distinct awareness of God's presence and that my prayer would be answered. I had my sign—I would survive!

Two days later I was sent to the hospital for a bone scan, and as I waited for the test I began walking the halls, finally realizing that what I was doing was looking for a priest. After three floors I knew that I wasn't going to find one that way, so I went into the Pastoral Care Center I had passed earlier and asked them to locate one for me. The lady behind the desk assured

me she could find a priest as there were four Catholic Churches in the immediate area.

Her first call was to the Front Desk. No priests were in the hospital or
scheduled to come that afternoon. At the first Catholic church, no priest
was available ... the second Catholic church, no priest was available ... the
third, none available ... the fourth, none available.

Devastated, I went into the inner room to wait and pray until they called me
for my bone scan. As I prayed, I got angrier and angrier at God. Frustrated,
I prayed out loud, "Why would You put me into a church that teaches that
I need a priest to come fully back into Your Grace, and then when I am
broken and NEED you, there are no priests available! WHAT KIND OF
GOD ARE YOU?!?"

Just then the phone rang, and I heard the lady say, "Oh YES! Send him
right down!" Minutes later, a priest walked into the room. He heard my
story, my confession (including my prayer of frustration), and allowed me
to verbalize my desire to make things right with God. I received commun-
ion for the first time in four years.

God was in that room.

Overwhelmed and with tears in my eyes, I said, "Thank you. You don't
know what a Godsend you are ..." And he replied, with tears in HIS
eyes, "No, YOU don't know what a Godsend I you are." Confused, I
looked up at him, and he explained: "I am a mission priest from up the
coast. I only came down to go to the Mall and shop. I began to feel sick
and was on my way back to Titusville when I heard, 'STOP. Someone
needs you.' I looked up, saw the hospital and kept going, and heard it
again even louder, 'STOP. Someone NEEDS you.' So I stopped, went
to the front desk, and asked, 'Who is it that needs me?' And they sent
me here to you."

God had pulled His priest right off the street to take care of me!

Six months later I was telling my story to a church group, and a lady stood up, interrupted me, and told the last half of my story. Surprised, I asked how she knew MY story, and she said, "He was our mission priest, and your encounter was the focus of our mission weekend—How God still uses His priests to heal his people, and His people to heal his priests!"

I want you to know that if God had not revealed Himself to me in the way He did that day my heart cried out to Him, I probably would have lost all faith in Him. I believe that there is great truth in the saying that He will never give us more than we can bear, and He knew that I could bear no more without sure knowledge of Him and His Love for me ... and WITH that knowledge, I could bear all that was yet to come. And there was much to come. Five surgeries, six months of chemotherapy, financial burdens, doing all this alone while my husband was going through military training in another state ... and yet NOT alone, for God sent "angels" daily to look after me in unexpected ways.

I was LOST ... Now I am FOUND.
I was SICK and He made me WHOLE.
Frightened, and He gave me PEACE of heart.
Full of PAIN and SADNESS, and He
gave me JOY, SO MUCH JOY!!!

So now my heart is bigger than it has ever been, full of Love—Love for Him and Love for my fellow travelers on this journey we call LIFE. I smile often, from the inside out. And I sing. A LOT. And I LIVE every day to the fullest. I no longer give time away ... I cherish every moment I am given.

And best of all, I know what the word JOY means and all because of the gift of my "angel priest."

THOUGHT TO PONDER:
Do you truly know what the word "JOY" means?

Life Lessons from the Upstairs room

By Barbara Mahany
The Works Fall 1999
Chicago, Illinois

Angels don't hide in churches. They work in homes, hearts, and dark alleys.
Heather Down, *Angel-grams*

IT WAS IN an upstairs room long, long ago. I have rarely talked about it, fearing I would too casually be dismissed, thought to be a little on the edge. In a word, crazy. A treasure to be guarded, to be kept ever so near my heart. I have, though, unfolded it once or twice, told my story when I thought it would be met with grace. Or at least not smirked out of the room. I am ready to tell it now. Ready to tell the story of what happened the night I knelt in a whitewashed chapel, all alone or so I thought.

I was 16. I was a believer, I mean I never missed church on Sundays, rode my bike every morning to 6:30 mass one whole Lent, and woke up plenty of days trying to figure out how I could be more and more like a saint. But then, too, I chose public high school over the one with the Sacred Heart nuns, I drove my mother nuts day in and day out, and once when I was seven, I dropped black shoe polish on the white carpet and I told my dad I had no idea how it got there.

Anyway, this particular winter weekend I'd gone with my mother on a retreat, a silent retreat. Me, the most talkative kid in my high school! I was not going to say a word for two days and two nights.

So, after dinner, I climbed a back stairs that opened onto a big white room. There were pews. There was an altar. There was a cross. I knelt and prayed for a while. I stared at the crucifix. And then it happened.

The face of Jesus started to change, a Kodak slide show of humanity, from a black man to a young, unblemished face. Asian to Indian to African, and back again. The more it changed, the harder I rubbed my eyes. I closed them, I wanted it to stop. I didn't want to be watching this. I was scared. But then I was not. Fear fell away and I was lifted. I fairly drifted from the upstairs room an hour or so later, tears dried in streaks on my own face, my heart feeling light, feeling changed.

The next afternoon, I was in the big chapel downstairs. I covered my eyes with my hands and peeked through my fingers. "Oh, Lord, what channel we watchin' today?" I was not quite sure I wanted the answer.

I saw only this: the face of Jesus softened. I saw a smile, a gentle one. I swear I did. I've never known just what it was that happened in that up-stairs room. But I called it my miracle. And I was sure it was meant to tell me how to live. To find the face of Jesus in every soul who crossed my path.

That was easy, most of the time, when I was a pediatric oncology nurse. The kids I took care of, the kids I loved, had bald heads and missing limbs and hobbled along with IV poles you would've thought were third wheels.

It's been easy, most of the time, being a newspaper writer, traveling the country, staring into the faces of people who've known long lives of misery, or who've just been catapulted into the wild terrain of unfathomable pain.

It's not easy when I walk across a street with my little boy, and a lady in an oversized SUV blasts her horn and waves her arms and then gives me the finger, only because she didn't want me standing there where I happened to be when she could have been, what, a yard or two closer to the stop sign that had backed up all the traffic anyway.

It's not easy when someone in the newsroom won't talk to me because I married a man who is Jewish, and I've done irreparable damage, the col-league believes, to his people. It's not easy when so-called friends talked about me behind my back because I nursed my baby for longer than two years, and didn't go out much without him in those days.

It's not easy, but that's when I have to grab hold of myself, pinch myself even, to think back to that night alone in the chapel when God gave me the Kodak slide show of my life.

Sometimes I have to stop the seething, count to ten, or maybe even 100, and then start to wonder where the pain could be coming from. Not mine. No, mine I can usually brush away after a while. The pain I wonder about, the pain that haunts me, is the pain behind the faces who can't be civil, who can't be kind, to a stranger or even a so-called friend.

I haven't told my little boy yet, haven't told him the story of what happened to me in the upstairs room. But my guess is he won't be surprised, and he won't go looking for folks in white coats to take me away.

I don't necessarily think it was such a miracle anymore. I just think God was tapping me on the shoulder, nudging me in the right direction.

And with the world the way it is these days, He can't afford to be subtle. Neither can we in our choices about how to inject His face into the ordinariness of our everyday lives.

Even when it means we can't growl back at the world when it treats us all wrong.

Can you find the face of Jesus in every soul you encounter?

Think of an "angel gift" you've received from someone. Please tell them again how much that meant to you. Then think of someone in your life who could use some encouragement—and remember, "angel gifts" don't have to cost any money. They simply say, "I care about you."

This is a beautiful poem about angels by Bob Bruce of Howie-in-the-Hill, Florida:

Guardian Angels

We all have guardian angels
That oversee each day.
They monitor our every step
And guide us on our way.

They watch our each and every move.
They know each precious thought.
They try to keep us safe from harm
Should we seek their help or not.

Their task is certainly not simple.
We challenge them each day.
No matter where our paths may lead,
Right by our side they stay.

They watch with us each sunrise.
Its beauty help us see.
And let us wish upon a star
That shines for you and me.

They share with us the raindrops
That nurture summer's flowers.
They understand each life must face
Some unexpected showers.

So when you're feeling lonely
And wish someone would care,
Remember your guardian angel
Will always be right there.

©2000 Bob Bruce

Every once in a while someone will touch your life and you will no longer be the same. You must have been touched by an angel.

Heather Down, *Angel-grams*

Chapter Two:

"Anonymous Gifts"

The stack of mail
Was filled with rejections, bills—
I wanted to throw the rest
Straight in the trash,
And avoid more bad news.
I rushed through piece after piece, tossing them down,
but the last one was a card:
my name handwritten;
dropped by the writer in my box,
the message read: You are my star;
signed: One who cares.
The writer left no signature, no address.
At that moment I began to realize
It is less important to know than to feel.

©Andrew Grossman 1999
Newton, CT

IN THE BIBLE we are told to do good things in secret, and when we give anonymously, there is a certain excitement and joy in wondering how the giver will feel and what he or she will do or say. Have you ever received an anonymous gift? I have been blessed with several gifts that are completely anonymous. I have no idea of the giver. I have spent many delightful hours trying to figure out who the dear person might be, almost a fantasy of imagination. And what fun it has been to surprise others when they didn't know it was me!

Last summer when I went to the front door to get the mail, I found a darling little basket in the door filled with 5 or 6 baggies of goodies— frosted cookie cutter cookies, brownies, Jordan almonds, and even herbal tea bags. On top was a little poem that read:

"THIS LITTLE BASKET COMES TO SAY,
YOU'RE A SPECIAL FRIEND IN EVERY WAY.
PASS IT ALONG, BUT DON'T GET CAUGHT.
DO IT IN SECRET AS JESUS TAUGHT!"

I was deeply touched! I enjoyed the treats and then refilled the basket with things I love and left it in another friend's door when I knew she would be away. I thought and thought about who sent it, but I never have found out who my special messenger was.

Sylvia Marshall writes about the impact an anonymous gift had on her life:

During a period of great personal despair, a subscription to a small monthly Prayer Book filled with special prayers throughout the calendar month was mailed to me for about a year. I never did find out who sent this to me, but I can tell you I valued that little book. I still have certain pages that I tore out and saved as a keepsake. Some days were harder than others, and the passages in each of the daily pages seemed to hold significance for me alone. It sustained me during those times. I'm so very grateful to that special person who heard my cry and answered my prayers.

Anyone could do either of these things in their family, workplace, neighborhood, or school. You may want to change the faith orientation in the basket poem to one which is comfortable for you, or make up your own poem. I loved filling the basket with things I treasured like little plastic chocolate-covered spoons, special small perfumed soaps, several wrapped Godiva chocolates, a tiny book of quotations, and Pepperidge Farm goldfish. The greatest joy, however, was in the thought of how delighted my friends would be and how much fun they would have trying to figure out who their benefactor was!

The Elf Foundation

To give without any reward, or any notice, has a special quality of its own. It is like presents made for older people when you were a child.

Anne Morrow Lindbergh

THIS IS A letter I received about a delightful anonymous gift that may become a foundation:

Dear Mrs. Glanz,

I recently heard you speak on the morning show of 99.1 in Lansing, Michigan, while I was on my way to work. I was so thoroughly impressed by your interview with Mark and Marcia Bashore that I went out that same day and purchased your book *CARE Packages for the Home*. I also ordered a copy of your book *CARE Packages for the Workplace*. I took the first book home and began to pour through it because I am a true believer that this world needs a big HUG and a LOT more CARING people like you in it!

Your book really touched my family and me. I was the first to read it, and I decided, as a result of your ideas, that I wanted to do something CARING for another family. I sat down with my Mom, and we decided to adopt the family of a woman that my Mother knew. The woman is a wonderful person with a heart of gold and pride the size of Texas! She would not have accepted the gifts if she had known from whom they had come.

We decided to adopt her family for the Twelve Days of Christmas. My whole family got involved in the project. Each night we would leave a package at her doorstep with a cute note about the items in the package. We left things like household items (cleaning supplies, shampoo, toothbrushes, laundry items. etc.), food boxes, gift certificates to local stores and events (movies, bowling).

In return, after the first few days, she would leave notes of thanks and home-baked goodies for us on the doorstep, so she became involved in the fun, too! We called ourselves the "Christmas Elves." From this beautiful experience, I plan to begin a foundation (namely the Elf Foundation) where throughout the year people donate different items or money to this cause. Then around the holidays, we would accept names of families who are too proud to ask for assistance but truly need it and anonymously deliver these packages signed from their "Christmas Elves."

Thank you for your wonderful book—it has truly touched my heart and will make a difference for many people!

Sincerely,
(Name withheld to protect the Elves' anonymity)
Lansing, Michigan

These are some of the poems the Christmas Elves left each day:

Consider us your Christmas Elves, bringing good cheer your way ...
Accept these gifts with love from us; we'll be back another day (eleven in fact!)
Don't try to understand or guess at who we are.
Just remember that you're cared for near and far.
Our identity is one that will never be revealed,
So don't peak out your window for we'll always be concealed.
Happy Holidays!!!
The Elves
(A box of various items such as peanut butter, bread, cereal, crackers)

On the second day of Christmas, some stamps to spread your cheer
And a Vg's Gift Certificate to welcome the new year!

Our identity is one that will never be revealed,
So don't peek out your window for we'll always be concealed.
Happy Holidays!!!
The Elves
(Stamps and a grocery store gift certificate)

Since we sent day number two straight through the US mail,
Today we're back to visit again, bearing things that won't go stale.
Here are some tools to help you clean …
The holidays—a time for you house to gleam!
Our identity is one that will never be revealed,
So don't peek out your window for we'll always be concealed.
Happy Holidays!!!
The Elves
(A box of household cleaning supplies)

On the fourth day of Christmas
A box of stuff to help you bake.
There's something good for all to eat,
Some holiday treats for you to make.
Our identity is one that will never be revealed,
So don't peek out your window for we'll always be concealed.
Happy Holidays!!!
The Elves
(Flour, sugar, brown sugar, etc.)

On the fifth day
We bring a box of "paper" your way.
Our identity is one that will never be revealed,
So don't peek out your window for we'll always be concealed.
Happy Holidays!!!
The Elves
(Paper towel, napkins, writing paper, toilet paper)

On the sixth day, we were feeling quite Christmassy …
We come bearing gifts from A to Z.

Today you'll see from A to M
And soon you'll see all the way to the end.
Our identity is one that will never be revealed,
So don't peek out your window for we'll always be concealed.
Happy Holidays!!!
The Elves
(Various food items starting with letters A through M)

On the seventh day of Christmas,
We finish the "Alphabet Soup."
You're sure to find gifts that will connect the loop.
Our identity is one that will never be revealed,
So don't peek out your window for we'll always be concealed.
Happy Holidays!!!
The Elves
(Remainder of alphabet—various food and miscellaneous items)

On the eighth day of Christmas,
You won't find us in your yard.
Instead we set you this "unusual" holiday card.
Our identity is one that will never be revealed,
So don't peek out your window for we'll always be concealed.
Happy Holidays!!!
The Elves
(Meijer Stores gift card)

On the ninth day of Christmas,
We bring you some general things.
We hope they make you feel good, too,
As joy to us this brings.
Our identity is one that will never be revealed,
So don't peek out your window for we'll always be concealed.
Happy Holidays!!!
The Elves
(General gifts—candles, stationery, etc., for everyone)

On the tenth day of Christmas,
A Target Gift Certificate,
Spend it on you and yours,
And it'll be a "perfect fit!"
Our identity is one that will never be revealed,
So don't peek out your window for we'll always be concealed.
Happy Holidays!!!
The Elves
(Local retailer—Target gift certificate)

On the eleventh day of Christmas,
A little something for fun.
We bought you a few because
We know there's more than one!
Our identity is one that will never be revealed,
So don't peek out your window for we'll always be concealed.
Happy Holidays!!!
The Elves
(Movie and dinner gift certificates for the whole family)

On the twelfth and final day of Christmas,
There's something for everyone.
We hope you've enjoyed our visits.
For us it's sure been fun!
We wish you a beautiful and prosperous new year. May you continue to grow and support
each other, and may better times soon be here.
Our identity is one that will never be revealed,
So don't peek out your window for we'll always be concealed.
Happy Holidays!!!
The Elves
(A bigger gift for everyone)

THOUGHT TO PONDER:

How might you and your family surprise someone for the twelve days of Christmas?

The New Clothes

By Barbara A. Glanz,
Sarasota, Florida

Blessed are those who can give without remembering and take without forgetting.

Elizabeth Bibesco

WHEN I WAS doing a television show about my new book, a very well-known, well-loved, beautiful anchor woman in Chicago shared a very personal story with me. She said she was the youngest of seven children in the family and the only girl. They lived in rural northern Minnesota, and times were very difficult for her family.

She said she was terribly distressed the summer before she was to start high school because she didn't have any nice clothes to wear, and her parents couldn't afford to buy her new ones. Late that summer she went out to get the mail one day, and in the mailbox was an envelope filled with money. On the outside it read, "For new clothes for _____ for high school."

As she told me this story, her eyes filled with tears. Even after all these years, she has never forgotten the generosity of her unknown benefactor. That anonymous act completely changed the way she felt about beginning a new school. Her feelings changed from humiliation and fear of embarrassment to joyful anticipation. New clothes created a new life! She says that now that she is successful, she tries to do the same thing for other young women.

THOUGHT TO PONDER:
The way we look can often impact the way we feel. A wonderful place to share your gently used clothes anonymously in the Chicago area is the "Bottomless Closet." They collect nice work clothing, and when a woman

on welfare gets her first job, she is allowed to pick five business outfits, complete with all the accessories. This is one way to help ensure her success and good self-esteem as she returns to work. Check your area for a similar group.

Food for the Pigeons

By Mary More,
Lakewood, Colorado

Most altruistic gift: an anonymous donor giving to an unknown recipient of some future generation.

Unknown

THE OTHER NIGHT when I was on the bus going home, it pulled up at a stop near the old dime store. There was an elderly man going through the dumpster. He looked like a well-dressed older gentleman with a cane, and I thought it was rather odd that he would be going through the trash. It made me sad because he looked so nice, and I wished that he had enough money to go across the street to Burger King.

I watched him go through about three bags of things that had been thrown out, and then he found a bag of French fries. He put his hand in the fries, and I thought he was going to eat them. But, to my amazement, he threw them up in the air and watched all the pigeons come to gobble them up. I thought that was so special, and was I ever surprised!

He had fun watching the pigeons and so did I. So, you can't tell about things—the way they look might turn out to be entirely different. Now when I see someone going through the dumpster, it doesn't make me sad as I think maybe they are looking for food for the pigeons.

THOUGHT TO PONDER:

Have you ever misjudged someone because you didn't take time to get to know the whole story?

The Pixies

By the Westmans: David, Lori, Tyler, Kayla,
Colin, Derek ... and Chester the Cat!
Naperville, Illinois

To enable others to look beyond themselves and their immediate concerns, and to give without expectation of fanfare represents the most vital contribution of the quiet hero.

Unknown

OUR FAMILY WAS in the midst of another Christmas season. In addition to the usual running around associated with four children and their involvement in various activities, there was the rush associated with Christmas shopping and planning for holiday get-togethers. Things always seemed to be out of control by the week before Christmas, leaving my wife and me exhausted and not always in the best of spirits.

Five days before Christmas, while sitting around the dinner table, we were interrupted by the sound of our doorbell. Upon opening the door we found no one there, but a shopping bag filled with presents and an attached note sitting on the step. The note read as follows:

> *PIXIES like sweet stuff, that's what they say;*
> *Especially on pretzels, they are better that way.*
>
> *The children are anxiously awaiting Santa, we're sure.*

We hope these treats will do until he arrives, all dressed in red fur.

We're having some fun spreading Christmas cheer.
This is really the greatest time of the year.

The shopping bag was full of surprises. There were chocolate covered pretzels and a wide array of additional goodies to put smiles on our faces. What a wonderful surprise! It was the talk of our family the rest of that night and into the next day.

As evening approached the next day the doorbell rang again. And again we were the subjects of a game of "ding dong ditch." Another package was on the step with a note reading:

PIXIES have a sweet tooth, oh yum yummy.
So here are some cookies great in the tummy.

We love Christmas trees, lights and ornaments too.
So we have selected this one, especially for you.

We love to come and we love to run, but ...
Please don't try to catch us cause it will spoil our fun!!!!

This time the various items in the package included an ornament, homemade cookies, and other assorted treats.

Each day that followed there was another package and note. One evening our children were playing in the side yard but never saw any one approach the door. Another night we followed footprints in the snow, but they ended at the sidewalk.

The hectic lifestyle and associated pressures continued to build as Christmas approached, but our collective mood was upbeat and full of excitement—wondering if the pixies would strike again. We were truly experiencing something unique, and we were continually speculating about who our benefactors were. The pixies obviously knew who we were and a lot about us. One night there was an outfit of clothes for each child—sized perfectly. Another night there were several gift certificates to our favorite restaurants. There were gift certificates for movie rentals, containers of popcorn and ice-cream with accompanying hot fudge and caramel toppings, a beautiful ceramic bowl, and holiday paper napkins and plates. Each day seemed to be centered around a theme:

> *We PIXIES give you ice-cream and hot fudge too.*
> *So you can make sundaes and top it with goo!*
>
> *PIXIES love to share good things to eat.*
> *But you must know we should never meet!*
>
> *It shall spoil our fun if we meet.*
> *And take away from your Christmas treat!*

And, finally …

> *PIXIES love popcorn and candy too.*
> *So now you can watch a movie and munch your way through.*
>
> *We hope the kids like the treats we are leaving.*
> *But be careful cause PIXIES don't like peeking!!!!*

On Christmas Eve our family has a tradition of riding around the city of Naperville looking at the Christmas lights adorning various homes. Sure enough, when we returned, there was one last package on the doorstep. This one read:

> *Here it is almost Christmas at last.*
> *And we are reminded of Christmases past.*
>
> *We hope you've enjoyed our Christmas sharing with you.*
> *No more running and hiding and secrets, WHEW!*
>
> *If by chance these gifts help reveal ourselves to you.*
> *Please keep the secret from others, for we may surprise them next year*
> *just as we did you!*
>
> *Merry Christmas,*
> *Love, the Pixies*

We never did find out who our pixie friends were (although we have narrowed them down to a few select people). What we DID find was a Christmas spirit that made for the most enjoyable holiday season we have ever experienced. And somehow, as we look forward to next Christmas, I think our family will have just as spirit-filled and enjoyable a holiday season as last year, as we take up the ball in playing pixies. We've already selected our target family!

THOUGHT TO PONDER:
How might you share Christmas or another holiday by playing pixies?

I Think You're the Greatest

By Tom Lagana
Wilmington, Delaware

That best portion of a good man's life,
His little, nameless, unremembered acts
Of kindness and of love.

William Wordsworth

ON VALENTINE'S DAY cut out red paper hearts and print "I Think You're the Greatest" on each one. Then anonymously distribute the hearts to the people you work with and your loved ones. Observe the reactions as people wonder who did this random act of kindness and caring. (I always send myself a heart, too, so that no one suspects it was me!)

It's especially interesting to see some of the guys post their heart on the wall of their office. A few years ago, someone "accused" me of sending him a heart on Valentine's day. Later he admitted it was the only Valentine he received that year.

THOUGHT TO PONDER:
Get out your scissors and red paper and make many people feel great!

The Gift

By Kim Mooney
Canton, Georgia

The greatest pleasure I know is to do a good action by stealth, and to have it found out by accident.

Charles Lamb

THE CHRISTMAS SEASON of 1998 was a real challenge for my husband, Mike, and me. He had lost his business that September and had only been able to pick up a few odd jobs during the next three months, just enough to squeeze in the bills with my income. We were facing a Christmas tree that had no gifts under it and only one week to go before Christmas.

The last three years we'd paid cash for Christmas gifts because of my business and hadn't had to charge anything. This year we decided we had no choice—there just wasn't an extra dime for any gifts. My mother-in-law let us use her charge card, but we tried not to put too much on it. We got a gift for each of our three children from "Santa" and one from us.

I was feeling very sad about this on the way home from the shopping trip. I knew it could have been much worse, but I kept thinking that Christmas morning there would only be one gift for each of the children under the tree after they had opened the one from Santa. Earlier in the year, we'd planned to take the kids to Hawaii on a trip that I'd earned through my company. However, that fell through when we had to use the extra vacation money we'd saved to help with bills that fall. The kids had been terribly disappointed, so I just wanted them to have a "normal" Christmas because everything else had been so pinched back for several months since then. It made my heart ache to think of how excited they were, and how it would all be "over" with one gift.

The next day I walked to the mail box and found a Christmas card with a return address from New York. I was puzzled because I didn't know anyone from there. I returned to my basement office and opened the envelope. Inside the card was a folded piece of paper around a small plastic bag. I didn't look at these right away, but I just put them on my desk while I read the card—I was just so curious to find out who this person was!

The note written on the card said that the giver had grown up as a very poor preacher's daughter, and at a young age she'd married an abusive man. She had had two little children when she left him, and she had to raise them on her own. However, since then she'd been blessed to marry a wonderful man, and her personal business as an Independent Consultant for The Pampered Chef had grown and prospered. She went on to say that she just felt led by the Lord to share her abundance with me at this time, that I could use it for whatever I needed and not to pay it back.

I can't tell you how "slow-motion" it felt as I reached for the folded sheet of paper on my desk. It was a check for $100! There was also a beautiful crocheted snowflake inside the little bag to hang on our Christmas tree. I sat there and cried out all the tears of fear, frustration, and hurt that I'd been holding in for so many months. I shared the card with my husband. We were both amazed that someone we didn't know would be so generous to us.

This money bought several more gifts for my children so they didn't have to feel yet another "pinch" on Christmas morning. But, the real value of that gift could never be measured in dollars. You see, there was no way Rebecca could have known of my situation. Her only connection with me was that we were both directors with The Pampered Chef. I had mentioned several months previously on an e-mail loop we were both part of, that my husband had just lost his job and how grateful I was that I worked with a company where I didn't have to worry about that happening to me, but I hadn't gone into detail nor mentioned it since. I didn't know her e-mail screen name nor had I ever corresponded with her directly—we were complete strangers. I don't even know how she got my address to send the card.

Rebecca was an acting angel of God. She taught me how giving and selfless a complete stranger can be. She refreshed my faith in the Lord's care for me when it was beginning to slip. She opened my eyes to a miracle—that special care "out of nowhere" that made me feel "touched by an angel." She shared of herself, and we have since become e-mail friends.

I have yet to meet Rebecca in person. I hope that someday I will. I'd like to hug her for all she's given me that money could never buy. And I'm looking forward to a time when I can be led by the Lord to pass on THE GIFT.

THOUGHT TO PONDER:
Who might you help today in your abundance?

Sharing His Birthday Joy

By Julie Garrett, *The Gainesville Sun*
Reprinted with permission
Gainesville, Florida

There is no better time than right now to start your own "family tradition" of helping needy children.

Debby Boone

THE LAST THING Lucas Heacock needed for his sixth birthday was more toys! Toys lined his playroom wall. More toys would be coming from his large extended family. The son of Bill Heacock and Rita Perez, Lucas started kindergarten the year before at J.J. Finley Elementary School.

"That was our baptism into the 15-birthday-parties-a-year mode," said Perez, a marketing consultant turned at-home mom. "These are all privileged kids. I thought, 'Why are we wracking our brains, going to Wal-Mart, looking for something these kids don't already have?'" So Perez came up with a cool idea: Lucas would keep the presents from his family and give away the presents from his friends. How did Lucas feel about that?

"I said 'yes' cause I had like a *pile* of presents," Lucas said. And maybe he's not too attached to toys, anyway. When asked, twice, to name his favorite toy, Lucas said, "My favorite thing to play with is a friend at school."

After giving it some thought, Perez decided they would donate the gifts to children in long-term care at Shands Hospital at the University of Florida. On the invitations they explained their plan and asked for travel games, play-doh, coloring books, markers, stickers, and Matchbox cars—toys children could enjoy while bed-bound. A few parents reacted with a touch of cynicism, but overall their idea was a hit.

On party day, Lucas' friends deposited their gifts in a laundry basket inside the foyer. A few days later, Perez, Lucas, and his brother, James, two, made the trip to Shands. "They received us like we had brought a million dollars," said Perez. "We were treated so well."

Shands child life specialist Marilyn Close-Battoe nominated Lucas as a hidden hero. "It may have been his mom's idea, but you could tell he was really into it," she said. "We do get donations throughout the year, particularly at Christmas time," she said. "But this was special because these gifts were from a child, for a child. We thought it was so great." Close-Battoe will pass out the gifts to hospitalized children on their birthdays. "It's hard enough for kids to be in the hospital, but to be here on their birthdays ... Lucas' gifts will really make a difference for these kids."

A postscript: After Lucas's birthday party his three year old brother took his mother aside and very conspiratorially announced, "But when I have my birthday, I want to keep ALL my presents, O.K. Mom?"

THOUGHT TO PONDER:
Do you have gifts you could give away?

The Gift of a Life

By Pam Johnson
Anoka, Minnesota

We should give as we would receive, cheerfully, quickly, and without hesitation; for there is no grace in a benefit that sticks to the fingers.

Seneca

I'VE JUST HAD an unbelievable weekend! You just never think anything like this could happen to you.

My parents were visiting us in Anoka from Alexandria (Parker's Prairie) this weekend because we were going to have a surprise 40th birthday party for my brother's wife. We were not going to start getting ready for the party until late Saturday afternoon, so my parents decided to go to the Mystic Lake Casino for a few hours that morning.

My father has had heart disease for about 20 years. His last major surgery was two and a half years ago when he had congestive heart failure. His major symptom was tiredness. My parents retired after that surgery and have been enjoying every minute of life that they can. We've all been pre-paring ourselves as much as possible, knowing that some day our dad wouldn't be with us anymore, but you can never be fully prepared for something like this.

On their way to the casino, while he was driving down highway 169, my father had a heart attack and died. My mom said that one minute they were driving down the highway and she was reading her book, and the next the car was swerving off the road. She tried to grab the wheel and keep it on the road, but couldn't. Unfortunately, Dad had his foot on the gas, and she couldn't get It off. This was in Shakopee, just south of the Minnesota River.

They went through a fence and plunged into a 10-foot deep embankment of water. My mom said she felt for a pulse and any signs of breathing by my dad and found nothing. (My mom is a nurse.) She said he looked terrible. By this time the water was coming in very fast, and my mother said she thought about her children at that moment, and knowing that she could do nothing for Dad, she tried to get herself out of the car. The car door wouldn't open, so she tried the window. The car had electric windows, but unbelievably, the window opened.

She was finally able to get out of the car through the window. (I can't imagine how she felt when she had to leave her husband in the car like that.)

My mother can't swim, so she tried to get on top of the car, but it started sinking very quickly. Fortunately, she could tread water and was able to do that while some people who had stopped their cars to help yelled if there was anyone else in the car. She told them my father was dead, and then they asked if she needed help. That's when she told them she couldn't swim. Two people immediately jumped into the freezing cold water and saved her.

Later when my mom was telling me this story, she told me how the trunk of the car had opened up, and the present she had spent a whole day making for my sister-in-law's birthday had floated out and sunk. Our birthday party had turned into a very different kind of family get-together.

Through all this we miss our dad tremendously, but we try to think of it the way his little four year old Grandson does: "He's with Grandpa Smith in

Heaven and he's no longer sick." Of course his other comment was, "Now he won't be able to give us any more gum".

We are just thanking God that our mom is still alive and with us. I don't know how we would have been able to stand losing both of them in one day. We have a very special place in our heart for the two people who saved our Mom. Now Grandma has taken on the very important job of "giving out gum" to her grandkids!

THOUGHT TO PONDER:
Has anyone ever anonymously risked their own well-being to help you or one of your family members? Remember this story when someone needs your help. You never know when it might be your mother or brother or child.

The Bike
As told by Penny Davoren
Chicago, Illinois

I am in the habit of looking not so much to the nature of a gift as to the spirit in which it is offered.

Robert Louis Stevenson

PENNY DAVOREN, MY former next door neighbor and good friend, is the single working mother of two boys. Not only does Penny always make me laugh, but she never wastes a single moment. If, for example, you have three minutes until someone is going to pick you up, that is enough time to put in a load of laundry. She has every single task timed to the minute!

Her application of this concept was never more evident than in her commuting to the train each day to go to her job in the city. She knew that it took her 12 minutes to walk the eight blocks to the train, but she could bike it in 4 minutes. To save those precious moments, she bought an old, beat up bike, and every day, rain, snow, sleet,or sun, one could find Penny pedaling to the train EXACTLY 4 minutes before it was due to stop in Western Springs. Each morning she would quickly stop and put her bike in the bike rack across from the police station, a half block away, and then run as fast as she could to catch her train.

Little did she know that after some time she became a legend at the Western Springs train station. All the commuters would watch for her to see if she were going to make it on time! In fact, she tells of one incident when someone who was walking to the station saw her bike past him and exclaimed, "Oh, my gosh. Am I <u>that</u> late?" And another time when she was in the local grocery store, someone said, "Oh, YOU'RE the 'bike lady!'"

One day as she was still a block away from the station, she saw that the train was already stopped there, so she knew she was in trouble! In her panic to catch the train she rode the bike right up next to the train and simply dropped it on the platform and jumped on the train just as it was going to leave. The conductor said to her incredulously, "Are you just going to leave your bike there?"

Penny replied, "Well, will you wait for me to put it away?" Of course, his answer was "no," so the train roared away from the station, leaving Penny's old bike lying on the Western Springs platform.

That night on the way home Penny said she began to have second thoughts about what she had done. Every penny was precious in those days, and she needed that bike to get to the train so she could have that extra eight minutes each day at home.

When she arrived at the station, just as she had expected, the bike was gone. No longer would she be the "bike lady of Western Springs!" As she forlornly walked towards home, she passed the Western Springs police station.

Lo and behold, there was her old rickety bike, placed neatly in the bike rack where she always left it.

To this day she has no idea who was kind enough to care for her bike. Some good samaritan took pity on the "bike lady!" Ever since that incident, Penny has made it a personal mission to try to pass this kindness on to others. And she STILL uses every single minute!

THOUGHT TO PONDER:
Why not do an anonymous good deed this very day?

All of these anonymous gifts made a difference in people's lives. Not knowing their givers allowed them dignity and the pure joy of receiving without obligation. It also was fun for the givers as they planned their secret gifts.

Chapter Three:

"Gifts of Friendship, Love and Support"

hello with a smile
hey, buddy
hey, pal
something of your story
something in your eyes
shines out in the crowd
something of me
comes out when we speak
enough to spend time
enough to connect
©Andrew Grossman 1999
Newton, CT

SOMEONE RECENTLY SHARED this thought with me: "Friends are angels who lift us to our feet when our wings have trouble remembering how to fly." How true that has been in my life! My husband had struggled with lung cancer for a year and a half, and I sometimes wonder how we could have made it through such difficult times without friends. They have brought in food, driven us to the hospital, visited Charlie when I have to be away, sent cards, notes, emails, faxes, flowers, treats, and of course, the very best gift of all—their prayers.

Two of the most touching gifts of support we received have come from my professional colleagues, other speakers. John Blumberg, a dear friend from

Naperville, Illinois, was asked to speak to a large group of men in a church last spring on "Beyond Empty Success." The night before, John, in his prayer time, dedicated that presentation to Charlie and asked for God's healing presence in Charlie's life. When he had finished, the contact person told John how deeply moved they were by his message and handed him a check. John called me the next day to tell me that he had sent the check back to the group with a letter telling them about his commitment to Charlie and asking them to pray for him as well. John's speaking business is the sole support for a family of five, so we were overwhelmed by the love and support he showed in his precious gift to Charlie.

Just after the first of the year Charlie contracted pneumonia and had to be hospitalized. Just four days before, he had finished his sixth treatment of a very strong chemotherapy drug, and just two months before that he had had ten radiation treatments for brain tumors in addition to the chemo. Needless to say, it was a very difficult time for us.

I had belonged for several years to a wonderful group called Professional Speakers of Illinois, a local chapter of the National Speakers Association. It is a group of speakers, consultants, and trainers who come together six times a year to network and learn more about the art of speaking. Usually at least 25% of the group are guests and brand new members. At their January meeting, just days after Charlie had been hospitalized, Mike Wynne, the president of the chapter, asked the entire group of over 80 people to stand and bow their heads as he said a beautiful prayer for Charlie and me. Even though this group is not a spiritually based organization, they gave us the most beautiful gift of friendship and support—their prayers! We were also put on the email prayer chain for the national group, and I was over-whelmed at the loving responses we have received—many from speakers I have never even met.

I have heard many times the statement, "Friends are the gifts we give to ourselves." And no matter where we are in life, whether in a time of crisis or simply trying to live each day in the best way we can, the blessing of friends lifts us up and helps us through. Many of the stories in this section are just simple things friends have done for one another, but their impact has been extraordinary. May they trigger in your heart and head even more ways that you can show your love and support to the people you meet to-day or tomorrow. We each are on a journey in this life, and if we can make the trip just a little bit easier for another, we have been a true friend!

The Angelic Choir

By Margie Martin
Annabella, Utah

Friendship consists in forgetting what one gives and remembering what one receives.

Alexandre Dumas the Younger

THIS LAST YEAR on December 23, I was wrapping Christmas gifts after returning from a church program when the doorbell rang and someone began singing "Jingle Bells." My husband and I answered the door to find friends who had lived in our neighborhood in another part of the state. They moved to a small town near where we now live with their twelve children shortly after we moved here. The whole family was on our front step! We invited them in, and they sang three or four more carols, had a hot chocolate each, told us how much our friendship meant to them, and returned to their outing to look at the lights decorating homes in our area.

It was like having an angelic choir in our home. A big part of the gift was that they took time at such as busy time of the year to be with us and share their talent and their love.

THOUGHT TO PONDER:
Do you have special friends you could thank in this way?

Give Me a Special Gift this Year—
Let Me Weep

By Fay Harden
Tuscaloosa, Alabama

If a friend is in trouble, don't annoy him by asking if there is anything you can do. Think up something appropriate and do it.

Edgar Watson Hovee

THIS POEM IS reprinted with permission from *The Compassionate Friends*, an international support group for parents who have lost a child, www.compassionatefriends.org

The mother of a dead child
will always weep
at Christmas-time.
On that, you can depend.
No matter how many people
or how many presents,
The pulsating void that seems
Too large for her heart to hold
Keeps on drawing her attention
Back to the child who's missing.
As others laugh and play
Her thoughts fly away
To Christmases past—
Or to a snowy cemetery:
To a face her heart aches to be kissing—
The face of the child who's missing.

THOUGHT TO PONDER:
Do you know a mother who has lost a child? Be sensitive to her loss and allow her the gift of grieving. Ask about that child, share your memories, and simply let your friend weep with you.

A CARE Package for Poland
By Rev. Howard White
Williamsville, Illinois

Learn from nature the profusion of her gifts. As you daily realize more and more the generosity of the Divine Giver, learn increasingly to give. Love grows by giving. You cannot give bountifully without being filled with a sense of giving yourself with the gift, and you cannot so give without love passing from you to the one who receives.

"HAMSTER" WAS HER nickname. Short, with chubby cheeks, you could say it fit Linda. But a 16-year old girl in Poland is not so different from a 16-year old girl in America. She knew hamsters were rodents.

After the fall of Communism, she had been able to study English in school. Other students in her class at the English Language camp that summer were all in their twenties, because they had not been allowed to study English until after the victory of "Solidarity." Linda's examples in class were not sophisticated enough, they thought. They would show by nonverbal language what a "pain" her stories about her little brother were. She could feel how out-of-place she was in that group every single day.

Dorothy and Bob were Linda's (Hamster's) teachers, volunteers through the Methodist Church. From America they brought gifts, or bribes, for their students—something new each day, mostly food. M&M's®, red licorice, real

American junk food, and one day—peanut butter. Linda took one bite and said, "Yuck! It's salty!" She had expected it to be sweet like all the other goodies. Peanut butter and jelly sandwiches were explained but to no avail. If Americans liked peanut butter sandwiches, Linda made it very clear that she was in no hurry to visit!

However, the next day Dorothy found some jelly, and what they couldn't explain in words, Linda could taste. She said it was "a little better." When she was caught making a second sandwich, Bob told her he was going to start calling her "Peanut." That name stuck to her like, well, peanut butter to the roof of your mouth! No longer an awkward teen, a "hamster," she became "Peanut."

Bob and Dorothy's example of making her special caught on among the other students, too. After the camp had finished, all of the students thanked their American teachers for everything they had done. But only one wrote them a note—Peanut! Bob and Dorothy gave many gifts to the students: food, souvenirs, education, and their time. But for one young lady, their most precious CARE package was a NICKNAME!

THOUGHT TO PONDER:
A true gift can be many different things! This was a gift that gave dignity to a hurting child.

The Healing Power of Prayer

Reprinted with permission from *Stressed is Desserts Spelled Backward*
By Brian Luke Seaward, Ph.D.
Boulder, Colorado

There are glimpses of heaven to us in every act, or thought, or word that raises us above ourselves.

Arthur P. Stanley

IN SPRING 1997, I was asked to make a presentation on mind-body-spirit healing for the American Occupational Health Association's annual meeting in Orlando, Florida. At first, the crowd of about a hundred physicians seemed less than interested as I stood at the edge of the stage, presenting information on the vanguard of holistic medicine, as part of a one-day stress-management seminar. But the crowd of seemingly uninterested general practitioners became a lively group of participants by the end of the session. As I made my way to the back of the room to pick up my slide carousel, I was politely ambushed by twenty-five physicians and nurses, business cards in hand, asking for more information.

One participant, who patiently waited until the group had dispersed, approached me and said, "You were the reason I came to this conference, but I wished you had talked more about the healing power of prayer. Do me a favor and call Dr. John Pfenninger." She quickly wrote down the man's phone number on the back of her business card, handed it to me, and smiled as she walked away. Intrigued, I placed a phone call to Midland, Michigan, a few weeks later. Dr. Pfenninger's remarkable story underscores the dynamic healing power of prayer. That afternoon, he shared these memories with me.

In 1994 John's son, Matt, a high school sophomore, was diagnosed with a brain tumor. The diagnosis wasn't immediate. In fact, Matt spent a fair amount of time in and out of hospitals, and if you were to ask him, he would tell you that he has seen more than his share of MRI (Magnetic Resonance Imaging) machines. Matt's mother's standing joke is, "The only specialists we didn't consult were those in obstetrics."

Eventually, the diagnosis revealed a brain tumor. It also revealed cancer cells isolated in the fluid of Matt's brain and spinal cord. Matt began to receive the typical treatment: chemotherapy. While often effective, chemotherapy is not infallible. It not only can kill cancer cells but destroys healthy cells as well. And it doesn't always work.

In the shadow of nearly every cancerous tumor lies the question of death. Matt's father decided to meet this shadow head-on. Knowing how much support the Pfenninger family had in this crisis, the thought occurred to John that if Matt were to die, those in attendance at his funeral would be in the hundreds. Rather than to have them come together for a funeral, John decided to utilize the energy and well wishes of their friends, colleagues, and family to heal his son, instead of grieving the loss of his life. John called them all to a "gathering to heal".

"I know if Matt were to die right now, you would all come to his funeral, but it makes more sense to me to use your prayers now," John said. "I would like to ask if you could pray with me and my wife for our son to be healed."

So the group of two hundred people sat in silence in an auditorium and prayed for Matt's recovery, some for over an hour. Sixty-five of the 110 physicians on staff attended the prayer meeting.

There are several ways to pray. There are intercessory prayers where we seek help and guidance. There are prayers of gratitude where thanks are given. Many prayers combine supplication for help with offering gratitude. Some prayers read like poems. Some prayers are spontaneous, like ad-lib conversations with God. What all prayers have in common is *intention*, the desire to work in collaboration with a higher source, a display of devotion to join the will of God, in whatever way you imagine that to be.

Several weeks later, Dr. Pfenninger made a grand rounds presentation at his hospital. By all measures, it was a short one. "Many of you have inquired about Matt's condition. As you know, we had a prayer session for him not too long ago. I'd like to show you something." As he said this, he illuminated two X-rays, before and after pictures. The tumor was gone. A hush fell over the crowd.

Jack concluded, "To those of you who understand the power of prayer, no explanation is necessary, and to those of you who do not, no explanation will suffice." With these words and a wave of his hand, Dr. Pfenninger left the stage.

Not only can faith move mountains, but when our will is aligned with the will of God, faith can make tumors disappear. It helps when physicians pray too!

© Brian Luke Seaward. Reprinted with permission

THOUGHT TO PONDER:
Have you ever attended a "gathering to heal?" What an amazing idea to consider for a loved one!

The Gift of a Phone Call

By Morgan Chambers
East Sussex, England

The only thing we can never get enough of is love. And the only thing we never give enough of is love.

Henry Miller

THIS YEAR I was going through my address book and reviewing it as I do every year and decided to ring a friend that I had not been in touch with for a couple of years. I rang only to find out that her husband had developed throat cancer and had just gone for surgery. The remarkable thing was that I was able to be there for my friend during a very stressful time and amazingly, at just the right time. I love the way the universe works for us all. We just have to listen!

THOUGHT TO PONDER:
Are you really listening when someone comes into your mind? How often we let the tyranny of the urgent keep us from acting on those messages!

The Friendship Ball®
By Barbara A. Glanz
Sarasota, Florida

When you find yourself overpowered, as it were, by melancholy, the best way is to go out and do something kind to somebody or other.

John Keble

GIVING A GIFT anytime is very special; however when we give gifts that are different and surprising and truly focus on the uniqueness of a person, the receiver is even more delighted.

My "second mother," Gail Flynn from Prairie Village, Kansas, gave me a most wonderful Valentine's gift. The beautiful cutout silver ball is called the "Friendship Ball®", and on the front of the attached card is a poem:

A ball is a circle
No beginning, no end.
It keeps us together
Like our circle of friends.
The treasure inside
For just you to see

Is the treasure of friendship
You've granted to me.

The inside of the card says:

In renewing an old English tradition, it is told how a special favor is tradi-
tionally passed back and forth as the occasion arises and exchanged through
the years by friends, sisters, and mothers.

Ours contains a luxurious French-milled almond beauty bar soap, along with
a Travel Puff Sponge to pamper and smooth. Maybe it will be returned with
special chocolates, seeds from your garden, a piece of jewelry, potpourri, or an
antique handkerchief for drying tears

In any case, use your imagination to fill your Friendship Ball® and pass it
back and forth through the years continuing the meaningful tradition.

In the spirit of the new Millennium as in countless ages before us, the timeless
treasures are as ever. The real treasure is priceless—the gifts of love,
forgiveness, grace, joy, peace, and the treasure of friendship.

The fruit of the spirit is love.—Galatians 5:22

What a lovely idea and beginning of a special "friendship tradition!"

I recently received a letter from an audience member who had purchased
one of the Friendship Balls®, Cynthia Kirker from Cincinnati, Ohio:

Dear Barbara,

Thank you so much for your CARE message. It's a great idea! I wanted to
let you know that I purchased one of the Friendship Balls® from you at the
Ohio Human Resources Conference a couple of weeks ago to send to a
relative that I hadn't spoken to in quite a while. The gift and short message

"broke the ice!" The relationship appears to be getting off to a better start this holiday season as a result of this small token of friendship.

Cindy

THOUGHT TO PONDER:
Is there someone in your life right now who can use a Friendship Ball® from you?

A Day of Pampering

Kindness is gladdening the hearts of those who are traveling the dark journey with us.

Henri-Frederic Amiel

WHEN RACHEL LACOMBE of Gainesville, Florida, was going to have a birthday, her older sister Rita had an idea for an angel gift that involved the whole family. Rachel had not had a day alone for over 18 months since her son Ryan was born, so the family planned a surprise day of pampering for her. At 8:30 they all met for breakfast to celebrate Rachel. Then while they watched Ryan, Rachel was gifted with a 10:00 am massage. At noon her husband picked her up to go out to lunch, and the afternoon culminated in a 3:00 pm facial. Everyone helped plan and pay for the surprise day, and it is one Rachel will never forget!

THOUGHT TO PONDER:
Who can you help to pamper?

Her Name Is Kirsten

By Cathy Hamilton
Holland, Michigan

You cannot do a kindness too soon, for you never know how soon it will be too late.

Emerson

I HAVE ALWAYS loved dolls! I collected them as a child and to this day I treasure those childhood gifts. But perhaps my favorite doll is one I received as an adult. Her name is Kirsten, and she was a gift from my parents who gave her to me for no reason other than that they loved me and they knew I would love Kirsten.

I'd been admiring her for years, but I had no realistic hope of ever owning her because she was rather expensive, certainly not in the budget of a young family with two boys. But my Mom knew that in my heart I wished for this doll. On the card she wrote, "Maybe someday you'll have a daughter with whom you can enjoy this doll. If not, may she bring out the little girl in you."

I cried for joy at this gift of grace—unmerited in every way. It wasn't even my birthday or Christmas. When I take her down now to carefully change her dress, I am overwhelmed by my parents' loving generosity in giving me such a perfect gift!

(Cathy is now the mother of twin girls, so she has the delight of doubly sharing her precious doll!)

THOUGHT TO PONDER:

Have you ever given someone a special gift "just because" ... for no special reason other than that you love them? What a fun way to bring joy to someone you love.

Ring of Reassurance
By Rochelle Prybylski
Fox Valley, Illinois

You cannot love much and give little. How much you love can be measured by how much you give.

Unknown

THERE ARE MANY ways that we get ourselves and our loved ones through stressful times. This is an example of a gift I gave to my husband.

At just forty years old my husband of 18 years was taken to the Emergency Room because he was so weak. He was diagnosed with heart disease. They placed him in Intensive Care and evaluated his condition. Here was the active, healthy, former fireman and Air Force veteran who served in Vietnam, who was being told he had a bad mitral valve. At that time, he and I didn't know the slightest thing about the heart—much less about a particular valve. We certainly learned quickly!

Jerry's mitral valve was not closing properly. The doctors called it a floppy valve. It needed replacing, they said, within 2-1/2 to 3 years. Their guess was very close! October 2, 1990, was the date of his open heart surgery. This was determined, of course, after regular checkups with his cardiologist, whom we have gotten to have much respect for after this many years.

Jerry and I talked about how he would feel, waiting in the room before surgery. He was very concerned since I couldn't be there with him. His wedding ring, of course, had to be removed. I knew he needed a way to feel close to me, since he was so scared, so I began to think of a way I could help.

I told Jerry when he needed to feel my love and support just to feel where his wedding ring would have been, and to know that I was there with him and I loved him.

The surgery was a success, and he said this way of calming him down really worked! He felt amazingly better after touching his ring finger with his thumb. He said he could feel me right there with him, even though I was down the hall. He also used this technique when he was recuperating from surgery, at the times when I couldn't be with him. What a small gift this was, but what a difference it made!

THOUGHT TO PONDER:
Is there a physical symbol you can give to someone in your life as a comfort and reminder of your love?

The Turn-Around

By Nancy Coey
Raleigh, North Carolina
Reprinted with permission from
Finding Gifts in Everyday Life by Nancy Coey

You will find as you look back upon your life that the moments when you have really lived, are the moments when you have done things in the spirit of love.

Henry Drummond

A LADY NAMED Lena made a big difference in my life.

Here's how it happened.

We had been living in the D.C. area for all of two weeks when we were invited to a neighborhood get-together. A lady asks, "Well, how do you like it here so far?" I'm feeling lonesome and overwhelmed and decide to tell the truth. To take a risk!!! So I open my heart to a stranger and tell this story.

When I was growing up, Aunt Helen and Aunt Marcy would come for Thanksgiving and Christmas and they would always bring Russell Stover candy. Russell Stover candy became for me the symbol of good times, of special events; it was then, and is to this day, the treat-of-all-treats.

With that explained, I tell her that just today the kids and I went to a nearby large shopping mall for the first time. The boys loved it, but I was intimidated. Then I remembered Russell Stover candy. And Aunt Helen and Aunt Marcy who always seemed rich and sophisticated to me. So I said, "Boys, we're going to get ourselves a treat!" And we marched into Bloomingdales and headed right for the gourmet section. A very well-dressed clerk looked down at us and said in a tone that still hurts, "Bloomingdales doesn't carry Russell Stover Candy. You might try the drugstore ..." Diminished, the boys and I left and went straight home.

I say all that, feel better just for the telling but, of course, she hears, "I'm not going to like living in a big city."

The party goes on; conversations ebb and flow; the evening ends. The next day, the doorbell rings.

It's Lena with a box of Russell Stover candy.

Things begin to look up.

© Nancy Coey. Finding Gifts in Everyday Life. Reprinted with permission.

THOUGHT TO PONDER:
Do you really listen to other's heartfelt needs? Does anyone in your life need a box of Russell Stover candy?

The Gift of a Fire
By Chelsea Chiodo
Millburn, New Jersey

Each of us will one day be judged by our standard of life—not by our standard of living; by our measure of giving—not by our measure of wealth; by our simple goodness—not by our seeming greatness.
                                                      William Arthur Ward

MY NAME IS Chelsea Chiodo, and I was the chapter advisor for Gamma Phi Beta sorority at Rutgers University in New Brunswick, New Jersey. On April 2, 2000, my apartment building burned down, and I lost everything I owned. I had no renter's insurance, and the loss was devastating.

The Gamma Phi sisters at Rutgers saw me on the news in front of my burning apartment building and immediately called the Province Collegiate Director, Nina Bonnet, who tracked me down at my parent's home. That phone call changed my entire point of view of the whole situation!

I was no longer depressed over the material things I had lost. Instead, I was touched and thrilled that I had <u>so many</u> people who were concerned with my health and well-being. My Gamma Phi sisters offered clothes, a place to stay, and asked for anything they could do for me. Their concern made me realize that everything was going to be O.K. because I had people who loved me, and that was the most important thing.

Luckily, my mother always taught me to count my blessings, and here is what I have learned from that whole experience:

• Material objects do not matter. They can always be replaced.
• Friendships, family, and loved ones are the truly important things in life.

These are the things we need to focus on. Your speech today made me realize my blessings, all over again! (NOTE: I was the keynote speaker for the national Gamma Phi Beta convention that year.)

THOUGHT TO PONDER:
How attached are you to your material possessions?

Chapter Four:

"Humorous Gifts"

Jennie came slunking by, feeling blue.
Henry said, "Jennie, that just won't do."
He flipped double loop, and briskly changed her mood.
Jennie said, "Half my smile belongs to you."

©Andrew Grossman
Newton, CT

Do your givin' while you're livin' ... then you'll be knowin' where it's goin'.
Ann Landers

WE ARE OFTEN so serious in our giving that it takes all the fun away. Sister Anne Bryan Smollin in her book *Jiggle your Heart and Tickle your Soul* says, "There's nothing like a good laugh. It tickles our very souls. Laughter is an activity of the heart. We scrunch our souls with negativity and a lack of enthusiasm. Laughter smooths them out." She goes on to say, "Research indicates that an infant laughs when she is ten weeks old. At sixteen weeks, an infant laughs almost every hour. When a child is four years old, he laughs almost every four minutes—unless we interfere with the child experiencing joy!" How often do you laugh a day? The average child laughs *hundreds* of times a day. The average adult laughs a dozen times a day. We need to *find* those lost laughs.

Just as grief and anger can suppress the immune system, laughter can strengthen it. Laughter creates a unique physiological state, with changes in the immune system opposite to those caused by stress. It lowers blood pressure, wards off colds, stifles the flu, helps you sleep better, lose weight, AND it's good for the soul! So, here are some ideas of FUN ways you can remember others.

The Gift of a Movie

By Barbara A. Glanz
Sarasota, Florida

God let it be known that it is better to give than to receive, but a lot of people failed to get the message.

Edmund W. Littlefield

UNCLE BRIAN IS the most delightful and unpredictable person in our whole family! He is the world's greatest storyteller and the world's most unreliable person when it comes to time. He has lived all over the world; he has been a hippie, a farmer, a college professor, a Buddhist monk, and an executive coach; and he makes friends wherever he goes, from Lord Spencer and Mother Teresa to an upstate New York cowboy/farmer who told my mother he had named a goat after her! He has taught my children to imitate an elephant, smoke a cigar, and play music through their nose.

One of the most special gifts Uncle Brian has given my children is that on every visit he made during their growing up years, they either made a movie or put on a performance with Uncle Brian as Producer and Director (and sometimes even an actor in the show—usually the "hero," of course!) Because we didn't have video cameras at the time, the first thing Brian would do when he arrived was to take the children downtown to buy a roll of Super 8 movie film. Then they would spend the entire next day in the basement writing the script, rehearsing their parts, and raiding the costume box. Later that day Uncle Brian would begin the filming.

The first movie they made was called "Count Garrettula," a takeoff on Dracula. Garrett slept in the toy box (coffin), attacked the beautiful princess (Gretchen), then turned into a bat when the hero (Uncle Brian) arrived. In another short movie segment of magic tricks, Garrett loved that he made his sister Gretchen disappear!

The second movie was "Cowboy Garrett Rides Again." In this movie Gretchen is Calamity Jane, the heroine, and Erin is Pocahontas, a beautiful Indian princess. The villain is the bad Indian chief (Uncle Brian) who tries to kidnap the beautiful Indian princess. Garrett, the cowboy, jilts Gretchen to rescue the Indian maiden from the bad chief, and the movie ends with Uncle Brian lying on the ground in our front yard covered in Ketchup, Gretchen miffed as the jilted lover, and Garrett and Erin riding off into the sunset on a wooden hobbyhorse with a brown paper sack head! While this one was being filmed, Brian ran around our front yard in his shorts with a brown towel hanging over the front and a giant tinker toy hatchet, chanting Indian chants and wearing shoe polish war paint. I wondered what people going by in our small village must have thought!

The children have watched those movies literally hundreds of times, and every relative, good friend, boyfriend or girlfriend over the years has been introduced to the "Legends of Uncle Brian." Finally, I did have them put on videotape and later DVDs as a Christmas present so each child could have a copy of his/her own.

Another year, much before the advent of "The Best Christmas Pageant Ever," Brian came for a Christmas visit. He immediately got all the children in the neighborhood together to put on a "show." They rehearsed all day in our basement, and that night all the parents were invited to the Christmas production in our backyard. They rigged up several scraps of wood and a string of Christmas lights to make a star in the basketball hoop, the garage was the stable, they filled the wagon with potting soil for the manger, and anyone in the neighborhood who had a dog brought it, and they were the "shepherds abiding with their flocks in the fields." Because there weren't enough boys, he chose the "three wise <u>women</u>," and for a camel they used the white car with a hump that belonged to one of the Moms. The cast was complete with Mary, Joseph, a Cabbage Patch doll Baby Jesus, and the Innkeeper (Uncle Brian, of course). As the Christmas story was read, each child acted out his or her part under Brian's direction. Then he lead us all in singing Christmas carols. It was a Christmas no one in the neighborhood will ever forget!

What a gift of memories he has given our children!

THOUGHT TO PONDER:
Grab a video camera and create a memory for someone today!

Bombardment Gifts

By Tracey Wolski
Villa Park, Illinois

He that bringeth a present, findeth the door open.
Scottish Proverb

TRACEY WOLSKI TELLS of a family birthday tradition started by her mother, Maureen Frost, of Villa Park, Illinois. Birthdays are very important in the Frost family. Whenever anyone has a birthday, at the beginning of the present opening, the birthday person gets a "Bombardment Gift" from each member of the family. These gifts are unique because everyone gives the person the same thing! Tracey told about some of the "Bombardment Gifts" that have been received:

* Her husband loves a certain kind of hair gel, so on his last birthday everyone gave him a bottle of it. Now that he has 10 bottles, his hair will look wonderful forever!
* On Tracey's birthday she received all different kinds of spoons. The last time her mother had visited her home for a party, she was nearly out of serving spoons.
* Her son, in Tracey's words, is a "super sucker fanatic," so on his birthday everyone got him some kind of a sucker. He has enough to have a sucker every day for weeks (and Tracey has to pay the dental bills!)
* Her 26 year old brother told them he wanted toys for his birthday, so his bombardment gift was a matchbox car from everyone.
* They got her sister rolls of film because she always takes thousands of pictures.
* Tracey's Mom got all kinds of knee high nylons, which she needed, and Tracey said that several other members of the family had also gotten socks.

Usually Maureen, the Mom, decides what the bombardment gift will be; however, when it is her birthday, Tracey gets to choose the gift. She says it is one of their most treasured family traditions and makes birthdays even more fun.

THOUGHT TO PONDER:
What a fun tradition to begin with your own family! What simple, everyday things do you love? I love new underwear and lots of Kleenex around my house.

A Potpourri of CARE Packages

By Gail Howerton
Las Vegas, Nevada

If it is more blessed to give than to receive, then most of us are content to let the other fellow have the greater blessing.

Shailer Matthews

WHEN THE OTHER college freshmen received their care packages from home, it was the usual candy, cookies, underwear and other goodies from their moms which contributed to what was affectionately known as the "freshmen spread"—the 10 pounds each person gained from all the midnight pizza and care packages from lonely mothers with empty nests and no kids to feed at home! My mom, however, was determined not to contribute to my figure and instead sent me running shoes, sweat suits, tennis skirts, a tennis racquet, granola bars, fitness magazines, and golf visors.

When I moved into my first house, she again sent me a care package filled with a leaf blower, purple flowered garden gloves, a purple t-shirt, nail polish, lipstick (I guess you have to look good and color-coordinated when you are blowing your leaves!), a garden book, a belt sander, a cordless drill, and an assortment of nails, screws, nuts, and bolts all in my old baby food jars she had saved for 38 years!

I can always tell when my mom wants to do more shopping guilt-free, or else clean out her closet so she can fit more clothes in it. I get mega-clothes care packages filled with 15 pairs of shorts the colors of the rainbow, tennis skirts, golf visors, tennis shoes, sweat suits, and t-shirts (some things never change!), and now the dog is even sending me items such as bath accessories and lotions under mom's assumed identity!

Finally, I decided to send a care package to my mom—my old 486 computer so she could learn email in order for us to stay in touch. It came with tech support by way of phone calls from me to teach her how to do it. After the first call of 2.5 hours and only learning how to control the mouse and how to turn it off and on, I decided the care package better come with personal consultation. I flew from Virginia to Phoenix for 5 days of computer lessons of 5 hours per day on that slow computer. Since she hadn't typed in over 50 years, we started from ground zero. Not 3 days after I returned home, she sent me an email with a photo attachment from her new super-duper Pentium II, hot-shot computer—I guess she thought she was now ready for the big-time and needed more power. Who knows who will get the "slow" computer now as their care package.

At one stage of my life, having lived overseas for 10 years without English-speaking television got to be a bit isolating. The best care packages were from friends in the States who would send six-hour videos with the best sitcoms and movies. We would all gather around for a video-fest and watch hours of shows from the States. Oddly enough, one of our favorite things was the commercials so we could see what we had been missing back home! Isn't it amazing to think about what strange gifts have been the best ones in our lives?

THOUGHT TO PONDER:
What wonderful, creative ideas Gail and her family and friends have had. May they be an inspiration to all of us! Who needs a care package from you?

"Appreciating Life's Gifts"
By Jill Bayer
Bradenton, Florida

'Tis much better to give than to receive—and it's deductible.

Unknown

EVERYONE HAS A relative in their family who is known for giving strange gifts. That infamous box comes at Christmas, and you are almost nervous about opening it. Will it breathe? Will it jump out at me? Will it be yet another weird thing that will live in the back of my closet forever?

Our great Aunt Emily is known for giving extremely unusual gifts. One Christmas we received a box of frankincense and myrrh. I had heard a song about it as a child but didn't know there really was such a thing. What do you do with such a gift?

Another year I rushed to open my gift, realizing that it was sure to be something I would never use. As I tore away the paper in which it was so lovingly packed, I realized it was a "You Are Special" plate. It was red and shiny and had the words "YOU ARE SPECIAL" in white letters around the rim. "What the heck do you do with this?" I thought. Later that day, I spoke with my brother and we shared the gifts we gave and received earlier that day. I laughed aloud when I learned that he, too, was now the proud owner of his very own red shiny plate!

You know we made fun of that plate for years, yet I carried it with me from place to place, thinking one day I would use it. I never did. Finally it ended up in the Goodwill box and was probably given to someone who just "needed" a plate, any old plate.

Well, I have my own family now and I realize that self-esteem is the most important gift you can give or receive. That night when my husband made a really big sale at work or tackled a tough-to-sell customer ... That day my daughter's friends made her feel left out when they said, "Three girls can't play this game" ... That time when I felt like I had been a great mom and wanted to say, "Hey, I'm the one who is special today!" Boy, I wish I had that red plate! I guess ol' Aunt Em wasn't so strange after all.

THOUGHT TO PONDER:
You never know when those "odd" gifts may come in handy!

The Spilled Milk Puzzle

By Lynn Durham
Hampton, New Hampshire

The Lord loves a cheerful giver, and so does everyone else.

Unknown

WHEN I THINK about fun, creative gift giving, I must tell you about some friends who moved out of the area. We gave them a nice going away party, a surprise at a restaurant. I don't recall what we purchased for them. I do, however, remember the gift they gave us—not the one they purchased to leave with us but another one which left a lasting impression because it was both creative and fun.

Do you know what a "spilled milk" puzzle is? Picture spilled milk, all white with an irregular border. It is a challenge as a jigsaw puzzle because there are no straight lines or pictures to help with the assembly. Suzy and Tom bought one, painstakingly put it together, and wrote clues for a treasure hunt, which they planned in advance, on the front of the puzzle. Then they proceeded to take it apart in sections and gave one group of pieces to each couple in the group.

Each couple was told to put their puzzle section together at home. Then, on a certain date, the couples were instructed to come together again to reassemble the entire puzzle by putting together all their individual sections. When that was accomplished, they could read the instructions their friends had left for a special treasure hunt "in their memory."

We each put our sections together and then planned the night for the rendezvous. All the sections were finally united, and the hunt began, using the clues we found there. I remember the hiding place ended up being in the doghouse, but I can't even think of what the treasure was. I just remember how much fun we had finding it!

Gift giving is not about money. The important gifts they gave us were:

- remembrance of them and their creativity and love of life,
- reconnecting their remaining friends together once again, and
- the laughter and joy we experienced that evening.

THOUGHT TO PONDER:
Any puzzle will do for this gift. It is the fun of "putting it together" that really counts.

An Everyday Survival Kit
Forwarded from Cindy Rispens
Villa Park, Illinois

We are here on earth to do good to others. What the others are here for, I don't know.

W.H. Auden

THESE ARE THE items everyone should have in their survival kit:

Toothpick	Chewing gun
Rubber Band	Mint
Band-Aid®	Candy Kiss
Pencil	Tea Bag
Eraser	

And, here's why:

Toothpick—to remind you to pick out the good qualities in others. (Matthew 7:1)

Rubber band—to remind you to be flexible. Things might not always go the way you want, but they will work out. (Romans 8:28)

Band-Aid®—to remind you to heal hurt feelings, yours or someone else's. (Col 3:12-14)

Pencil—to remind you to list your blessings everyday. (Eph 1:3)

Eraser—to remind you that everyone makes mistakes, and it's okay. (Gen 50:15-21)

Chewing gum—to remind you to stick with it and you can accomplish anything. (Phil:4-13)

Mint—to remind you that you are worth a mint to your Heavenly Father. (John 3:16-17)

Candy Kiss—to remind you that everyone needs a kiss or a hug every day. (John 4:7)

Tea Bag—to remind you to relax daily and go over that list of God's blessings. (1 Thess 5:18)

This is a gift to you. May you be richly blessed.

To the world, you may just be somebody ... but to somebody, you may be the world.

THOUGHT TO PONDER:
Make several survival kits for your friends and loved ones today. You'll touch their hearts!

Krikit's Gifts

By Shannon R. Johnston
Oceanside, California

It is with narrow-souled people as with narrow-necked bottles: the less they have in them the more noise they make in pouring it out.

Alexander Pope

Krikit's Breakfast Frog

ONE NIGHT I was awakened about 1 a.m. by a squeaking sound. Since there are various animals that visit in the night outside the patio, I didn't think much about it. However, when it became clear that the squeaking noise had moved from the typical "somewhere out there" to inside the house, I got curious. I got up and turned on a light for the living room. As I moved into the dark room I evidently disturbed Krikit's work, for as the light came on the squeaking stopped and she was staring intently under the black cabinet that houses all the music in the living room. I figured she had dropped whatever she was carrying, and it had escaped under the cabinet.

What to do, what to do. She had evidently decided to provide breakfast for us all, but being the wuss that I am, I decided to go back to bed, closing the door so that she could not bring her catch in to show me. I would deal with it in the morning.

As I entered the living room the next morning, forgetting all about Krikit's problem, I was surprised by the sight of Krikit in exactly the same spot and position that she had been in 6 hours ago. She was crouched low, peering intently at whatever she was observing. Her eyes were a little droopy, having spent all night watching. Her head occasionally bobbed a little, as if she was drifting off, but no. Back to the job of one of the following: 1) saving her master and mistress from a terrible scourge, or 2) waiting for her live breakfast to give up and come out, or 3) forgetting totally why she was there, but answering to some strange call of the wild.

I went about business as usual, feeding our dog Missy and putting food out for Krikit, then walking Missy. When I returned and invited Krikit for her usual morning walk, she turned me down. Couldn't leave her post, oh no. This is a cat for whom food and walks are true pleasures, but she wouldn't budge.

While we were eating a breakfast Krikit had not caught for us, she got the idea of sticking her paw in and around the cabinet, and dislodged, would you believe, a fairly large FROG. She sat with it in her mouth until I approached, but then decided to tell me all about it. She opened her mouth to say something and out it hopped! (A great hunter would never talk while capturing its prey ...)

I took a paper towel and unceremoniously dumped it out the front door. Big mistake. I didn't show Krikit what I had done, and she naturally assumed it had returned to its hiding place. She took the position again and sat down for another wait.

I went off for tennis, returning a couple of hours later. Had she eaten her breakfast? Had she gone out on the patio to Ken to get her morning brush? Oh, no. There sat Krikit, low to the ground, her head drooping, eyes half closed, looking even more tired than she had been.

Now, I know cats are fairly near-sighted, so she couldn't really see if the frog was there or not. However, since she had originally brought it in by mouth, there was probably a little blood or something in its spot and she could still smell it. I finally decided to spritz a little air freshener where the frog had been, on the hopes that it was the smell that kept her there. Good guess. Krikit left, ate her breakfast, and immediately went soundly asleep in the sun. When a friend stopped in, she asked why Krikit seemed so tired. I replied, "She was up all night with a new friend."

Krikit and the Lizard

Krikit walked up to the sliding glass door on the patio with a very large lizard in her mouth. She looked at us through the doors to say, "You brought lunch; I'm bringing dinner." Unfortunately, she opened her mouth to tell us about her contribution, and of course the lizard scampered away—not fast enough, however, because, lightning-fast, she grabbed it again. I decided to go out and see if I could get her to give it up. She dropped it again and I picked it up in a paper towel.

Remembering her all-night vigil with the frog, I decided to show it to her, so that she'd know I was taking it out and so she would not continue to look for it. I held it up to her face, thinking she would see and smell it. Again, I had forgotten that cats are very nearsighted, so she had no idea what I had in my hand. Well, the lizard didn't care for that close up at all— it probably thought I was going to feed it to the cat—so it opened its tiny toothless mouth and bit her squarely on the nose. In my surprise, I dropped the lizard, and Krikit jumped. Back to square one.

This time I didn't fool around, and grabbed the lizard and dropped it outside on the bushes. Once again Krikit's owners were not going to share in the gift of her "kill!"

THOUGHT TO PONDER:
What special gifts our pets can be! They love us unconditionally and entertain us constantly. No one who has a pet can ever be bored.

The Plate
By Barbara A. Glanz
Sarasota, Florida

When some people give their old clothes to charity, they should stay in them.
Unknown

ONE OF OUR favorite family memories was a running gag between my husband and my grandmother. When they first met, they always enjoyed good-humored political discussions. My grandmother was a dyed-in-the-wool Republican who would never think of voting any other way, regardless of the circumstances. Charlie liked to consider himself an Independent, and that drove my grandmother crazy! He loved to tease her during their discussions.

On our honeymoon we went to Washington, D.C. (We even stayed at one of the honeymoon resorts in the Pocono Mountains, advertised in *Brides* magazine!) While we were there, Charlie decided to buy my grandmother a very special souvenir—a plate with a picture of John F. Kennedy, a Democrat of course, on it. It was such fun to watch her, the staunch Republican, open that silly present! Of course, she pretended to be offended—just what Charlie wanted.

For the next seven or eight years on their birthdays and Christmas, that plate went back and forth between Charlie and my grandmother, always disguised in the wrapping, so that the receiver thought he or she was getting something else—sometimes in huge boxes, sometimes inside something else, sometimes beautifully wrapped, and other times in newspaper. What FUN they had with that "gift" until it finally got broken in the mail!

TOUGHT TO PONDER:
Think of fun gifts that you can start as family traditions in your home. We all need more laughs in this stress-filled world!

Roscoe G. Simpson

By Brian Bauerle
Chiang Mai, Thailand

The Lord loveth a cheerful giver. He also accepteth from a grouch.
Notice in a Church Bulletin.

ONE CHRISTMAS MY big sis and her family came back to Iowa to share the usual extended family holiday. My older sister, Barbara, and I have a history! I was the ultimate obnoxious little brother spending a great deal of time, thought, and energy into finding a way to torment and embarrass her. She was the ultimate foil that reacted to each prank in a way that gave me the greatest satisfaction. I knew I had mastered the art of driving my sister crazy! In fact, this history we shared had become a part of family legend with her children often asking to hear "Uncle Brian stories," most involving some form of tormenting their mother.

One of the family tales involved a car trip to Colorado during which I bugged my sister with constant repetition of a very stupid song about "Farmer Alf." "Happy Anniversary, Farmer Alf to Thee ..." I repeated this song endlessly until I only had to hum or even silently mouth the words to make my sister hysterical and myself utterly delighted.

It was out of this myth that I created a conspiracy with my nephew, Garrett, and nieces, Erin and Gretchen, to join me in again driving their mother crazy with a new ditty about, "Roscoe G. Simpson coming to town." Of course, they had no idea who Roscoe G. Simpson was. The song extolled the wonderful virtues of Roscoe and was great for add-ons and ad-libs. The chorus was so simple it can still be sung by all of us to this day:

"Roscoe G. Simpson, he's a comin' to our town.
Roscoe G. Simpson, he's actin' like quite a clown.
He's a great guy to come to your house;
He'll make you so happy you'll squeak like a mouse!
Roscoe G. Simpson, he's a comin' to our town."

The Roscoe G. Simpson song was a roaring success and added great fun to our family holiday, but I explained to the kids that it would <u>really</u> work best in the confines of their small car on the road trip back home. What a fitting legacy from the ultimate obnoxious little brother—<u>eight full hours</u> of "Roscoe G. Simpson, he's a comin' to our town!"

After a wonderfully chaotic ride back with mother reacting this time with good-natured annoyance that made everyone laugh, they arrived home to an extra special Christmas surprise from Uncle Bri—a small cock-a-poo puppy with a card attached that said, "Hello! My name is Roscoe G. Simpson." Roscoe became a much-loved family member for the next four-teen years. What a final fitting legacy for the ultimate obnoxious little brother!

THOUGHT TO PONDER:
Think of a gift you can give that creates a family legend. With a little creativity, foreshadowing, and a lot of fun, you can give a gift whose memory lasts through generations!

Our Laughing Place

By Lynn Durham
Hampton, New Hampshire

Charity begins at home, and generally dies from lack of outdoor exercise.

APRIL IS HUMOR month. Have you found a laughing place? I have found one at my sister's home. We always have a great time. On Easter weekend we have a tradition called "Eggstravaganza."

Aunts and Uncles, cousins, and Grandma have our religious ceremonies and go to church together on Good Friday afternoon, and most of the group goes together again on Saturday evening. We also take the festivity of egg coloring, etc., to another level of joy. The etcetera has kept expanding over the years.

How have you decorated eggs? Are they bejeweled, have hair, or kilts? Is anyone sanding, gluing, wrapping? Has anyone named categories, described the eggs in detail or had secret ballots for the winners? Uh, oh, are we the only ones?

The children's friends join us. Some of the children are in their late 20s (actually some are in their 50s and 80s). Their friends truly enjoy the time of creating and laughing. Colors, glue guns, a box of "stuff" and blown out eggs are among the items that are on the table. Imaginations run wild! Joshua, my 12 year old, had decided what he was going to do for his egg last October (and it won the gold medal this Easter, I might add). We all have an "eggcellent" time!

Someone has decorated "Eggraham Lincoln," "Queen Egglizabeth," and even "Eggstream skier." We immediately get down to the serious funny business of designing the most intriguing of creations. The "McGreggor egg" was complete with tam-o-shanter and plaid kilt. "Steggosaurus" was a real hit! There was even a bike in the two egg category along with the orange, twin pod, cloud car from the "Empire Strikes Back." Headlines on the "Eggstra, Eggstra" newspaper egg detailed events of the day.

We give "Eggcadamy" awards to the finest. After the entries are in, John, my brother-in-law, categorizes, shows them off, and describes them in "eggquisite" detail. Some of the groupings have been the Sparkle Category,

Commemorative Eggs, and Animate Objects in Humanoid Form. John is always the Burt Parks of this ceremony. He is so "eggacting" and "eggciting" in his descriptions that someone suggested he apply for a position on the shopping channel!

The competition was fierce this past Easter, as I am sure you can tell, so we decided to have secret ballots. We were trying to decide which engineer should do the spread sheet for tabulation or if we needed to do a pie graph. But with only paper and pen, the calculations were made that named the winners in each category. Then another vote for the grand prize winners.

Kerstin was very disappointed her "front end discharge cement mixer egg" only came in second, and Brett was lucky that as a first timer, he took third with a rock island sunbather under a palm tree, or was it a "sunbegger?" Joshua was in his glory because he got to stand on the chair in the middle of the room for the photos because he took first place with his yellow "Volksweggon Beetle." For sure, all want to return next year.

There might be some of you who wonder at the sanity of this group. However, I prefer to be around the people that wish they could have joined us because our hearts were merry and all our cells were happy. We were in our favorite laughing place! Just do what brings you joy, or put more joy into all you do. All it takes is a little imagination.

"You will show me the path to life, fullness of joys in your presence, the delights at your right hand forever."—Psalm 16:11

THOUGHT TO PONDER:
How will you decorate your Easter eggs this year?

The Garden Mister

By Donna Cutting
Asheville, NC

As the purse is emptied, the heart is filled.

Victor Hugo

MY BIRTHDAY ARRIVED about a month after I began dating the man who was to become my husband. I was thrilled to be spending the day with him! He bought me several lovely gifts that I opened with anticipation and relish. It was the last gift, however, that he seemed particularly excited about. It was an inexpensive, plastic garden mister.

I wasn't quite sure what to say. Not really having a green thumb, I wasn't sure why he gave me this gift ... but he seemed so excited about it! "Do you like it?" he asked eagerly.

"Oh, uh, yes", I said, bewildered.

"I have one, too!", he said, with bright eyes.

"Really?" I asked.

"Yep", he said. "Too bad mine is FULL!" he laughed. He whipped it out from behind his back and started squirting water at me. Stunned, I stood there, laughing and getting drenched. Finally, I got my wits about me and ran to the sink to fill up my mister. We carried our fight out to the lawn until we were both drenched and loving it!

My husband, Jim, has given me many gifts since then—some tangible, some intangible—some expensive, some inexpensive—but this is one that I always look back on with love and laughter. It's been nine years and we're still laughing!

THOUGHT TO PONDER:

How long has it been since you've given someone a "silly" gift?

Chapter Five:

"Labors of Love"

LABORS OF LOVE
Doesn't matter,
I would do it for free.
I'm a poor baseball player
But the play pleases me.
Andrew Grossman 2000
Newton, CT

He who gives to me teaches me to give.

Danish Proverb

SOMETIMES THE BEST gift we can give to another is the gift of our time. Material gifts can be lost, stolen, broken, used up, or even discarded. However, the gift of one's time is a memory, an experience that will never be forgotten.

There are certain "labors of love" that people gave me in my life that I will never ever forget, even though in one case I cannot remember the name of the person who gifted me with her time. But I will never forget the love she gave to me in that act of helping. As a young mother with two children under the ages of six and a brand new baby, I was struggling with my self-image. Not only was I continually exhausted, but I was also quite overweight from my last pregnancy. Having struggled with weight issues all my life, I decided to return once again to Weight Watchers, although I dreaded the time and effort I knew it would take to stay "legal."

I attended my first meeting with a baby and a toddler in tow—not the ideal way to listen to a lecture on losing weight! Each of the new people was asked to introduce themselves and tell why they had come to the meeting. I shared my desires and concerns about all the extra planning, shopping, and preparation I was worried about with no time to myself as it was. Yet, I was determined to lose weight and feel good about myself again.

When the meeting ended, a lovely woman came up to talk with me. She told me that she understood where I was in my life since she had three children of her own. Her children were now in high school and college, and she said she had some extra time and she wanted to help me get started on the Weight Watchers program. I was amazed and a bit skeptical, I must admit! She said she would call me that afternoon.

Later in the day when the children were napping, she called me and asked what vegetables I liked. She was going to go shopping for me and asked if she could come by the next afternoon during naptime and help me parboil all the vegetables, weigh them, and package them in freezer bags so they would be all ready for my lunch or dinner in just the exact amounts the diet called for. That way I wouldn't have to worry about extra preparation time for my special meals.

True to her word, she arrived the next day with several grocery bags of fruits and vegetables. We scraped, cut, peeled, boiled, weighed, and bagged for several hours, and at the end I was left with a full freezer of Weight Watcher-sized portions. That small boost of encouragement gave me the incentive to keep on the diet, and six months later I reached my goal weight. I am ashamed to admit that I did not keep in contact with that wonderful lady and I don't even remember her name, but her gift of a labor of love will live on as I try to give of my time, without any expectations, to others in need.

CARE Packages that made a difference

By Michelle Porchia
Trumbull, Connecticut

After the verb "to love," "to help" is the most beautiful verb in the world.
Bertha von Suttner

IN 1996 I was separated from my husband of 10 years, and I was moving into an old home of a co-worker. The house needed a lot of work and cleaning. My very dear friend, Debbie, came over every day and helped me clean, paint, and do whatever needed to be done. We had never seen such dirt! During the day, while Debbie was out, she would pick up blinds, throw rugs, and whatever else she felt I needed to help make this place my home. She gave not only her love and support during a difficult time, but she also gave of herself—through manual labor. Her unselfish gift of time and love got me through a very difficult time.

During this same time, a former co-worker of mine, Yolanda, came over a few evenings after work and helped put in shelf paper, paint, and other fix-up jobs. Since I commute from Connecticut to New York City every day (3 hours round-trip by train), she would meet me at the house with food for Debbie and me. The three of us would work until we were about to fall over! Keep in mind, we did about 4 hours manual labor cleaning this house <u>after</u> we had worked 9 hours a day! These are true examples of unselfish love and caring.

In 1997 I moved into a two-bedroom apartment from that 3 bedroom, two-story house. I had gone through a divorce the year before, moved twice in one year, and was having trouble trying to find a place for everything. A friend and coworker, Rolande, came to my apartment with a huge gift bag. Before entering my home, she blessed my home and all who dwelled in it.

Rolande then proceeded to pull items out of the bag, which seemed bottomless. She had made two pillows for my new futon. She had made potpourri and shared with me the importance of each ingredient. She gave me a tool box. (I love practical gifts.) Then she gave me the gift of the heart: "Cookies, so you will never go hungry. Tea, so you will never be thirsty. Salt, so that your home will be filled with the spice of life." After giving me the gifts with this blessing, she hugged me, and I cried. We then proceeded to roll up our sleeves and put the futon together.

This gift of time, love and carefully selected items is still precious to me years later.

THOUGHT TO PONDER:
Is there someone in your life who needs your gifts of time and love?

A Builder's Gift of Love

By Bette Price
Dallas, Texas

There never was a person who did anything worth doing who did not receive more than he gave.

Henry Ward Beecher

MY GIFT OF love came with a hammer, nails, and a saw. He came at a time when disaster and despair had become commonplace on a daily basis. Thank God, he came!

Early in the morning on July 8, 1997, I received a shocking phone call. I was on a business trip to Williamsburg, Virginia, thousands of miles from my Dallas home. My husband, likewise, was out of town on business. The call came from my brother-in-law, so I initially assumed that perhaps something had happened to my elderly mother-in-law. "No," he said, "Mother is fine. But at 3 o'clock this morning an airplane hit your house." That was the beginning of what would day-by-day become a chain of devastatingly stressful events!

The plane, a twin engine Aero Commander, carrying a load of freight, had been in the air only fifteen minutes when it descended upon our house, hitting it twice before turning completely backwards and crashing through the entire back of the neighbor's house. While the damage was less visual at our house than the neighbor's, it was equally as serious because we suffered what they called "hidden damage."

After dealing with insurance adjusters, structural engineers, contractor's bids, and an array of other so-called experts whom we trusted and relied on, we moved from our home to a furnished apartment so work could start. The recommended contractor began by tearing the front half of our roof off so that re-framing of the upper structure could begin. That's when the problems also began.

Inferior plastic tarp, shoddily draped over the open roof wasn't enough to keep pouring winter rains at bay. At first a portion of the tarp formed a holding cup for the rain water until it could no longer withstand the pressure. Breaking the weakened rafters that had temporarily restrained it, wood fell through the ceiling below, the sharp-edged remaining wood punctured the tarp, and water poured down into the house, drenching the walls and carpet and eventually flooding the entire back half of the house. Since no workers were on site, it was hours before the damage was discovered.

As bad as this day of damage was, it was only the beginning. The contractor who had been recommended so highly turned out not to be the unique restoration contractor he'd been stated to be. For the following two months, one disaster after another prevailed until our home became a shell of what it had been—void of ceilings, walls, and carpet, leaving nothing but wooden studs in many areas. Finally, there was enough cause to legally fire the builder. But, now we had to start the quest all over again. Once again, we had to try to find a reputable contractor.

In the state of Texas, contractors are not required to be licensed. We had already experienced the horror of a supposedly reputable expert. Our trust had been severely diminished. Our confidence was eroded, and my nerves were wearing mighty thin. Where were we to turn? We simply did our earthly checking as best we could and left the rest of the mission to God.

I truly believe God responded by sending a gift of love and caring in the form of a kind and gentle man named Charles Lancaster. Well into his 60's, Mr. Lancaster had retired from the corporate world where he had dealt with overseeing the hiring of commercial contractors. When he and his wife set out to build their retirement dream house, with Mr. Lancaster acting as the general contractor, they experienced a horror of their own. The experience led them to start a small construction firm that would perform in an ethical manner, with quality craftsmanship and with honor and integrity. That was the story he told. But could I believe that? Even though his references checked out with rave reviews, my head was skeptical. My heart, on the other hand, hinted that I could believe him. We took a chance.

From the moment they started, I could tell the difference. Knowing the horror I'd been through, his entire family nurtured me through every tiny, picky question and concern I expressed. During one particular phone call I became quite nervous and distraught over concern for some special painting. "Bette," Mr. Lancaster said, "Could you meet me at the house this morning?" "Yes," I said, with some annoyance. "Good," he responded. "I think it's important to meet you there. I need to show you some things."

I had been crying. The pressure of months of stress had built up in me. He knew it. I left the apartment and drove straight to the house. As I drove up, the cab door of his old, red weathered pickup truck opened, and Charles Lancaster stepped out. He was sporting a familiar tweed sport coat, neatly pressed blue jeans and well-worn cowboy boots.

He reached for my hand and grasped it tightly. A warm smile brushed across his weathered face and his gentle eyes, twinkling like a Santa Claus, connected strongly with mine. "You've been through a lot he said," in a fatherly tone. "I normally wouldn't point out some of the things I'm going to show you. But, I want you to know, we're going to do everything we can to put your house back together with the quality you deserve."

Then he guided me to the side of my house to show me how they had put an extra layer of trim beneath the roofline—not because they had to, but because it looked better and they thought it was the right thing to do. Next we climbed the ladder to the attic, and he pointed out all the extra supports they had built in—not because they were required, but because they felt it provided better quality and it was the right thing to do. He proceeded to walk me through the entire house and point out areas where extra attention had been given beyond the requirements, and, while I instinctively knew it but had been afraid to really believe, it was clear to me that I had been given a special gift in Mr. Lancaster. Not only had he truly cared enough to ensure that quality workmanship was provided, but he had also provided it with pride and care, and even love.

Today, we live in a house built stronger than it was when we bought it, with many finishing touches that only we might know about, but also some quality touches that even visitors see. Charles Lancaster not only restored our shattered house; he left behind a precious gift—memories of a uniquely honest, loving, caring soul that we shall always cherish and whose memory helps to keep our house a strong and loving home.

THOUGHT TO PONDER:
How much care do you bring to the work that you do? Charles Lancaster certainly went above and beyond the skill requirements of his job. His was a labor of love.

A Precious Friend

By Mary Torgler
Western Springs, Illinois

All the beautiful sentiments in the world weigh less than a single lovely action.

James Russell Lowell

IN JANUARY OF 1997, my husband Bill was in the hospital with double pneumonia. We did not know if he would live. Every day during that time Jean Corson came to our house and walked our puppy so that I could stay at the hospital and meet with doctors. In addition, I came home late one evening and found all our exterior Christmas lights neatly wound and placed for me to store. She knew that I had no time to remove them, so she did it for us. What a precious friend to share her labors of love!

THOUGHT TO PONDER:
The smallest acts of helping can become lifelong memories of love.

Brightening the Lives of Others

By Rose Henson, Executive Director
Life Care Center of Brookfield
Brookfield, Missouri

"Help thy brother's boat across, and lo! Thine own has reached the shore."

Hindu Proverb

DIXIE SHARPE BECAME a Licensed Practical Nurse fifteen years ago and came directly to work at Life Care Center of Brookfield. Dixie is a very special person. She raised four children on her own after the death of her husband and even put them all through college! She has always worked the 100 hall as well as helping wherever she is needed. She knows all the residents—their wishes, dislikes, discomforts, and what makes them happy. They are her family.

Ronnie Hines has worked at Life Care Center of Brookfield for almost ten years. Her primary hall is the 300 hall. Both her hall and Dixie's are on the south side of our building. Ronnie is also a very special person. She knows her residents' every need as well as knowing their families and histories. Ronnie left us for about nine months and came back as our Admission/Marketing person about a year and a half ago.

Last year Ronnie and Dixie came to me and said they wanted to do something special for their residents: they wanted to decorate their halls. Our facility was build in 1982 and still had the same drab, big old pictures with no special significance on the walls, and the halls were very plain. I told them I would love to see this done.

About four months went by, and I was beginning to think they had forgotten about their project. One Monday morning I came to work and was met at the door. "Close your eyes," said Ronnie and Dixie. "We have a surprise for you, and we will lead you to it."

They led me to the 100 hall, and when I opened my eyes, it was the most beautiful sight I will ever see! By each resident's room there was a grouping on the wall—something special that pertained uniquely to that resident. If they liked birds, the theme of the grouping was birds. Other themes were Bible verses, flowers, farming, angels, cars, children, England, and fishing, and each grouping was artistically and perfectly hung.

Those two women went to garage sales, antique shopping, bought home interior magazines for ideas, refinished, stained, painted, framed, and laid out each grouping in Dixie's basement until they had something special for each resident's wall. They even included the Nurses Station, the sitting area at the Nurses Station, the front entry hall, and the south entry. Their whole families came with them on Sunday night and helped hang all the groupings!

Everyone was amazed at the beauty, and the difference it made was over whelming! As a result, the North side of the building decided that their halls had to be just as beautiful, so the whole staff became involved, and every hallway was decorated to the hilt in just one month. The only thing the facility purchased was a chair, two hutches, and one table and a lamp. Everything else was done by the staff.

The amazing part was that everyone thought that the groupings in our Special Care Unit which is for behavioral problems would get broken or that the residents would take things off the shelves. To this day there has been less damage on that unit than on any other!

These women wanted to do something for their residents because they are their family. They truly went above and beyond the call of duty. I have the most beautiful nursing home in the <u>world</u> because it was done totally with love!

These pictures were taken after the decorating was done. The first woman loved flowers, the second person was a bird watcher, the third had lived on a farm. and the last person was a Christian. What a precious personalized gift of caring these women gave to their residents!

THOUGHT TO PONDER:

Two women took their own time to brighten the lives of those around them. What might you do in your workplace or community to bring joy to those who so desperately need it?

The Gift of Giving

About Rita Perez
Gainesville, Florida

Time is not measured by the years that we live,
But by the deeds that we do and the joys that we give.

Helen Steiner Rice

RITA PEREZ OF Gainesville, Florida, has taught her sons, Lucas, 6, and James, 2, the real gift of giving. Rita has ensured that they have been involved in acts of community goodwill. Lucas and his mom drove a food route for Gainesville Harvest, a group that gleans leftover food from restaurants and stores and delivers it to the hungry. Rita and her boys have volunteered at an Alzheimer day care center. "The elderly people just loved the kids," she said. And they've served lunch to work crews building houses for Habitat for Humanity.

Every Thanksgiving Rita and her children serve Thanksgiving dinner to the residents of a halfway house. "There's a lot of opportunity out there to help people." Perez said. "You can live in a void, but I don't think that's why we're here. I want my kids to know that."

THOUGHT TO PONDER:

Are you teaching your children to the gift of giving?

Ways You Can Help a Sick Mom

By Wendy Bergren

Reprinted with permission from *CARE Packages for the Home*

By Barbara A. Glanz, Andrews McMeel 1998

Service is nothing but love in work clothes.

Anonymous

WENDY BERGREN WAS a married young woman with three children, a baby, a preschooler, and first grader. In her struggle to beat cancer, people asked many times over the months how they could help. In an issue of *Focus on the Family* magazine before she lost her battle, she shared several ideas:

1. **Cook a dinner for my family,** but offer a choice of two entrees. One week we got tuna casserole four nights in a row from well-meaning friends! Bring the food in disposable containers or marked pots. If I can't return your casserole, I will cry at my powerlessness and confusion.

2. **Bake homemade cookies or brownies** and bring them frozen so I can have the delight of sending off fresh goodies in a lunch box the next morning. This will give me the fun of feeling like a mama.

3. **Make your offer specific.** Say, "I want to come over Monday at 3:00 to clean your pantry shelf or do your laundry." Otherwise I won't know what you want to do or when you are free.

4. **Offer to baby-sit**—even if my husband and I stay home. This gives us the freedom of a private adult life in a place my illness can cope with.

5. **Help with holidays, birthdays, and anniversaries.** Ask if there are any special gifts or cards or wrapping paper you could pick up for me. How many times I have wanted to give my husband a special "Thank You" card or put up a holiday decoration but have been unable.

6. **Help my children attend birthday parties** by bringing some pre-wrapped children's birthday party gifts to our home for future use.

7. **Call before you visit, but drop by for 20 minutes** when you can. Don't assume sickness requires rest at the expense of communication and friendship. (Loneliness is the greatest interrupter of sleep).

8. **Ask me who you know that I might like to see and bring them by.**

9. **Take snapshots of my children** over the months. This gives me a feeling that there are permanent records of the temporary happenings I must miss.

10. **Offer to run two meaningless errands** a week for our family— otherwise the small stuff like no hair ribbons, the cleaning, or cologne fall by the wayside.

11. **Allow me to feel sad,** or to prepare for the worst. One of the most difficult problems of serious illness is that everyone wants to encourage the patient. But sometimes, having a good cry with a friend who allows it will let the tension escape.

12. **Even if the joke is terrible,** tell it! Read something funny to me or describe a funny story. Speak to the part of me that is more alive than dead, for that is the real me.

13. **Touch me.**

14. **Offer to watch TV with me** some afternoon when an old movie is on. Bring a book or a magazine in case I fall asleep.

15. **Say the word "Cancer"** around me and talk about the *real life* you are living. This helps me feel less like an untouchable and more like I am still involved with the world of normalcy. One of the hardest things for me as an invalid is the problem of conversation with my husband. If you don't talk to me about the life outside, I am left with only illness and TV to talk about to him, and this is hard.

16. **Tell me how great I look considering** what I'm going through. I know I look sick, but I still need to feel honestly attractive.

17. **Encourage your husband to come over to visit my husband** in the evenings. My illness has eliminated many of his pleasures. How happy I am when I hear him laughing with a friend!

18. **Pray for me** and say you are doing so. The fact that you have faith gives me faith.

19. **Talk to me of the future.** Next week, next year, ten or twenty years! The power of planning is incredible. If you look ahead, I can too.

20. **Remind me of the abundant life** that awaits me and is promised, but also recall that there is comfort to be had here and now, in the midst of my illness. The fact that you could care so much in this moment tells me how much God cares for me in all moments.

THOUGHT TO PONDER:
Since every person is different, these ideas may not be helpful for all sick mothers; however, you can use these ideas as guidelines. If your offer is specific and sincere, you can show your caring in your own special way. When I had to be in bed for 9 weeks before our middle daughter Gretchen

was born, a friend came over and rubbed my feet and put polish on my toenails. To this day, the memory of that special gift fills my heart with love for her.

The Quilt from Hell that Went to Heaven

Jody Morgan
Valdez, Alaska

Deeds of giving are the very foundation of the world.

The Torah

LAURA WAS A brand new quilter, pregnant with her second child, when she attempted to make a "Tumbling Blocks" quilt as her first project. The quilt was to be a gift for her sister, who was also expecting a baby.

This is not exactly an easy quilt to make, especially for a new quilter. Laura had lots of trouble putting the pieces together and often recruited another friend, Janai, and me for help. This quilt was referred to as "The Quilt from Hell" for several months as we all struggled to make the pieces fit and the quilt lie flat.

Before the quilt was completely finished, Laura's son was born. Sadly, he died just a few hours after birth. As our gift of love and support for our friend, Janai and I took the quilt, finished it, and gave it back to Laura to bury her baby son in. We are all confident that this quilt is now in heaven with that precious little boy.

THOUGHT TO PONDER:
This labor of love was truly a heavenly gift.

Slave for a Day

By Christine Corelli
Morton Grove, Illinois

God has given us two hands—one to receive with and the other to give with.
Billy Graham

EACH YEAR ON Mother's Day, my son Jeffrey takes me to dinner with his wife and my darling granddaughter and presents me with a lovely rose and a nice card. As much as I appreciate and enjoy this, I always remind him of the best mother's day gift I ever received.

When he was eighteen and the month of May came around, he asked me what I wanted for Mother's Day. I didn't want him to spend money, so I said, "Jeff, there are so many things I need done around here. Why don't you help me out around the house for a few hours? That would be a great gift and what I would love the most. In fact, I'd be THRILLED if you agree. I've been so busy with my job, I simply haven't had time to do everything. You can be my 'Slave For a Day'."

Being a single woman for many years, I can tell you that there are certain chores a man can do better and faster than a woman! That day, Jeff moved the furniture from the walls in the living room, vacuumed behind the couches and chairs, and moved it all back. He scrubbed down the bathrooms and kitchen floor and took the light fixtures down and wiped them clean. He even cleaned the refrigerator! Then he moved everything from the garage, power-washed the garage floor, hosed down the lawn furniture and my bicycle, and then scrubbed down the barbeque grill. After all that, he gave the yard a good spring raking. We cooked dinner on the grill and had a great time together before he went off with his friends. I looked at all he had done in just a few hours and was ecstatic!

I will always remember the best Mother's Day I ever had. Oh, how I wish he'd be my "Slave For a Day" again. His wife would love the same gift, too!

THOUGHT TO PONDER:
Is there someone you know who would like a "Slave for the Day?"

Valerie's Happy Restroom
By Barbara A. Glanz
Sarasota, Florida

People need to give who they are, not just what they have.

RECENTLY, I WAS flying home and had a layover in the Charlotte, NC, airport. My next flight was going out of Terminal E, so the first thing I did after arriving there was to find the Ladies Restroom. As I walked in, a lovely lady greeted me loudly and enthusiastically with a huge smile on her face, "WELCOME TO VALERIE'S HAPPY RESTROOM!" I was certainly taken aback but also delighted and all I could do was to smile.

She then said, "If you be happy, you'll pee happy!" Laughing out loud, I began to head toward a stall. She stopped, looked at me, and responded, "You have a lot of stuff, so I am going to give you the VIP section" … which was the Handicapped stall!

I smiled the entire time I was in that bathroom and so did everyone else as they got the same "happy" greeting from Valerie. Another of her greetings was, "Don't worry. Pee happy!"

As I was leaving, I told her about my work and asked if I could share her story in my presentations and books. Her response—"I already have four videos on YouTube!" So, if you google "Valerie's Happy Restroom," you can see her in action. Her final comment to me was, "My Mama told me, 'If you can't have fun at work, then just stay home.'"

She certainly WAS having fun at work and so was everyone else who came into that restroom that day. She gave a gift of joy in a very unexpected place and lightened everyone's day. If you are ever in the Charlotte airport, head for Terminal E and look for Valerie. She is truly making a difference.

THOUGHT TO PONDER:
How can you add more fun to your work?

Chapter Six:

"Little Things Mean a Lot"

blossoming tulip
by the pile of road cinders
sways in the breeze
©Andrew Grossman
Newton, CT

DO YOU REMEMBER the song "Little Things Mean a Lot" by Gogi
Grant in the 1960's? So often we think that we have to do big, important
things to make a difference in this world, yet it is the little day-to-day
blessings that make up the fabric of our lives and give us hope. How often I
have been encouraged by a phone call, a note, a fax, or an email that took
the sender very little time but made a big difference in my day. And
sometimes just a smile and a kind word can turn a cloudy day to one filled
with sunshine. In fact, my idea of Heaven has become that we will see all
the people whose lives we've impacted through those little gifts of kindness
that we knew nothing about.

In my speaking I always share with my audiences this little model I call the
"Three Column Chart" which has a minus column, a zero column, and a
plus column.

In Any Interaction

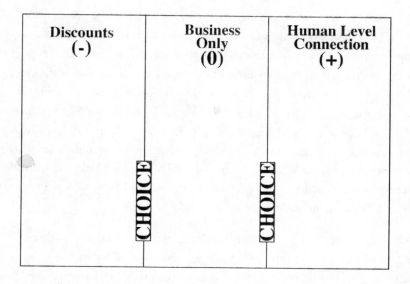

You will notice that it says beneath the model, "Your choice in any interaction." I created this model for myself a number of years ago because I wanted to be able to see and measure in a concrete way the difference I could make every single day. In every interaction we have with anyone, we have the choice of creating for that person a minus, a zero, or a plus, according to how we treat them. If we discount them and make them feel less important than us or our organization, we will leave them with a minus. If we simply go through the motions of an interaction, just doing the business at hand with no real connection, we will leave them with a zero. However, if we connect with them on the Human level, recognizing them as a living, breathing person of value, then we will leave them with a plus, feeling a little bit better because they interacted with us. This is the gift we can bring to every interaction we have with anyone.

In my presentations I often tell the following story:

Several months ago I walked into the Ladies Restroom at O'Hare Airport en route to one of my speaking engagements. There was a lady there who was cleaning. She was all hunched over with a grim, down-hearted expression on her face, ever so slowly going through the motions of cleaning the sinks and mirrors. I walked up to her, touched her on the arm, and said, "Thank you so much for keeping this washroom clean. You're really making a difference for all of us who travel." She immediately perked up, smiled a huge smile, and began cleaning with zest! By the time I got ready to leave, she was handing out towels to all the women who were washing their hands. It brought tears to my eyes. What was the little thing I did? In that one statement I told her she was of value and her work was important, the gift we all desperately need in our world today.

I challenge you to keep this little model in your head as you go through the daily routines of your life and make it a mission to try to create as many pluses as you can by truly noticing human beings—the person at the checkout counter at the grocery store, the child selling Girl Scout cookies, the server in the cafeteria at work, the money-taker at the toll booth. You never know when the little kind, caring thing that you do may change a life.

The Dog Bite

By Barbara A. Glanz
Sarasota, Florida

Such a simple thing as the giving of yourself—giving thoughtfulness, time, help or understanding—will trigger the cycle of abundance.

Norman Vincent Peale

THIS IS A true story, a story of a whole series of CARE packages that powerfully impacted my life. None of them were big things, but they made a huge difference in my memory of what could have been a horribly traumatic experience. Because of the little things a handful of people did, I only have POSITIVE memories.

I grew up in a small town in the Midwest, the oldest of four children. We did not have a lot of money—my father was the Postmaster in our little town. One of the things I remember vividly in my growing up years was hearing my Mother talk about wishing she could go to see a favorite uncle who lived in Wyoming.

My mother and I had birthdays only two weeks apart, and for my fifth birthday, my Dad gave us two train tickets to go to Wyoming while he stayed home with the other children. It was the most exciting moment in my whole life when we got on that train!

The very first thing my uncle showed us when we arrived was his brand new Pointer hunting dog. He was thrilled with the dog, it had all kinds of special papers, and he had wonderful plans for hunting and fishing trips with it.

Evidently, the dog didn't like me very much. We were about the same size, and all of a sudden, this cute little girl began getting all the attention that the dog had been getting just hours before. So, the second day we were there, he lunged at me, bit me in the head, and almost tore my whole scalp off!

They quickly got me to an emergency room, but it was quite a long time ago, and they didn't have many of the medications they have now. For some reason because the wound was so close to the brain, they felt they could not give me any kind of an anesthetic, so they literally did hundreds of stitches without being able to give me anything for the pain. Unbelievably, I have no memory at all of any pain. All I remember is the doctors and nurses holding me, talking to me, touching me. My whole memory is simply being enveloped by love!

Two days later I began to run a 105 to 106 degree fever. The wound had gotten infected. They rushed my father out and told my parents that I had a 75 to 1 chance to live, and that if I did live, I would never look "normal." During that time in the hospital in that tiny little town in the mountains of Wyoming, the doctors and nurses somewhere found a 16 millimeter movie projector, the kind that sort of shook as you watched the movies! They brought it into my room, and they brought as many films as they could find—Abbott and Costello, the little Rascals, Casper, the Friendly Ghost. At that time my parents didn't even own a TV set, so can you imagine the thrill of my having movies in my hospital room? In fact, one of the reasons I think I fought that infection and lived was I DIDN'T WANT TO MISS THOSE MOVIES!

In the end, I did survive the infection, but I was literally a freak—I had huge chunks of scar tissue sticking out all over my head. The following two summers my parents decided to take me to Mayo Clinic in Rochester, Minnesota, to see if they could do plastic surgery to help me.

When we would go to Mayo Clinic, my mother and I would have to be there for 7-8 weeks at a time. In those days they tried to create a "family" experience, so they did not keep children overnight in the hospital unless they absolutely had to. Instead, they assigned each family a driver who would pick the family up at the hotel each morning, drive them to the hospital, and then pick them up at the hospital each evening and drive them back to the hotel.

The driver we were assigned was really just a taxi driver, but he became our friend as he drove us back and forth each day. In his car, he had an ugly little furry thing which hung from his rear view mirror. Every day when he would pick us up, he would say to me, "Barbara, say good morning to Fred. He's my good luck charm. Nothing bad ever happens to me when Fred is around. I've never had an accident because Fred takes such good care of me. He is my best friend in the whole world." As a result, I thought Fred was pretty special!

On the day of my first surgery (it was elective—they didn't know for sure if they could help me), the driver picked us up at the hotel, drove us to the hospital, and let my mother and me out of the car. Then he said, "Now wait a minute," and he walked around to the front, opened the front door, and took Fred off the rear view mirror. He came over to me, got down on his knees so he was eye level with me, and he said, "I know it's your operation today, and I know you're kind of scared. But you remember how Fred takes such good care of me and never lets anything bad happen? You take Fred with you, and you're going to be just fine." I remember going into the surgery clutching that ugly little furry thing, whatever it was, and knowing I was going to be "just fine!"

The doctor who did my surgery was the best-known plastic surgeon <u>in the world</u> at the time. Can you imagine how busy that man was? After the surgery, I would be bandaged from the top of my head to the bottom of my neck for weeks at a time. When I would come in to get my bandages changed, he would never let the nurses do it. He would always bring me into his office, sit me up on the table, and tell me all about his children. As he changed the bandages (they were cloth in those days), he would tear the ends of every one, and then he tied LITTLE BOWS all over my head. My only memory is how pretty I was! People would even stop me on the street and in the hall to tell me how lovely I looked. There was a man who was changing people's lives very day (they only get the very worst cases at Mayo Clinic), and yet he still had time for a little six year old girl.

So, none of those things were big things, but each small CARE package served to change what could have been a horribly traumatic experience into one that only has POSITIVE memories. I am not afraid of doctors or hospitals, I love dogs, and although I still have scars on my forehead and in my hair, that whole experience is a joyful one in my memory. In fact, today I make my living by standing up in front of hundreds of people in my audiences, never even thinking of the miracle of how I look.

My belief is that we all have this opportunity to give CARE packages every single day. We can never know when the extra kind, caring thing we do for someone might make such a difference in their whole life. I have tried to go back and find these people years later, and of course, they didn't even remember me. However, that is a true CARE package when we give without asking for anything in return.

THOUGHT TO PONDER:
When I tell this story to my audiences, I have to tell it in the third person as if it happened to someone else, because whenever I try to tell it as my own story, I cannot get through it without crying. It is simply awesome to me to think of the difference these few people made in my whole life. The beautiful thing is that each one of us can make that same difference for other people as we send our CARE packages every single day.

An Ordinary Day

by Jeanne Arbet
Woodridge, Illinois

Small deeds done are better than great deeds planned.

Peter Marshall

WHILE TRYING TO think of the greatest gift of love I have ever received or seen, I realized how lucky I am because I have received and witnessed so many gifts. I truly enjoyed just remembering all the wonderful experiences! This made me realize how important it is not to overlook the simple gifts of love that are given each and every day. So instead of telling one of the greatest gifts of love I have ever received, I'd rather just tell you about the gifts in one ordinary day.

* It's in the "love ya" that ends each one of my husband's telephone calls.
* It's in the full tank of gas that I can always count on when I get in the car.
* It's in the constant chatter about the latest recess chase going on at school.
* It's in the patient explanations my six year old gives my one year old about the things he needs to know.
* It's in the hug my one year old gives for no reason at all.
* It's in the wagging tail of our dog, greeting me, whether I have been gone for ten hours or ten seconds.
* It's in the way our dog follows me wherever I go, from room to room, though his age poses special challenges.

These things are all just ordinary things, but these ordinary things are the greatest gifts of love.

THOUGHT TO PONDER:
Do you notice these ordinary gifts in your life each day? We all need to be reminded to be thankful for the small things.

Small Gifts of Love and Remembrance
By Barbara McCauley-Lovejoy
Salt Like City, Utah

We are here to change the world with small acts of thoughtfulness done daily rather than with one great breakthrough.

Rabbi Harold Kushner

BARBARA MCCAULEY-LOVEJOY writes about several special gifts that are small but can make someone's life just a little bit better:

* I received a wonderful gift from a cousin in Michigan. Most of my father's family is from Michigan, but I have never been there. My cousin, Matt Kennedy, recently sent me a map of Michigan, highlighting some cities where my family lives. He also sent me a sample of the Michigan State rock. If you have friends or relatives who have never been to the state where you live, a fun gift is to send some items representative of that state.

* One of my former students, Kim Morrell, just stopped by our house to visit with me for a few minutes and to give me an update on her life. It was a reminder to me how much a simple visit can mean to someone. Is there a former teacher, church leader, neighbor, scout leader, Sunday school teacher who has made a difference in your life who enjoy a visit, phone call, lor letter from you?

* When my mother passed away last November, one precious friend, Vickie Sleiman, called me and invited me to lunch with the invitation to spend the entire time talking about my mom. Vickie was true to her word, and it was the most wonderful healing experience! My mother was buried in a small cemetery about 3 hours away from Salt Lake City. She had requested only a viewing in Salt Lake. Therefore, I had told family and friends not to make the trip to the cemetery because we were only going to have a short dedication of the grave. One friend from my ward—church—did not pay attention to me and she made that long drive from Salt Lake to be with us at the graveside service that only lasted about 5 minutes.

* One year while I was teaching school in Salt Lake, I wanted to go home to Washington state and be with my parents for the summer. My father would not hear of me driving home alone, so he flew down to Salt Lake so he could help me drive home. No

big deal? Well, it is when you realize that in spite of the fact that my father was a non-commissioned officer in the Air Force, he hated to fly in airplanes—and would not under any condition—except for me.

* While I was attending BYU, my grandfather who lived in Salt Lake which was about an hour away from BYU in Provo, would drive to Provo whenever I wanted and pick me up so I could spend the week-end with them, and then he would drive me back.

* One year while I was teaching, someone gave me an anonymous gift every month or so. One of the gifts was a small pin that said, "You are loved." To this day I don't know who that person was, but I wear that pin almost every day as a reminder that there is someone who loves me.

* My Aunt Relia always seems to know when I need a little extra money. When I have been working on special project that has stretched me financially, she will compliment me on my efforts and then give me $50 or a $100 and tell me to go spend it on myself.

* The first Mother's Day after my mother's death was especially hard for me. There were two people who remembered that it would be. My dear friend, Connie Frisch, sent me a card in the mail telling me that she would be thinking about me and my mother on this Mother's Day. Then at church a little 11 year old girl gave me a card telling me that she loved me and that she knew this day would be hard.

* I have three aunts who have always believed in my potential, Millie Leonard, Ida McCauley, and Carolyn McCauley, who incidentally married into the family. Two have now passed away, but I could not talk to them without leaving their presence feeling like I could conquer the world. They complimented me

on everything possible and told me what a difference I had made in their lives.

* It is so fun to share a first name with someone else like Barbara Glanz. She has sent me the cutest things with the name "Barbara"—stickers, a necklace, etc. These have been spontaneous gifts that have reminded me that someone is thinking of me and is glad to be my friend.

* I have never met Judy Engel in person. I had read something by her that I liked so I sent her a note. We have now talked on the phone various times and written letters back and forth. She has a subscription to my newsletter and when she sees something that fits something I have written, she sends me a little treat. One time I wrote about leadership, and she sent me a little book about leadership thoughts.

* Kate Asbill is another person I have not met in person. In fact, Judy Engel introduced us. Kate has become a very dear friend, and we have talked on the phone, written letters, and sent many, many e-mails. She is another who sends me little "treats" when she finds one that fits. She knows that my "personal signature" is hearts, so she sent me a tape called "One Heart At A Time." She has been my "balcony person."—someone who cheers me on!

* I have started to work on my genealogy. I found one man, Glenn Martin, quite by accident who had some information on my family although he was not related in any way. He made great strides to get in touch with me so that he could send me the information.

* When I was serving a 1 1/2 year mission in Ecuador for the LDS Church, I received notice that my father who was not LDS had been diagnosed with pancreatic cancer and was not expected to live more than six months. I still had more than a year left of my mission when I received this notice. Needless to say, I felt

for sure that my heart would break, and I just did not know what decision to make. I spent the night at the mission home praying and crying. The next morning I was informed that my father was on the phone. Choking back tears, my father told me that after much soul searching he felt strongly that I needed to stay in Ecuador and finish my mission. I was given special permission to call my parents every week, but my father did die six months later, and I never saw him again. This was not only a sacrifice for my father, but it was also a sacrifice for my mother, because I was an only child, and she had to experience the depth of her sorrow with a daughter who was thousands of miles away.

* I was serving this LDS mission with young men and women who were19-23 years old. Many did not know how to deal with the news about my father. It actually frightened some, and they stayed away from me. Yet, there was one young man, Elder (this is the title male missionaries have) Tracy Crowell, who was only 20 at the time who knew exactly what I needed. He wrote letters to my father. He let me cry when the sorrow became unbearable. He bought gifts for my mother. The day my father passed away, we were holding a conference for all the missionaries in Quito, Ecuador. Our mission president gave Elder Crowell and me per-mission to meet alone in the living room of the mission home so I could just cry and share my feelings. Then Elder Crowell stayed by my side throughout the conference.

* Two former students that I had taught in fifth grade, Layne Simmons and James Marchant, took me out for breakfast fifteen years later when they both had professional careers to thank me for being their teacher.

Barbara writes, "As I looked over these stories, I realized that there were some common denominators:"

1. I did not ask for the gift.
2. The gift was given spontaneously.

`3. The person did not expect anything in return.

4. The gift was tailored to me.

Here are some of her ideas for little things you can do to help others:

Think of a magazine subscription that would bless someone's life. Then think of some way to save money during the month to pay for the subscription. Then subscribe to the magazine for the person anonymously. It's true that you may never know what it will do for the other person, but it is amazing what it will do for you!

The next time you see a mother struggling with her children, think of some way to help her instead of thinking, "Why doesn't she have better control of her children." There is a woman in my church who is a beautiful example of this, and I have learned from her. I held back from helping Moms because I wasn't sure I knew what to do. Then one day I saw a Mom **really** struggling with her two youngsters. I just offered to sit with her. No big deal!—but it worked. Now, I am not quite so intimidated by the situation.

Introduce people to people. I cannot believe how many times my life has been blessed because someone thought I should meet a certain person. We all know people who could bless the lives of other people in some way if they just knew who they were! Think about this. I challenge you to do this for at least one person this next month.

THOUGHT TO PONDER:
How simple most of these gifts are, yet they will add so much joy to the days of both the giver and the receiver!

The Stranger Who Cared

By Mary Louise More
Lakewood, Colorado

How far that little candle throws his beams! So shines a good deed in a naughty world.

Shakespeare

THIS WAS WRITTEN in a letter to her sister, Carolyn Baker:

I had the nicest surprise this noon! I went to McDonald's for lunch and stood in line for about 15 minutes. When I finally got up to pay for my food, I realized I didn't have the purse with my money in it. I told the lady I would be right back with the money ($2.46). A nice man in a good-looking suit was behind me, and when I went to leave, he said he would pay for it, but I told him I was parked just down the street, and he didn't have to do that.

I left to get my money, and when I got back to McDonald's, the lady told me that the man had gone ahead and paid for my lunch. I looked for him but didn't see him. I thought that was really nice of him—he made me happy. I hope he realizes that that little act of kindness made a big difference in my day.

THOUGHT TO PONDER:
Be on the lookout to "treat" someone in your life—especially a complete stranger.

Hidden Gifts

By Suzanne Wermes
Sioux City, Iowa

The smallest good deed is better than the grandest good intention.

Duguet

MY MOTHER WAS a terrific mom and friend and daughter, a caring and giving person at all times. She passed away five years ago at the age of 68 because of a bad blood transfusion in 1965 which doctors only discovered in 1994 when they operated on her gall bladder. Her death was a terrible loss. But Mom's habit of giving has continued in our family even after her passing.

When I graduated from high school, I went to college not far from home. I continued to work at my job at home on the weekends, so there was a great deal of travel back and forth between the two towns. My folks would pick me up at school on Fridays and bring me back on Sundays.

At Christmastime I was particularly dreading my return to school. Nonetheless, my parents dropped me off at the dorm as usual. I was dejectedly unpacking my bags when I discovered an eight-inch-tall dime store Santa Claus with his bright red suit and a note from my mom in the bottom of my suitcase. I will never forget how special that little gesture from Mom made me feel—very warm and loved! She did these things quite often—little surprises when we least expected it.

Now the tradition is continuing. When friends or family members visit me, I always manage to sneak a little token of love into their bags without their knowing it. Then I get a call when they get home, with a thanks for remembering them and questions about how I managed to sneak the surprise in.

When my daughter graduated from high school, she joined the Navy, and I loved to tuck things into her duffle bag without her knowing it. Doing so gave me great joy just to know I could put a smile on her face even from many miles away. Kristin would tell me that the other girls wished I were their mom! I learned a wonderful lesson from my mom. It is so much fun to give!

Kristin is now out of the Navy, married to a Navy man and stationed in Chicago. She has two boys, and whenever they all come home to visit, I love to sneak "I love you" gifts into their bags. Now my grandson looks forward to discovering what Grandma put there. Every time I do this, I think of that little Santa and my mom.

Last spring I was at my daughter's during a big snowstorm. I went out in the storm with a friend and bought a baby walker and brought it home for her. My daughter was in the other room and my grandson, Brody, was standing in the doorway and saw me with the walker. "Oh no!" I thought. "Now the surprise will be spoiled!" I put my finger up to my lips and said, "Shhh! Don't tell Mommy!"

Would you believe that five year old kept the secret and didn't tell his mother? When I got home from the airport, I called my daughter, but she hadn't discovered the walker yet, even though they live in a small place, with not a lot of room to hide things. The next day, she called. She couldn't believe that Brody had kept our secret. We hope he will remember the fun and keep the tradition going!

THOUGHT TO PONDER:
What a special family tradition to start at your house!

Kindness

By Nancy Coey
Raleigh, North Carolina
Reprinted with permission from *Finding Gifts in Everyday Life*

So many paths that wind and wind,
While just the art of being kind,
Is all the sad world needs.

Ella Wheeler Wilcox

IT'S THE MIDDLE of August and very, very hot. I'm driving home from a speaking engagement. It's a six-hour drive and I'm exhausted. Not just from the drive, but from very little sleep the night before. Anticipating the talk, and unable to get the motel temperature right, I was awake most of the night.

Groggy and spacey, now. Driving in a fog.

Pull into a rest stop and head right for a soda. Fumble forever with the coin changer: first put the bill in upside down, then in the wrong direction. Finally get change, then stand in front of the drink machine and cannot figure out where the coins go. It's as if my battle with the coin changer has taken every last bit of mental energy I have. Tentatively move my arm once or twice toward the machine, then just stand, confused.

A voice says, "Here, ma'am, this is where the coins go." And a very large hand points to the spot. I look over and in front of me is the sort of person I usually ignore: diesel cap; large belly hanging over his belt; cigarette dangling from his lips. He sees my surprise—or fog—and says almost contritely, "I didn't mean to be smart, ma'am. It's just sometimes these machines can be tricky."

Yes, sometimes they can.

And sometimes even putting one foot in front of the other can be tricky. And sometimes we are showered with kindness in unlikely places, in unlikely ways, by unlikely people.

Is there a lesson here?

© Nancy Coey, *Finding Gifts in Everyday Life*. Reprinted with permission.

THOUGHT TO PONDER:
Be open to kindness in the strangest of places—and be a carrier!

The Gift of a "Complete Picture"
By Suzanne Aiken
Arlington, Massachusetts

The accumulation of small, optimistic acts produces quality in our culture and in your life. Our culture resonates in tense times to individual acts of grace.

Jennifer James

WHILE SORTING OUT family pictures in an attempt to organize and preserve cherished memories for myself and my children, I noticed that there were very few pictures of my husband and me together. This was mainly because we were on trips with each other or with the children, and naturally someone had to take the snapshot so someone was always left out. This made me very sad since my husband had died recently, and I deeply regretted not capturing the memories of us together. I decided that part of my personal quest to be an "angel on earth" would be to give couples and families the gift of a "complete picture." As they grew older, families would be able to sit down to a whole album with every member included.

Soon after, I happened to see a couple with their three young children at the Nutcracker Ballet at Christmastime. They all looked so beautiful together—coordinated outfits, bows, and ties all matching. The father was about to snap a picture of them on the stairs, so I offered to take it for him so that he could join them. He hemmed and hawed so much that his wife stopped coaxing him and looked rather embarrassed. I quietly and gently told him about my small mission: that my husband had died suddenly and how sad I was that I didn't have more pictures as a family. I told him how beautiful they all looked together and that some day when they were old and gray, they would cherish this memory. I could see by his face that I didn't make him sad so much as I made him stop and think about his initial resistance.

Now, wherever I am, going about my day locally or traveling in a different city or country, when I see a couple or family taking a picture, I offer to snap it for them. I stop whatever I am doing, especially for couples. It brings me great joy, and the happy look on their faces is rewarding, too! I also pass on pictures that I have taken of friends and family for their collections, since I have learned the hard way how precious a photo can be.

THOUGHT TO PONDER:

Suzanne's story has really come alive for me since my husband died and I have realized, like her, how few pictures we have together. I am a convert! Now whenever I see someone taking a family or group picture, I always ask if I can take it for them. How delighted people are! Thanks, Suzanne, for your wonderful idea.

Love Heals

By Sue Rusch
Bloomington, Minnesota

Small things, done in great love, bring joy and peace.

Mother Teresa

I'D HEARD IT said hundreds of times: count your blessings and don't miss opportunities to tell people you love them, because you never know what tomorrow will bring. It wasn't until February 7, 2000, that I fully understood the wisdom behind those words.

Who would guess that grocery-shopping could be a life-threatening activity? On the way out of the supermarket, an out-of-control vehicle struck me as it jumped onto the pedestrian walkway. Some memories of the accident still bring a chill to my bones: the squeal of the tires, the frightening ambulance trip to the trauma center, and the frenetic pace of the emergency room doctors and nurses. Yet the memories that warm my heart stem from the overwhelming expressions of love and kindness shown by family, friends, and acquaintances during my recovery.

The accident served as a strong reminder that life is fragile. I am thankful that my injuries were limited to bruises and broken bones, all of which will heal in time. I'm grateful that the toddlers that walked into the store just seconds before I walked out were not hit. Most of all, I feel deep gratitude to my friends and family who have showered me with concern and kindness.

I suspect that most people don't know the impact that a small gesture of kindness can make. Until this accident, I certainly didn't. As friends have called and stopped by, I have been reminded of times I meant to send a card and didn't get around to it. I've recalled a few times I waited so long to take the right action that I took no action. I even remember times I didn't offer to help in a time of illness because I didn't want to get in the way.

Of the gifts this accident has delivered, one has been a first-hand lesson of how to show love to others in a time of need. I now know the power of even small expressions of kindness, and this experience has demonstrated the easy ways to offer help that make a difference. I know that the next time I know of someone recovering from an accident or illness, or facing a personal tragedy, I won't stop and wonder what the right thing to do might be. I won't wait. I'll think less about my need to do the best thing and more about the person's need to feel my concern and my love.

The next time, what will I do? Right away, I'll do one of these things:

* Say a prayer each day, and tell her I'm praying for her.
* Send her a cheerful card.
* Send a crossword puzzle book.
* Send a plant or colorful bouquet of flowers.
* Offer to run errands.
* Offer to help her wash her hair.
* Bring a casserole or easy-to-warm dinner.
* Videotape a children's program or event that has to be missed.
* Bring a cheerful balloon.
* Bring a plate of individually wrapped sandwiches.
* Send a movie rental gift certificate.
* Offer to help with housework.
* Send a favorite snapshot in a bedside frame.
* Stop by for a brief visit.
* Stop by to play cards or a quick board game.
* Send something to read.
* Bring lunch.
* Offer to drive children to activities.
* Send a gift certificate to a take-out restaurant.
* Water her plants.

* Care for her bouquets of flowers.
* Bake cookies for the family.
* Offer to take her on an outing when she's ready.
* Help her to sit outside on a sunny day.
* Tell her I love her and I'm glad she's ok.

Next time, I'll remember the friends and family who have warmed my heart and put a smile on my face. Next time, I won't wonder how I can help the most. I'll remember this: the greatest gift of any gesture is the love it shows.

Love heals.

© Sue Rusch, March 6, 2000. All Rights Reserved.

THOUGHT TO PONDER:
Let's learn from Sue's traumatic experience that we will all be in need at various times of our lives. By encouraging and helping one another, we get through those difficult times. Love IS the greatest gift! May each of us bless others with our love and caring.

The Gift of a Smile

From "Smiles," *Tampa Tribune*, March 25, 2000

Life is made up, not of great sacrifices or duties, but of little things, in which smiles and kindness, and small obligations given habitually, are what preserve the heart and secure comfort.

William Davy

Important lessons from life

DURING MY SECOND month of nursing school, our professor gave us a pop quiz. I was a conscientious student and had breezed through the questions, until I read the last one:

"What is the first name of the woman who cleans the school?" Surely this was some kind of joke. I had seen the cleaning woman several times. She was tall, dark-haired and in her 50s, but how would I know her name?

I handed in my paper, leaving the last question blank.

Just before class ended, one student asked if the last question would count toward our grade. "Absolutely," said the professor. "In your careers, you will meet many people. All are significant. They deserve your attention and care, even if all you do is smile and say 'hello.'"

THOUGHT TO PONDER:
Do you know the name of the cleaning person where you work?

Goin' Fishing
By Linda Lenore
Redwood City, California

We can do noble acts without ruling earth and sea.

Aristotle

Jeff: "Mommie, Mommie. When are we going fishing again?"

Mother: "I don't know, Jeff. When I have time."

Jeff: "Can we go tomorrow?"

Mother: "No. I have a class."

Jeff: "How about the next day?"

Mother: "No, Jeff. I have a meeting to attend."

Jeff: "Saturday?"

Mother: "We can't do it then because Melanie has an orthodontist appointment."

Jeff: *"Mommie, I want to go fishing. When can we go?"*

Mother: "Jeff, I don't know. Why is it you want to go fishing so badly? I don't understand. First of all, you don't like to use worms for bait because you don't want to hurt the worms. And you don't want to use marshmallows because they aren't healthy for the fish. Next, you don't like to eat fish so you usually release them back into the water almost as soon as you catch them. So tell me, Jeff, why are you so insistent on wanting to go fishing?"

Jeff: "Because, Mommie, that is the only time that you and I are alone with nature, and we talk a different kind of talk."

Jeff, you died long before I truly understood your powerful words of wisdom. Although we spent a lot of time together going places and doing things while you were alive and healthy, I didn't realize the quality of the place where we spent our time together would have such an impact on our communication and the memories I hold dear. What a gift I've received from some of those locations.

I cherish the times we sat at the mouth of the river or side of the lake, talking about anything and everything ... and NOT A THING! LISTENING ... to the silence and that "still small voice" within us. I can hear it clearly now, and I hear you as well. Thank you, Jeff, for the gift of fishing!

THOUGHT TO PONDER:

Is there a special place in nature that you can share with those you love?
Have you ever tried fishing?

M&M's®

By Donna Cutting
Ashevillle, NC

Youth expects fun in the getting, age reflects on the fun of having given.
Milton Murray

M&M'S® HAVE ALWAYS been my favorite candy. Every year at
Christmas time I received a big bag.

When I went away to college, I was moving out of my parent's house into a
dorm room, at a college where I knew nobody. I was trying to be brave, but
I was terrified. I'll never forget saying good-bye to my parents, and sitting
alone in the dorm room, wondering what my new roommate would be like,
and secretly wishing for the comfort of my own bedroom back home.

I opened my suitcase to unpack, and on top of the clothes that I had
packed, my Mom had sneaked in a big bag of Peanut M&M's®. It was a
little bag of love from home, and I've never forgotten it!

THOUGHT TO PONDER:

So often it is the little things that we remember. Do you know the
"favorites" of the special people in your life?

Little Things

Most of us miss out on life's big prizes.
The Pulitzer.
The Nobel.
Oscars.
Tonys.
Emmys.
But we're eligible for life's small pleasures.
A pat on the back.
A kiss behind the ear.
A four-pound bass.
A full moon.
An empty parking space.
A crackling fire.
A great meal.
A glorious sunset.
Hot soup.
Cold beer.
Don't fret about coping with life's grand awards.
Enjoy its tiny delights.
There are plenty for all of us.

Author Unknown

Chapter Seven:

"Life-Changing Gifts"

in a shell, like a shy
sea creature dug into the ocean floor

all windows curtained, all doors
closed to keep out the chance of sunlight

a hand touched the glass, lifted the night
out of my eyes and the heaviness from my heart

see us dance the bright morning cartwheel, see us part,
then come together again in a flashing melting brilliance

©Andrew Grossman, 1999
Newton, CT

The richest gifts we can bestow are the least marketable.
                                      Henry David Thoreau

SOMETIMES WE HAVE changes in our lives that we certainly do not
view as gifts at the time, but as we look back on those experiences, we
realize that they were, in fact, gifts that taught us about ourselves and
helped us live better lives. I will always be grateful to my piano teacher,
Ruth Potter, who gave me the gift of believing in myself. For many of the
years I took piano lessons I certainly did not appreciate Ruth's pushing me

to play in contests and recitals all over the state and constantly insisting on perfection. I can so well remember that sometimes if my lesson was at dinnertime, she would go out to her kitchen to check on something in the oven, and I would always hope against hope that she wouldn't be able to hear my mistakes. But, time after time, she "caught" me when I hadn't practiced enough or I had missed a note or a bit of expression—even when she was in the kitchen!

She changed my life because she taught me the importance of attention to detail and the belief that I could do anything I set my mind to. When I was in high school, there was a terribly difficult Liszt Etude that I had wanted to play for years. I think Ruth probably gave it to me before I was really ready, but I can remember being so engrossed in my practice of it that I would sometimes be at the piano for three to four hours after school and feel as if only moments had passed. (In fact, that is the feeling I have now when I am engrossed in my writing!) After several months of intensive practice and lots of encouragement, I played that piece in the Iowa State Piano Contest—and I got a First. What a sense of accomplishment that was! I will always be grateful to Ruth Potter for teaching me to work hard toward a goal and for standing beside me all the way, always urging me on to be better and better.

Another life-changing experience which was the most painful I have ever had to face and yet taught me the most important lessons in my life was losing our infant son. I had had a perfectly normal pregnancy, and when I started to have some labor pains in the night two and a half weeks before my due date, the doctor decided to induce labor. Gavin Wayne Glanz was born at 11:26, December 21, and weighed seven pounds two ounces. It was not until the next morning that the pediatrician knew something was wrong, and of course, by then we had called everyone with the news of the baby's arrival. The first diagnosis was a congenital heart, but we later learned that he had hyaline membrane disease, a condition that he would have survived today. Perhaps the most difficult thing for me at the time was that our little son was buried on Christmas Eve, the celebration of the birth of a baby.

Not only did I receive the gift of empathy for others who had lost a child, but I learned three important lessons that have impacted who I am, how I live my life, and the focus of the mission I have in my work. First, I learned that every day is a gift. None of us has any guarantees that we will wake up tomorrow, so we must rejoice in today, whatever that day may bring, for WE ARE ALIVE!

Second, I learned to live five minutes at a time. Some days my depression and sense of loss were so great that I did not think I could make it through the next hour, let alone the rest of a day, but I could always get through five minutes. I love the thought that even climbing the highest mountain must begin with a single step. As a result of this lesson, I have learned to be fully present in any situation in which I find myself. Certainly I have learned from my past, and I do make plans for the future, but I live my life in the present. When I began to travel in my speaking career, a good friend told me to always keep this thought in mind: "Surrender to the moment." No matter how long the delay at the airport or how many hurdles I have to go through to get where I need to be, that thought is a constant reminder of the lesson I learned from the short life of my son. And it is amazing what wonderful people I meet during all those delays!

A third gift I received from our son's short life was that never again would I pretend to be someone or something I am not. I was hurting so deeply during that time that I knew no one could ever hurt me that much again, so I vowed to always be my authentic self, regardless of what others thought. That gift has served me well in my speaking career because I am the same person off the platform as I am on the platform, and I try to live my message with my whole being.

I know each of us has experienced life-changing gifts. Often they are painful, and we do not see their value at the time. In fact, we often resent them, yet we become more beautiful and real with suffering. As the old skin horse tells the velveteen rabbit in the lovely book, *The Velveteen Rabbit*, "When all our hair is rubbed off and our eyes fall out, and we are truly loved, that is when we become real."

A Boy Named Jose

By Jay Leon
Oak Lawn, Illinois

There is no greater joy nor greater reward than to make a fundamental difference in someone's life.

Sister Mary Rose McGeady

AS A TEACHER for 28 years, I've taught every grade from kindergarten through high school. All my years of teaching, however, could not have fully prepared me for the '86-'87 school year when I taught the infamous "Jose!"

Jose was infamous because of the reputation he achieved his first five years at his school in Chicago. I would hear from other teachers who taught other grades, "Wow, is he something!" "You'd better pray you don't get Jose in 6th grade!" "What happens when he gets to be *that* age, if he's this bad now?" You might say that Jose was an "industrial strength" gang-banger. Not only was he in a gang, but he flaunted it at every opportunity for hell-raising, misbehaving, and anti-social behavior in school.

Despite all of the warnings from my colleagues, I was not fully prepared for what Jose had in store for me. You know how it takes awhile to know all of your students' names? I knew Jose by 9:10 am the first day of school! Within his first month in my sixth grade division, he:

* Marked up another child's brand new jacket with a "Magic Marker."
* Pulled down another child's pants on the way back from physical education—in the hallway.

* Cut Social Studies class for two weeks straight and hid out in the balcony of the school auditorium.
* Continually cursed female students, both in the lunchroom and on the school grounds.

After Jose returned from his third suspension for these infractions, I told him that I did not trust him (this was a private conversation) because of his many infractions—and I listed them all, specifically and chronologically. I asked him to think about if he were a teacher with a student who had done all of these things, would he trust him? He answered "No", while in tears.

I felt Jose was crying because he cared how I felt about him. We had a good relationship with each other. He knew I cared because I listened to him when he had something to tell me without judging, criticizing, or offering unsolicited advice. I established consistent, specific, immediate consequences for his behaviors—as well as for the rest of the class. I only reprimanded him for behaviors related to school. (I never got "in his face" about irrelevancies. I dealt specifically with his behavior and how it affected myself and others, and each time, I did it privately.)

I had established clear boundaries within the classroom for Jose's behavior. I enforced those boundaries each time they were violated, whether it was by Jose or any other student. Possibly, for the first time ever, Jose had some consistency in his life. He had been shuttled from living with one relative to another throughout his young life; at that time, he was living with his grandmother. I didn't know the specifics, but I knew Jose was a child faced with difficult challenges every day of his young life.

I told Jose it was okay to cry, but I wanted him to look at me while he was crying. Once we made eye contact, he found out from me what "not trusting" him would mean:

* From that point on, Jose would need an adult guardian for field trips. It could be his grandmother, an uncle, or anyone else he chose to escort him. The reason? I didn't trust him to behave if he went by himself.

* He would only be allowed to go through the school—to use the washroom, or for any other reason—with an escort (another student)—and that was only in the case of emergencies.

* For the next two weeks, Jose was on an in-school suspension, to be served in my classroom. He would receive his work from his other subjects during the day, but he would stay in my classroom the entire day. This was directly related to his cutting Social Studies. Lastly, if he forgot something in the classroom, another student would need to retrieve it, again because I didn't trust him.

I asked Jose if he understood everything I had said. He nodded his head, "Yes." I asked him again to look at me—he was still crying, holding his head down and looking at the ground. I asked him if he would like to regain my trust. He said, "Yes."

I asked him to write down all the things he needed to change about his behavior for me to trust him again. Upon completion, he would give it to me, and we would go over its contents together. If we agreed that the list was complete, we would both keep a copy.

Every other Friday after that Jose could ask me to go over the list with him to see if, in fact, he was following what he had written. If we agreed that he was on target for three consecutive Fridays, then I would begin to give him back my trust. However, I said I wasn't going to "hold my breath" for this to happen, considering his "rap sheet" with me up until then.

As the school year progressed, Jose began to drop his anti-social behaviors; he acted more and more like a regular kid. By the end of the school year, he had changed so much that he was voted the most improved student in the 6th grade! His grades and his behavior had improved. He had actually become a joy to be around!

Jose taught me an important lesson: I must always open myself to the possibility that someone can change for the better. However, I need to be grounded in the reality of the situation and deal with them exactly as they are, not how I would like them to be, while still giving them the opportunity to change. Thank you, Jose!

THOUGHT TO PONDER:
Is there a Jose in your life?

Champion Blood Donor

From *Encyclopedia of 7,700 Illustrations*
By Paul Less Tan

Perhaps the world little notes nor long remembers individual acts of kindness—but people do.

H. Albright

JOE KERKOFSKY IS America's blood donor champion. The American Association of Blood Banks will honor the 62-year-old retired security guard at a special presentation in Chicago.

Mr. Kerkofsky lost an arm in an accident when he was six. He was thence rejected for military service in World War II. Since then he has donated nearly 31 gallons of blood. The human body contains 10 or 12 pints of blood. Joe has donated more than 20 times that amount!

"Giving blood makes you feel like you are contributing life itself," he says. "There's no more precious a gift than life. Money can't buy the joy of giving to help someone who needs it."

THOUGHT TO PONDER:

Have you given the gift of blood? Are you an organ donor? These are the true gifts of life!

A Christmas Miracle

By Randall Steadman
Salt Lake City, Utah

Give as the sun gives light, a glad outpouring of the best that is in you.

Anonymous

WHY ME, LORD? Why me? Of all the days to work, why Christmas? I know. I know, I'm single. I'm the one without a family. But, that's just the point—at this rate, I'm never going to have a family!

Just look at this hospital ward. Four patients, count them, four. I guess someone has to be a nurse at Christmas, but why does it have to be me? After all, three of these women could care less. They're all but ready to go home anyway, and that just leaves Suzan. And, well, Suzan is never going home. A coma ... it's funny what we don't know about medicine. All we know is the body kind of goes to sleep to heal itself and the longer we stay comatose, the less chance there is we will ever wake up. For four months the doctors have been trying, for four months. I think they're about to give up. But, her husband will never give up, and each of her seven kids refuse to believe she's not coming home.

I think about Suzan a lot—every time I drive my car. One little accident and it's over, her whole life, over! A loving husband—boy, what I would give for a guy like that—and seven kids. One accident and it's over. Why doesn't someone tell them? With every passing day the chances go down that she will ever wake up, and after four months it's just not going to happen. Why do they just let them go on believing? Wouldn't it be kinder to tell them the truth?

Suddenly I hear footsteps. All of the visitors have gone, but, the sound I hear is still the sound of footsteps on the long hospital hall. And then I see them, seven beautiful children dressed in Sunday best. The father, carrying the baby, and each of the children, carrying a present for mother.

"Don't do it, Sandy. Don't start crying. Don't let your tears dampen their holiday. Be strong. Nurses deal with death every day. After all, it's part of my job. Just smile, Sandy, and wave like you always do. Don't let them know." But, as they pass, I turn and one small tear drops across my cheek. Just one little tear ... maybe they didn't see it. No, I'm sure they didn't see.

Down the hall I hear the voices. I imagine the embraces. I wonder what it would be like to be loved like that.

Then it started. One of the children began to sing, "We wish you a Merry Christmas. We wish you a Merry Christmas." First softly, and then louder, one by one the others joined in. I thought I must be hearing things because after a moment it was not the voice of a family I heard, but the voice of thousands.

Quickly I rose to my feet and made that somewhat long trek from the nurses' station to Suzan's room. I thought, "Dear God, why not me? Why Suzan? She had so much to lose and me, well, there is just me, and I'm not so sure anyone would really miss me anyway."

Suddenly, there was silence. The sound I heard was the sound of my heart beating and then the children screaming. Run, dear feet, run. And I was there. Six children, one husband, and a baby, all embracing mother. "Where am I?" she asked. "What are you doing here? And what are all these presents for?"

Somehow, some way, in God's own grace, He had seen fit to wake this sleeping beauty from her sleep. A miracle, a genuine Christmas miracle.

Slowly I found my way to the nurses' station. Slowly I found my way to my knees, to pray, to give thanks this Christmas day.

Being a nurse, I probably should have called first, so each of the doctors could congratulate themselves on another job well done. But, maybe, just maybe, the singing I heard was the voice of a heavenly choir. Maybe, just maybe, it was a wake-up call from heaven.

There was a handwritten note at the end of this story that read:

> *Dear Margie,*
>
> *This story happened fourteen years ago at LDS Hospital. Sandy was a friend of mine. I wish I had more to give to you this Christmas season, but all I have is the gifts of the heart.*

Margie told me that her friend was very apologetic that this story was all he had to give her for Christmas. Yet, she said, "This gift had the most value of any Christmas gift I've ever been given." She has used it many times over the years at Christmas when she has taught adult classes in her church, so this is a gift that has continued to bless many, many people.

THOUGHT TO PONDER:

Are you aware of miracles in your own life? Have you shared them with others? I have loved giving the book *Small Miracles* by Yitta Halberstam and Judith Leventhal as a gift. In it they say, "When a coincidence takes place, it is nothing more and nothing less than God tapping us on the shoulder, whispering, or at times even shouting, 'I'm here! I'm with you!' 'Coincidences,' the writer Doris Lessing once said, 'are God's way of remaining anonymous.' *Small Miracles* attempts to strip away that façade of anonymity and demonstrate that these seemingly random moments are instead the full and vital expressions of God's handiwork." Be on the lookout for the small miracles in your own life.

A Gift of the Soul

By Robin Maynard
Fridley, Minnesota

Giving of ourselves is the way we change the world at the end of our fingertips.
Richard F. Schubert

HAVE YOU EVER received a gift that was so beautiful that it touched your soul? Try as you may there is no way to repay this life-changing gift. I received such a gift through Mother Teresa. After many years of feeling that I was being called to see Mother Teresa in person, in November of 1996, I traveled to Calcutta to serve the poorest of the poor and hopefully meet her.

When I deplaned in India, I was amazed at the power of God. He had built a bridge to Calcutta for me by providing everything I needed for the journey—a traveling companion, money, time off work, and He even helped my husband and me through a crisis just days before departure.

Gerrie, my traveling partner, and I were thrilled when we arrived at the Mother House—the humble home of Mother Teresa and the Missionaries of Charity. Gerrie pulled a long string that was attached to a bell. Momentarily, a Sister opened the door, welcomed us and directed us to the chapel. We walked through the courtyard and then up the staircase. During the first few steps, I was compelled to look up at a crucifix of Jesus on the wall between the first and second flights of stairs. I had never seen a crucifix that showed blood from the wounds He bore. Once on the landing, I stopped and took a good, long look at Jesus. He had suffered! For some reason, seeing the blood brought His pain to life.

As I stepped into the chapel, I felt a tingle all over my body—the sensation of a dove flying so close that the flutter of the wings brushed me lightly. My burden and fears seemed far away upon entering this spirit-filled room. I immediately searched the room for Mother Teresa and was jolted when I realized Mother Teresa was only about ten feet away from me! After years of following her, admiring her, and thinking she was so unreachable and untouchable, there she was, sitting a few feet from me. I noticed she was deeply concentrating, and her gaze was set. Mother Teresa was not the least bit distracted by the new volunteers and visitors who were fixated on her. I followed her stare, curious to know what had her completely captivated. Mother Teresa was staring at Jesus on the Cross.

I watched the way she looked at Jesus—her entire body immersed in fervent, interactive prayer. I could see the love she had for Him and could feel that love emanating from her. There was something in the way Mother Teresa looked at Jesus that told me I was missing a very important piece of my faith. She looked to Him in a conversational way, as though He were answering her question. Her body language conveyed a living interaction between them and undivided attention. I was moved by the unwavering manner in which she beheld her Lord.

I could not help looking to the crucifix in a state of wonder. What was I missing? This cross was similar to the one on the landing of the staircase. It showed blood flowing from His wounds, but in addition, it had a message in big, black letters, "I THIRST." The words "I THIRST" struck me as if I had walked into an invisible brick wall and then stepped back to look at it. I was stunned. Without saying one word, Mother Teresa had led me to Jesus. She radiated Christ so fully that I couldn't see anyone but Him.

Immediately, I was given a soul-level revelation. I thought I had traveled to India to volunteer and possibly meet Mother Teresa; however, my soul knew a higher truth. My journey was for a spiritual reason. I was really thirsting for Jesus, for my faith, and for strength beyond my human body.

In that instantaneous moment, I felt touched by God. A tingle covered my body as new understanding and wisdom entered my mind: I could have an interactive, moment by moment relationship with God. I needed to be in communication with God for all my concerns, big and small. Jesus could help me with my daily problems. After all, He had taken human form and knew what being human was all about. I realized that the way to get closer to God was to understand Him through a relationship with Jesus.

While in the chapel, I prayed with new understanding. I believed that all of the adversity in getting there was part of a higher plan. My heart was flooded with gratitude. I felt God bless me with renewed strength and a deeper faith through Jesus Christ—all this only in the first minutes of my arrival to the Mother House chapel.

After the Mass, I put my shoes on and headed down the staircase. Once again, I stopped and looked at the Crucifix of Jesus on the landing. This time, I noticed the words "I THIRST." Just an hour before, I had been blind to it, but now, through Mother Teresa, I could finally see.

We all have received many gifts. The ones that matter most touch our heart and soul. You remember the kind word in your darkest hour or the smile someone gives you at a moment that is too sorrowful for words. Praise God for giving us these beautiful soul gifts, miracles performed, through people that we love, admire, or perhaps don't even know. Jesus, the hand of God, and the faithfulness of Mother Teresa eternally touched my life.

If you would like to read more about Robin's journey of faith, look for her book, *I THIRST: A Journey Toward Unconditional Faith.*

THOUGHT TO PONDER:
Is there someone who has deeply influenced your life who is still alive today? Write them a letter, or better yet, see if you can arrange to meet them in person.

A Gift From Above

By Carlos Conejo
Thousand Oaks, California

Every good gift and every perfect gift is from above, and cometh down from the Father of lights, with whom is no variableness, neither shadow of turning.

James 1:17

THE WORDS PIERCED me to the quick! They took my breath away … I was scared. I was mad. I felt betrayed! I had damaged goods. How could this be happening to me?

My wife's doctor had just referred us to an oncologist. I'd started out pre-med in college, and I knew that Oncologist meant … cancer!!

The two weeks we waited for an appointment seemed like an eternity. If it was cancer, wasn't two weeks too long? My God, what's wrong with these people?!

The Doctor told us: it was hydatidform-mole, a type of uterine cancer. This was the reason Diane couldn't stay pregnant. This was the reason she had miscarried four times. He told us he would try methyltrexate, a powerful chemotherapy drug that unfortunately would kill the good cells as well as the cancerous ones.

It might cause hair loss. Diane might not be able to tolerate different odors. He would monitor Diane for about six months, and, at the end of that time, he would give us an updated prognosis.

About the third dose or so, clumps of hair began to fall out of her head. Her beautiful eyebrows disappeared. Her olive skin took on a ghostly white pallor, and sure enough, she couldn't stand the smell of food cooking. I cooked while she stood outside on the patio or took a walk. Thank goodness it was summer, because many of our meals were eaten outdoors that year.

Six months into the treatment her bloodwork showed no progress. Meanwhile, our oncologist had taken on a new associate, a recent graduate from UCLA. This associate reviewed our case and gave us the good news that this type of cancer could be beaten. The bad news was that he had to double the dosage.

More hair loss followed, along with huge, nasty-looking sores in her mouth. There was a foul odor when she spoke. Was this the smell of death?

How could this be happening to me? How could God be giving me such a burden?

One day, Diane just looked at me with tears in her eyes ... "You know, you're not the one who's going through this. You're not the one who's dying!"

BAM! It hit me like a two by four across the face! How could I have been so insensitive, so selfish, so self-centered?

"Please forgive me. We're going to beat this together!"

"I don't think we can beat this together, she explained ..."

Did she want to divorce me because I'd been such a jerk?

"This is too big for the two of us," she continued. My heart stuck in my throat. I was waiting for the final blow. How could she manage this on her own?

"We need help," she said. "We need God's help. I'm going to the church down the street on Sunday. Let me know if you want to come along."

We hadn't been to church in five years. That day the sermon pierced our hearts like a giant bolt of lightening. We sobbed the entire time. Time after time, we returned, hand-in-hand sobbing like babies together. We found God ... and our marriage began to grow stronger. We got involved in a Bible-study group. People began praying for us, and laid hands on us.

About four months into the new dosage, we began to see definite improvement. It had been about ten months now—we were tired, but now there was some promise, a ray of hope. Diane was given a clean bill of health at the twelfth month—but she still had to be monitored every month for the next year. At the end of the year, the doctor gave us the "green light" to try for a baby if we wanted to. This seemed really far-fetched after the road we'd traveled.

We got pregnant on the very first try!

At the age of 37 my wife had Carleigh, who at this writing is now nine. Last year at the age of 46, my wife had Lucas who at this writing is now four months old. These are God's miracle children, His gifts to us. God is great!

THOUGHT TO PONDER:
In my mind all children are miracle children. Do you feel that way about yours?

The Gift of Feng Shui
By Linda Lenore
Redwood City, California

Give a man a fish and he will eat for a day. Teach him how to fish and he will eat for the rest of his life.

Unknown

WE NEVER KNOW when our flat-line, everyday existence is going to take a turn or a tumble, sending us down a different road or over the crest of the roller-coaster and down out of control. And are we going to refuse the ride, try to abort it, or go to the finish looking back with wonderment at the blessings which have occurred in our lives? Such was the situation on that eventful day when I walked into a workshop at a trade show, expecting to gain more design ideas.

It was the last day of the trade show—six long days walking in 4" pointed-toe shoes, sitting in seminars, and five nights of drinking and partying. My body, mind and spirit were not ready for much of anything that day, especially for what was about to transpire. The only saving grace was that I was ignorant of the event which would change my life forever.

Having checked out of the hotel, I was prepared to spend a few hours to attend another workshop or two and reconnect with a couple of the vendors before heading home. Perusing my catalog of the day's events, I found there wasn't much left which interested me, so I walked into the auditorium to hear a design program which could fill time. I was so early there was only one other person sitting in the auditorium.

At that point in my career I was a sponge for information, so I eagerly sat down in the front row in order to limit distractions once the program began, then pulled out a recently purchased book to keep me occupied. I was vaguely aware of the commotion from people entering behind me as I continued to read. Glancing at my watch, I realized it was about time for the lecture to start.

Turning my head to see how filled the room was, I discovered I was one of only a handful of people not of Asian descent. A strong feeling of discomfort engulfed me. Although I thought I was open-minded and non-judgmental, my background to that point had kept me from being in minority situations. I was literally surrounded on three sides by more than 400 people from different Asian cultures. It was so unsettling to me, I started to pick up my belongings to leave. Just then, the side door opened and a gentleman dressed in all black robes entered, followed by six people in a processional. I was trapped on all four sides!

Raised to be respectful of other people, I never considered getting up at this point. Most of the lectures had been 75 minutes long, so sitting for that period of time should not be a problem … so I thought. Then a gentleman came to the podium and began to speak, but it was not in English. What was I to do? I couldn't get up without everyone seeing me. I felt a sense of panic starting to overwhelm me when another person arose to his feet, translating the Mandarin words into my familiar English. I breathed a sigh of relief, <u>especially</u> when I discovered the lecture was to last three hours.

The Master discussed the use of mirrors and some furniture placement. He suggested the use of mirrors to bring in the sunlight, making the room feel bigger, brighter and more alive, connecting us with nature. This was familiar because we use mirrors in interior design for that purpose all the time.

He continued by stating that a negative situation would be created by placing the sofa close to the door with its back to the door; the "chi" would be blocked from entering the room, and people would feel uncomfortable having their backs to the door while sitting in the sofa. I didn't know what he meant by "chi", but again I could relate to this as "traffic flow". Through our common language of interior design, this Master was drawing me gently into <u>his</u> world, the world of Feng Shui.

Next he talked about a house, referring to the children, family and partnership areas within it. I assumed he was referring to a child's bedroom, the family room, and the master bedroom. I was wrong, but this assumption allowed me to follow along with an open mind. (He was referring to the subtle energies we have and can find in a dwelling through the use of a Ba-Gua map.)

Toward the end of this presentation, the discussion turned to placement of beds. I distinctly remember getting ready to leave while glancing up at the new transparency on the overhead. The floor plan resembled the floor plan of my house. There was only one room drawn and the placement of a bed within that room.

During the course of the morning I had been hearing the words "Good Feng Shui" and "Bad Feng Shui" without understanding the meaning of either. When the Master commented on this overhead in his native language, there was a loud gasp uttered from the audience. The translator began, "If this is a house with a child's room in this particular location and the bed is placed on this wall within the room, it is 'Bad Feng Shui.' It could be harmful to the child's health. In fact, it could be so bad for the child's health, the child could even die!"

I couldn't believe my ears! My heart started beating faster. My hands were sweating. I felt sick to my stomach. I wanted to scream, run, cry and throw-up all at once. On that overhead was a picture of my house and my son Jeff's room. Jeff had died just a few months before from a brain tumor at the age of 13 years.

What is he talking about? How could this be? How could he have known this? Any of this?

I grabbed my things and ran out of the room looking for a place to hide. Tears were pouring out of my eyes. I couldn't see where I was going. People were staring at me. I was having trouble breathing I was crying so hard. I went to the restroom thinking I might find a place to hide, but there were too many people. No privacy anyplace! I finally found a very dark secluded corner by a back security exit where I continued to sob for what seemed like hours.

An emotional wreck, I slowly calmed myself. Jeff's death had been a terrible shock to me. Basically a healthy teenager, Jeff had suffered a headache over Labor Day weekend which was finally diagnosed as a blood clot. After surgery, he recovered rapidly, but the swelling in his brain continued to increase to the point that he required a second operation.

It was during this second hospital stay that they discovered the malignant tumor. The doctors tried to remove it, but could not remove it all without leaving Jeff paralyzed. Before the surgery, a discussion had occurred between Jeff and the doctor regarding the possibility of paralysis. Jeff had told the doctor, "I want to be able to do everything I've been able to do". So the decision to play it safe in hopes that radiation and chemotherapy would stop this insidious disease had been made.

It didn't work. Jeff slipped into a coma six hours after the surgery was complete, only to be pronounced "brain dead" the following day.

Now, having somewhat composed myself, I was sitting on the cold cement floor of a foreign building in a strange city. Weak from the emotional drain and stunned by what I had heard, I looked at the program of events for the remainder of the day. There, in the same auditorium where this shocking information had been stated, was another workshop on Feng Shui—a continuation of the earlier program.

Every part of my body and mind said, "Get out of here! Run! Don't enter that building again." But some part deep within me which I had never known before, drew me back to that place.

Rather than sitting in the front row this time, I hid in the back by a door, able to leave at a moment's notice. It was in this second three hour seminar I heard weird suggestions such as placing beads in doorways to prevent money from flying out of the house and arranging beds differently to reduce the risk of a divorce. Neither of these made sense to my logical, skeptical Western mind.

Yet there was something about this person or the philosophy which was so profound it had touched my soul, a connection beyond all reasoning or experience which felt as though it must be both forbidden and sacred at the same time. Why did I stay? This was contrary to my Judeo-Christian upbringing. Was this the work of the Devil? Was I getting involved with a cult? I didn't know. I left the conference with an unquiet feeling and many questions.

A few months later I discovered a class on the topic of Feng Shui at a local university. As I signed up and entered the room, there he was again, the same man in a black robe—Professor Lin Yun, Master of the Black Sect

Tantric form of Feng Shui. Again the feelings of discomfort arose within me, my "flight syndrome" urging me to run, but the "fighter" part of my Being was telling me to stay. I sat in the back of the room, watching this man with the eyes of an eagle, noticing every movement, reading his body language.

Many weeks and months passed. I didn't believe him or the things he said. I questioned it all. It made no sense. But some part of me was "getting it". My design clients were benefiting from this information. The rooms were more humane and harmonious, the buildings more beautiful. My business increased from "word-of-mouth" referrals. The design awards followed.

For many years I studied under this incredible, spiritual being, trying to make sense of all that he said. It wasn't happening.

Life was getting more absurd. In the middle of a divorce and having to sell the house that I had poured all my love and energy into since Jeff's death, we had a 6.3 earthquake in Northern California. The town of Los Gatos, the town where we lived and where my daughter worked, was the epicenter.

That night I experienced the longest drive of my life, although it was only 10 miles. On the radio they told of the buildings that were down. Melanie, my daughter, was working in one of those buildings. People were trapped and feared dead. Having been late for my previous appointment, I hadn't stopped for gasoline for my van.

Now the gas stations were closed due to lack of electricity. I had to stop at the houses of several friends who raced cars in order to have gas to simply get home. I couldn't even drive to the downtown area where Melanie was.

Never have I been so relieved as when I rounded the corner of the driveway to see Melanie's car and her face, although pale from the trauma, greeting me. That sense of "coming home" and finding all I really needed in life, my loved ones, was there waiting for me.

That night I learned the deep, spiritual meaning behind Feng Shui, its amazing power. The words may respectively refer to "wind" and "water," the elements that have helped create this land on which we live and the elements without which we as human beings cannot exist, but it's more about the power of what is natural and how we as human beings live with nature.

As a culture, we generally are not in tune with the energies of nature. We ignore the fact that we live in desert areas which lack water unless we import it or it rains. Or we live close to water, ignoring the fact that the forces of water, combined with wind, could destroy our homes through floods, hurricanes, tidal waves or erosion.

I was living in an earthquake area, not paying attention to the power which might erupt at any time. On one level, I valued objects more than the priceless gifts which surrounded me, my family, including pets, friends and the health of all of us. That night a Higher Power decided many of the things I was to take with me into a new life and which items were to be left behind. Yes, it was very painful during the evening to clean-up and throw away the collections of a lifetime, but the memory of what is really important remains with me to this day.

The real meaning of Feng Shui is to learn about, and honor, the energies of the land on which we live plus honoring the energies of the people in our lives. Our homes, both our physical dwellings and the planet Earth, are but vehicles with which to do this. We are not in control of the Universe, but we do have a say in how we care for our lives, including the resources which surround us.

It took several more years for me to realize the profound message I was given that day in an auditorium in an unfamiliar city by a gentle man in an all black robe, through a language I didn't understand. But he communicated through another language we all do understand, the only language we all intuitively understand—that of spirit.

That day, and those words, changed my life forever. It challenged every one of my beliefs and led me into areas of discovery I could never have imagined. The journey encompassed body, mind and spirit.

Today I help others discover and explore Feng Shui in a gentle fashion, bringing richer experiences to the meaning of their lives. This can be accomplished through developing a home filled with love and light, creating a home with "Good Feng Shui".

Many objects were taken away that night in October, 1989, but something far more valuable was given to me—the gift of learning what really mattered. I learned to love, honor and respect the power and energies of this land and to love, honor and respect the living creatures that live on this planet, plants, animals and people.

Through the tragic death of a child and an earthquake, both of which shook the grounds of my existence, I was guided to a much stronger foundation for my life—a spiritual connection to my Higher Power. I lost a child and many possessions but I found my life purpose, sharing the beautiful, magical "Gift of Feng Shui".

THOUGHT TO PONDER:
Have you been blessed to find the gift of your life purpose?

Chapter Eight:

"Memorial Gifts"

When you were here
The constant smile you carried,
The song in your words and handiwork
Was a treasure shared with many, and with me.
We take new roads, never leaving you,
We are the spokes of your encircling spirit,
Open to all that we meet, taking joy
From your greater and greater reach.
©Andrew Grossman 1999
Newton, CT

ONE OF THE best ways to help overcome one's grieving is to find something to do in memory of a loved one or a friend. And the best gift we can give a grieving friend is to talk about that person, to keep his or her memory alive. When our second child died at Christmastime, I thought I could never survive, but the gifts of some wonderful friends made that time just a little bit easier. In this section you will read about the white rose and how much that meant to me.

The David Schulz family of Downers Grove, Illinois, gave us another precious gift. Each year, on December 21, Gavin's birthday, they picked a special book that would be appropriate for his age and dedicated it to our town library in his memory. On the year he would have been twenty one, I received a letter from them saying, "Now that Gavin is an adult in Heaven, we have decided to donate money to Habitat for Humanity in his name so that a family on earth can be helped in his memory." Not only did they acknowledge his life, but they kept his memory alive over all those years in such a dear and meaningful way.

As a family we, too, decided to do something in Gavin's memory. Through Compassion International we sponsored two little boys in Colombia, one from age seven until he graduated from high school, and another young man to age eleven when he left the program. We kept their pictures with our other family pictures and wrote to them regularly. It was a great comfort to know that even though we couldn't do anything materially for our son any longer, we could help another young man to have a better life here.

You will read some touching stories in this section about how both parents and friends have found precious ways to remember those who have passed on. My prayer is that they will trigger ideas for you so that when someone you know and love is grieving, you will not feel so helpless. No matter how strong one's faith, the desolation and loneliness of never again being able to hold and touch someone we love can only be healed by the gifts of love from others around us and from the assurance that that person's life DID make a difference. We can help by honoring their memories. Please remember as you read these difficult stories not to focus on the tragedies that occurred but rather to celebrate the legacy of love these precious ones have left behind. Use the memorial gift ideas as ways to help others who are grieving remember their loved ones in visible and concrete ways.

A Single White Rose

By Barbara A. Glanz
Sarasota, Florida

To live in the hearts we leave behind is not to die.

Thomas Campbell

IN 1971 I faced the most difficult experience of my life, one which has changed me forever. I had grown up in a small town in Iowa where families were the center of our lives, I loved dolls and babysitting, and I could hardly wait to be a mother! I even became a high school English teacher because I loved working with young people. In 1965 I graduated from the University of Kansas and began teaching in LaGrange, Illinois, in 1966 I married a wonderful man named Charlie, and on April 2, 1969, we were blessed with our first child, Garrett Wayne Glanz.

I felt in control of my life and filled with thanksgiving and anticipation for the future. We had saved all of my teaching paychecks and were able to put a down payment on a small English cottage in Western Springs, Illinois. Charlie was doing well in his work at the Chicago Tribune, and I found out I was pregnant again in early 1971. We were ecstatic!

I had a perfectly normal pregnancy, teaching adult swimming two mornings a week at the YMCA, and loving each moment of teaching our little son Garrett about our beautiful world. Our second child was due January 3, 1972. On December 20 I began having labor pains in the night, so we took Garrett to the neighbor's and went to the hospital. Since I was nearly fully dilated and only 2 1/2 weeks early, the doctor induced labor, and our second child, Gavin Ward Glanz, was born at 4:45 pm December 21, 1971. We spent the evening calling all our family and friends to share our joy, and both of us tried to get a much-needed good night's sleep. The next day the nightmare began!

When our pediatrician and personal friend, Dr. Allen, walked into my room early the next morning, I immediately knew something was wrong. With great difficulty, he told us that he thought our baby son had a congenital heart defect and they were taking him by ambulance to Cook County Children's hospital to the best pediatric cardiologist in the area. However, he said not to give up hope because often open heart surgery could be performed and the children could be fine, so Charlie followed the ambulance, and I began the awful waiting.

Later that afternoon, Charlie called to tell me that our baby had died. The problem turned out to be with his lungs, and there was no way they could have saved him even though he weighed over 7 pounds. He was buried on Christmas Eve.

I know that never again in my life will I feel so helpless and so completely empty—I would have traded my life for his in an instant! Because none of our family or friends ever got to know him, hold him, or even see his picture (the hospital didn't take one), they had a difficult time relating to our grief, and although they were sad for us, they really felt little connection to our son. As a result, much of the time Charlie and I felt alone in our deep love for him and in the terrible loss of not being able to watch him grow and become an adult.

I tried to go on with my life, especially since we had a young son who needed me; however, there were days that I didn't think I could make it through until noon, so deep was my grief and sense of loss. Someone about that time gave me a copy of a book called "I Ain't Much, Baby, But I'm All I've Got!" that has forever influenced my life and helped make my recovery possible. It was by Jess Lair, a wonderful Christian man, who talked about living five minutes at a time. Many days I could not face even one more hour, but I could always get through five minutes! I consciously held onto that thought plus my faith in a loving God as the means to my survival. That was one of the most beautiful lessons I learned through all my pain—

to be fully in the present and to treasure every minute of every day. However, I still struggled with people's reluctance to talk about our son, their lack of memories of him, and the terrible void there was in my life.

On December 21,1972, the day which would have been Gavin's first birthday, the doorbell rang, and there at the doorstep was a deliveryman from the florist. He had a small bud vase holding one single white rose. With it was a card from some very dear friends that read, "This is in memory of a very special life, one which we know will make a difference in this world—Gavin Ward Glanz." And each year for many years on December 21, that single white rose has arrived on our doorstep—a symbol that someone in this often indifferent, rushed world of ours does remember the life of our little boy.

And they were right—he has made a difference in this world through me, the person I have become because of his life and death, and the abiding message of hope I am able to share with others as I speak all over the world.

A beautiful post script to this story is that on May 17, 1998, our first little grandson was born, and what did they name him? Gavin William Glanz. How very blessed we are! Our son lives on through this precious gift of new life, and we will always celebrate our new little Gavin's birthday with one single white rose.

THOUGHT TO PONDER:

This story exemplifies how a simple gift of remembrance and caring can help heal a broken heart and become a family tradition. The giver of this single white rose will never fully know the difference she has made in a family's life. Yet that is the ultimate CARE package—when it is given with no thought of any reward.

Down to Earth

By Penny Wallace
Battle Creek, Michigan

It is not how many years we live, but what we do with them. It is not what we receive, but what we give to others.

Evangeline Booth

I HAVE AN angel who is always looking over me—my son, David. On May 25, 1989, David was killed in a head-on collision caused by a reckless driver. David was 8 years old.

David was in the second grade with only 3 weeks to go before the summer vacation was to begin. He was a very active eight-year-old, involved in ice hockey, soccer, and baseball. He was especially looking forward to his first year in rocket football.

His death was devastating to the entire community. We received an overwhelming response and support from his classmates, teachers, fellow teammates, coaches, and friends.

The parents of his classmates collected money and purchased benches for the playground at the school in Memory of David. The Ice Hockey Association, David's teammates and parents, had a dedication ceremony on his 10th birthday. A flag pole and bronze marker was permanently laid outside the hockey rink in Memory of David.

With those big blue eyes, smiling face, and shining personality, David made a lasting impression on all those he knew. Over the past 10 years, I have had contact with David's friends and classmates and watched them grow into young adults, in my heart, always wondering what David would have grown to be.

May 25, 1999, was the 10-year anniversary of David's death. This year has been especially difficult to overcome. On June 1, 1999, David was supposed to graduate from high school. Another milestone missed, another hurdle to overcome.

As graduation neared, those around me were planning celebrations for their graduates, and graduation announcements were being sent. What would have been David's senior year was coming to an end; the air was filled with excitement. As I tried to share in the excitement of those around me, inside my heart was breaking. One of the most exciting times for a child and his or her parents was one of the most miserable for me—I had nothing to celebrate.

Then my earth-bound angels appeared—a day never to forget. It was a Sunday, May 15, only 16 days till graduation. I had just returned home when several cars pulled into the driveway behind me. I turned to see what all the commotion was and there before me stood my son's classmates. As they approached me, they tearfully presented me with a beautiful bouquet of flowers and a 1999 Yearbook—dedicated to my son. There in the pages of the senior class portraits was an enlarged picture of my son, David. Beside it was a special poem written by his girlfriend from the second grade. Each page was signed by his classmates with poems, stories, and goodbyes.

His classmates gave us special passes to attend the Baccalaureate and Graduation ceremonies. On graduation night David's best friend tearfully gave me a graduation tassel to keep to honor David. A unique Senior tradition in our community is making a video which includes snap shots of special events, special times, and special friends during the school years of that class. The video is shown during the Baccalaureate ceremony. To my surprise, the video included pictures of David with his classmates in their younger years, together with a special dedication in his memory.

Words cannot express the heartfelt joy and pride these individuals have brought to me. They have grown to become very exceptional young adults; how proud their parents can be! I, too, am proud of my son for becoming the person he was in eight short years. His classmates demonstrated how special he was to them by celebrating and commemorating his eight short years of life and the impact that life had on them.

These individuals made a very difficult, almost unbearable, time for me very special. They made me feel very much a part of this milestone in their lives, as well as in what would have been a milestone for David. Thanks to my Earth-Bound Angels for making the impossible ... possible.

THOUGHT TO PONDER:
Is there someone in your family, workplace, or community who has suffered a loss? One of the best gifts we can give them is to help keep the memory of their loved one alive.

A Commitment of Love

As told by Hanthip Amornsing
Phuket, Thailand

The monument of a great man is not of granite or marble or bronze. It consists of his goodness, his deeds, his love and his compassion.

Alfred Montapert

ALL HER LIFE Hanthip (nicknamed "Jang") wanted her father, Somsak, to quit smoking. She offered him good grades, being on her best behavior, and many other bribes over the years. However, nothing worked. He sometimes quit for a short while but always started again. In the summer of 1999 Jang married a young man from the United States and would be leaving her family to come to a new land. She said her father never cried in front of her, but her mother told her that on the day she was leaving, while they were at the airport, her father went into the men's room and wept because his precious daughter was going to be so far away. At that moment he threw his cigarettes in the toilet.

He came out and told Jang that he had decided to never smoke again as a memorial to his love for her, and each time that he thought about wanting a cigarette or when he saw someone else smoking, he would think of her and how much he loved and missed her. That was the last time she saw her father and that was his very last cigarette!

Her mother tells her that whenever her father meets a smoker, he tells them how much he misses his daughter in the USA. Her mother is amazed that he has been able to quit. But this time he says it was easy—because it was a tribute to his daughter and his undying love for her!

THOUGHT TO PONDER:
What a beautiful way for a father to show his love for a daughter! When my father died of a heart attack at age 62, my husband and I decided to give up smoking in his memory. He had always been a heavy smoker, and we knew this had contributed to his early death. Even though we had tried to quit several times, this time was easy because we had made a commitment. It was a gift to my dad. Is there something harmful in your life that you could give up as a gift to those who love you?

A Celebration of Mom

By Laurie Trice
Kenosha, Wisconsin

What we do for ourselves dies with us—what we do for others remains and is immortal.

Albert Pike

(THIS WAS PART of a letter to me from Laurie after the death of her mother. In 1998 I had shared a story about her mother and how she had made button dolls along with a story she wrote about them for each of her grandchildren in my book CARE Packages for the Home—Dozens of Ways to Regenerate Spirit Where You Live.)

My mom's funeral was beautiful. It truly was a celebration of her life. One of the church musicians, a dear friend of mom's for years, sang the Ray Bottz song, "Thank You." It was so very fitting. My mom mentioned near the end of her life that she felt she hadn't been bold enough in sharing her faith. She felt she didn't make much of an impact in doing the Lord's work. She was so wrong! It was obvious at her funeral that she was wrong. So many people shared with our family all she had done to impact their lives. She changed many lives.

Something very special took place at mom's funeral. Our family had asked my mom's dearest friend, Midge Harter of Stratford, Wisconsin, to say a few words. Midge decided to share mom's "claim to fame," her published story about the button dolls in your book CARE Packages for the Home. She held up the book and read the title and author. She then took the time to read the entire story. Everyone laughed as she read through the details of buttons on clothes for each one of us kids. However, none of us remembered that the story ended the way it did:

"Someday when the grandmother is in heaven, she will look down and see the grand-daughters smile at their little boys or girls when they hang you on the Christmas tree, and she will know that love is passed on to future generations."

Barbara, I'm so glad you encouraged me to share my family's ideas for the book. It truly is a wonderful family legacy. When mom's story was published and the book was out, it was at a time when she was already experiencing serious physical problems. It was such a lift for her. This year she bought a copy of the book for each granddaughter for their birthdays. She wrote something for each granddaughter inside the book. Now that she's gone, I know the granddaughters will cherish their button dolls and books even more. What a blessing your book has been to our family!

Here is the original story from my book, *CARE Packages for the Home-Dozens of Little Things You Can Do to Regenerate Spirit Where You Live:*

Give Handmade Gifts

THE IDEA:

A handmade gift has always communicated to me someone's special caring. It is as if they put a little bit of their own spirit into the gift, so the gift becomes a valued treasure.

THE IDEA IN ACTION:

Laurie Trice tells how her mother, Doris Kunkel of Stratford, Wisconsin, made each of the grandchildren a special Christmas ornament:

"It was a doll with buttons for arms and legs and a cute dress and hat. While the doll was darling, the story she put with it was even cuter. Mom's button box was always a treasure to all of us kids and grandchildren. Now each grandchild has some of those treasures in their ornament. The story includes the names of all of us kids which makes it even more special to the grandchildren."

Cute as a Button

Many, many years ago we were big globs of plastic in a place called a factory. We were poured into molds, and we came into being in all shapes and sizes. They punched holes in us and called us "buttons." They put us on cards and then in boxes—my, it was dark in there! Then we were put on a truck and taken to a place called Marshfield, Wisconsin.

Some nice ladies put us on a rack, and we were able to watch all the people come and go. We were very sad when no one picked us. One day the store lady threw us in a bin and put up a sign, "10 cents a card." How humiliating! We were worth much more.

One day a very nice lady came in with two small children. She didn't have a lot of money and seemed very pleased to see us. We were so happy when she picked us and took us home with her.

She began to sing and sew, and soon some of us were on a dress for a girl named Sandy. Sandy was the oldest and looked out for the other two. She liked to play school, and maybe that is why she's a teacher today.

Then the lady made a shirt for Dale. It's a good thing we had a "spirit of adventure" because we walked beams, climbed trees, and crawled under barbed wire fences. Life sure wasn't dull for us!

The lady then made a dress for Theresa. Theresa liked to play with pill bottles and bandage up our broken arms and legs. I suppose that's why she is a nurse today.

Soon we were cut off all these garments and put in a box. It was sad to be in a dark place again, but one day the lady opened the box, and what was this—two new girls, one named Laurie and one named Susie.

The lady began to sing and sew, and pretty soon we were on a shirt for Susie and a shirt for Laurie. It was fun in the sun again. Laurie had a friend named Sara, and they liked to take a picnic lunch and go to the woods. They let Susie tag along because she had no one to play with. They did 4-H projects, and we all went to the fair. They did a lot of fun things, and we were all very happy. When Susie's brothers came along, she played ball with them, and we called her our "little tomboy."

Now, with 3 boys, the lady opened the box again and began to sing and sew, and pretty soon we were on shirts and pajamas for 3 boys, David, Mark, and Scott.

David liked to wrestle, and his favorite sport was to wrestle his brother Mark. He liked baseball, too, but we weren't too happy when he slid into base on his stomach and almost popped his buttons!

I guess the best word for Mark was "impulsive." He went out the door so fast he ripped of his buttons. He liked to step on nails, ride three wheelers, and knock down football players and then help them up. Life was never dull for us, and those of us on pajamas were glad for a quiet night's sleep.

Then there was Scott. We felt sorry for him because he was so little and his brothers were so big. They liked to take him along to play football with the neighbors, and I think the only thing they didn't knock out of him was his music. He liked to go to his room and lock the door for some quiet time, and even the nice lady sometimes wished she could find a room where no one could find her.

Soon the house was quiet, and we were all back in the box again—and we still didn't like the dark. We were there a long time, but one day the nice lady opened the box and dumped us all out on the bed. She began to sort and line us all up. We were happy because we were going to have some fun again.

But, what was she doing? She was stringing us up and laying us in piles. We watched while she made a doll with just a head and a body and then put a dress on it. To our surprise, WE were the arms and legs! She wasn't singing when she put the hair on because the glue gun and the hair were not cooperating. Soon she put on a hat and a flower, and then she smiled and said, "You're as cute as a button!"

Then she lined us all up and said, "You are going on a new adventure. You are going to Granddaughters who will love and care for you. You will hang on their Christmas trees, and you will watch them grow up and graduate from high school and go off to college and marry and start a home of their own. As each Granddaughter places you on her tree, she will remember she had a Grandmother who prayed for her and who loved her very much."

"Someday when the Grandmother is in heaven, she will look down and see the Granddaughters smile at their little boys or girls when they hang you on the Christmas tree, and she will know that love is passed on to future generations."

THOUGHT TO PONDER:

What a wonderful gift this Grandmother gave of herself! Anyone can create a similar story and gift to give to family members as a special treasure that will communicate their love and live on forever and ever.

Four Mothers with Love,
A Millennium Tribute Calendar

By Carole Copeland-Thomas
Milton, Masschusetts

The dead hold in their hands only what they have given away.

Carl Sandburg

OUR LIVES CHANGED forever when each of our precious sons died accidentally in 1997. The impressions of their fatal moments are permanently etched in our souls and have marked a new direction in the way that we think and what we do. Our families have learned how to pick up the pieces and only skip one heartbeat when our beloved boys' names are called out.

Although we have collectively cried an ocean of tears and continuously utter silent prayers for the safety and welfare of our living children, we will never forget each golden moment that we shared with Keone, Harvard, Deshaun, and Mikey.

"Four Mothers with Love" was a millennium tribute calendar published in 2000—dedicated to the lives of our children who lost their lives between June and July of 1997. Rather then silently suffering their deaths, we have decided to celebrate the gifts that they brought to the world. All were in school pursuing their life dreams. All made mistakes like other young people on their journey to adulthood. All had a passion of being the best and developing to their fullest potential. All had reached a certain level in life where their real purpose was being fulfilled. All believed in the awesome power and grace of God.

Unlike other stories about troubled African American young males prone to violence, excessive drugs, and social unrest, it was important for us to tell the other side of the story so often withheld from newspapers and television reports. Our sons were not troubled, managed to stay away from criminal activity, and in many ways were role models for others. Their loss leaves an empty hole for humanity to fill with the decency and compassion that they shared with others. Their smiles, jokes, teen pranks, and intellect will be sorely missed. Their love for their families has kept us from falling apart.

Keone Jamel Glover, age 19, died on June 22, 1997, in Boston. He was a student at Newbury College. Keone drowned while trying to save another teenager. That young man also drowned. Keone lived in Boston, Massachusetts.

Deshaun Raymond Hill, age 20, died on July 3, 1997, in California. He was a rising junior at Harvard University. Deshaun was accompanied by Harvard Stephens and another young student in the automobile that crashed as the three began their Fourth of July holiday weekend. The third passenger survived the crash. Deshaun lived in Milwaukee, Wisconsin. Harvard Clarence Nabrit Stephens, age 19, died on July 3, 1997, in California, in the same crash as Deshaun Hill. He also was a junior at Harvard University. Harvard lived in Brentwood, Tennessee.

Mickarl Darius Thomas, Jr. (Mikey), age 17, died on June 14, 1997, in Boston. He was a recent Milton High School graduate and would have started his freshman year at Morehouse College. He died in a single car accident in Boston. Mikey lived in Milton, Massachusetts.

The Mothers are Rhonda Glover, Mary Ann Hill, Dr. Barbara Nabrit-Stephens, and myself, Carole Copeland-Thomas.

"Four Mothers with Love," Carole explained, "was my personal idea which I felt would best express the joys and sorrows I felt as a mother who had lost a child. Realizing that I was not alone in my journey, I reached out to three other mothers who had also lost their sons."

The calendar was filled with family stories and pictures of each young man and described the personal legacies that they left behind. Important Black history dates and events were highlighted each month, as well as information about Student Safety Month observed each June. There was something for everyone in "Four Mothers with Love." Contact Carole at www.tellcarole.com for more information on this process.

THOUGHT TO PONDER:
These beautiful women have found a way not only to memorialize their sons but to help others in their memory. We give the most precious gift when we use our pain to help others. What might you do as tribute to someone you have lost?

Life Goes On

By Suzanne Aiken
Arlington, Massachusetts

What a man does for others, not what they do for him, gives him immortality.
Daniel Webster

Life goes on and so do we
Yet softly with your memory
Tucked fondly in a special place
Our hearts remember your sweet face
With smiles, with tears, at times with pain
But with memories of your love we gain
The strength and faith to go on through

The trail you blazed to lead us to
Our heavenly destination where we will be
Wrapped in your arms eternally!

THOUGHT TO PONDER:

Suzanne wrote this poem as a tribute to her husband who died suddenly at age 38, leaving her with three young children.

The Memorial Brick

By Kathy Pacey, Tommy's loving Mommy
Woodridge, Illinois

Love is the only thing that we can carry with us when we go, and it makes the end so easy.

Louisa May Alcott

ON SUNDAY, JULY 11, the Downers Grove Public Library dedicated a new brick. (As a fundraiser, you could buy a single or double brick and have it engraved with your message). Tim and I pitched in with Dave and Karen Putnam, John and Sue Freeman, and Mike and Maribeth Kavanaugh to buy a double brick bearing all of our sons' names. What follows is my "brick story":

"One Paver Stone, Four Sons and the Mothers Who Love Them"

Every brick does indeed have a story, though I doubt there is another quite like ours. Our brick is not simply in memory of a special occasion or person. Our brick represents so much more. It's about beginnings and endings; joys and sorrows; loss and survival; mothers and sons; the young and the old; the past and the future; love of this world and the next. Our brick represents the yin and yang of life itself.

It represents the beginning of our grief journey at the ending of our son's lives; the joy of friendship borne of life's greatest sorrow; the loss of four sons and survival of four mothers; the young preceding the old in death; honoring the past while preparing for the future; our love shared in this world and extending into the next. Our brick represents a bond formed between four women from four decades of life who see no differences, only commonalities in their relationship with one another.

When one reads our brick, "Forever Loved, Ken Putnam, William Kavanaugh, John Freeman, Tommy Pacey," one might think these boys were related, or were friends, or perhaps died tragically together. Our children are not related, nor were they friends. Our children did not live together, nor did they die together. In fact, our sons were total strangers in this life, but within eight months they passed, one by one, from this life into the next.

Prior to the deaths of our sons, only two of us were acquainted. I am a pharmacist and knew Karen Putnam for years, as she frequented my pharmacy. I'll never forget the day in June, 1995, when she came in to inform me that their youngest son, Ken, age 28, had died in an auto crash out west on May 23rd. It knocked the wind out of me—I was shocked and filled with disbelief. "Oh no! This can't be happening to someone I know!" I thought. My heart went out to them, but I didn't know what to say. Little did I know three short weeks later we'd receive the ominous news that our only child, Tommy, age 2 1/2 years, was terminally ill with a degenerative brain disease, with no treatment prospects. A true medical mystery—in this day and age!

While Karen mourned her loss and I attempted to accept my fate, Maribeth Kavanaugh's firstborn, William, died in a vehicular accident on July 4, 1995. At the time, she was eight months pregnant with their second child. Along with the shock and the pain came premature labor. However, Maribeth was blessed with another son, David William.

As Maribeth tried her best to resume parenting amidst her heartache, we kept trying to obtain a specific diagnosis for Tommy. We knew it was a leukosystrophy, we just wanted to know which one. Tommy was recovering from a diagnostic brain biopsy as Sue Freeman's eldest son, John, age 23, died on October 2, 1995, due to a non-traumatic cerebral hemorrhage. Although John was a hemophiliac, this tragic turn of events was quite unexpected.

The holidays came and went, and another year began. Karen, Maribeth and Sue tried to find the strength to begin a new year without their precious sons, as I sat holding our comatose son in my arms, not knowing which day would be his last. That day came January 7, 1996. His diagnosis came six months later: vanishing white matter disease, a brand new leukodystrophy, with only 16 diagnosed cases worldwide. It was a relief to know.

In less than eight months' time we four mothers had experienced the unthinkable—the most difficult loss imaginable: the death of a child. We all attend a monthly grief support group, Bereaved Parents of the USA, www.Bereavedparentsusa.org. On the first Friday of each month, one has a good chance of finding us "Four Musketeers" at Redeemer Lutheran Church in Hinsdale, Illinois, from 8 to 10 pm. We all became acquainted through this group, and over the years our friendship has blossomed. We support each other, not just once a month, but on a daily basis, being especially attentive on those very difficult anniversary dates.

We're fond of saying that our children are hanging out in heaven together as a result of our friendship here on earth, but who's to say—perhaps it was THEY who orchestrated our friendship down here from up above. Either way, it's a comforting thought.

Since all of us are avid readers, we thought it extremely fitting to acknowledge our very special bond of friendship by honoring all our children on one brick. Thank you for giving us a "concrete" memorial to our four very precious beloved children. Thank you for taking an interest in our story—for giving us a chance to tell it, and for listening. You have no idea what a gift that is to a bereaved parent, particularly as the years roll by.

Please, the next time you meet a bereaved parent, or see one you already know, DO mention their child. It's music to our ears!

THOUGHT TO PONDER:

For many of us, the comfort of a concrete memorial is a very special gift. When our little boy died, a wonderful friend dedicated a book to the library in his name each year on his birthday. The book was always appropriate to the age he would have been. Even years later, I loved to go to the library and check out those books. I know that each child who reads them will think about our little boy! Always remember Kathy's advice and share memories of loved ones with those who are left. They will appreciate that gift more than you can ever know.

Luminaria for Jason

About Nancy Stein
Naperville, Illinois

When the oak is felled the whole forest echoes with its fall, but a hundred acorns are sown in silence by an unnoticed breeze.

Thomas Carlyle

NANCY STEIN FROM Naperville, Illinois, whose teenage son Jason was killed in a boating accident, shared how she keeps his memory alive in a beautiful way. Every year at the beginning of December, she buys special luminaria bags. Then she sends one to each of her son's friends and family who are scattered all over the country.

She asks them to decorate the bag in a way that helps them remember their friend, Jason. Sometimes they attach a photograph taken with

Jason, others write letters of remembrance or poems, and some even make a picture or collage of things they loved to do together. They then send the decorated bags back to her, and on Christmas Eve she puts them around Jason's grave at the cemetery. It becomes a healing for them all—a special celebration of Jason and what his life meant to each of them.

Nancy says that she receives close to 100 bags each year from many people who knew Jason. She invites anyone who wants to come to the cemetery on Christmas Eve night where they each light a candle as music is played, and they sing "Silent Night." This year the young woman who had received both Jason's lungs sent a luminaria bag to thank Jason for giving her life back to her. Nancy and Jason's ten-year-old brother Corey make a copy of each of the bags and put the pictures in a binder as an ongoing memory.

THOUGHT TO PONDER:

The holidays are the most difficult times for those of us who have lost a loved one. Ignoring our pain and trying to make things "normal" is not helpful. One of the best gifts you can give to someone who is grieving, especially at the holidays, is to encourage them to share memories of the person they have lost. We need to know that the lives of our loved ones has made a difference in this world:

So for now I'll wipe away the tears
And join with loved ones dear
To celebrate this Christmas time,
For I know that, in my heart, you're here.

Forever Frogs

By Holly Wright
Lakewood Ranch, FL

When we grow old, there can only be one regret—not to have given enough of ourselves.

Eleonora Duse

IN EARLY 2006, Payton Wright, age 4, began complaining of a pain in her knee. Thinking at first that it was nothing more than growing pains, her parents, Holly and Patrick, took her to the doctor, where they were told that the pain would probably go away on its own. When the pain persisted, The Wrights were told that it was probably juvenile arthritis, or perhaps diskitis.

After a few weeks with no improvement, Dr. Bob Morelli, the ER doctor at All Children's Hospital in St. Petersburg, FL ordered an MRI. On May 17, 2006, just weeks after her 4th birthday, Payton was diagnosed with cancer when the MRI revealed a tumor on her spine and pelvis. Always worried about everyone else, as she was wheeled into her first surgery Payton looked at her worried father and said, "Don't worry Dad. It's gonna be a good day."

Payton fought her entire battle with the attitude that everyday was going to be a good one. Doctors determined that Payton had Medulloepithelioma, a very rare form of brain cancer, and one for which there was no treatment protocol and very little hope for recovery. First at All Children's and later at Duke University Medical Center in Durham, NC, doctors pieced together Payton's treatment, which included intense rounds of chemotherapy and radiation. In August of 2006, Payton was paralyzed from the waist down due to the tumor's compression of her spine. She received as much radiation as a human body can tolerate, but the tumor continued to grow. Payton continued to fight, and she was able to graduate with her pre-school class in May of 2007. However, the cancer continued to spread, and on May 29, 2007, Payton Wright passed away at the age of 5.

Forever Frogs is a company founded on the strength and determination of a 5-year old little girl with brain cancer named Payton Makenna Wright. Frogs were always part of Payton's life. She loved to follow them around outside and talk to them as if they were her buddies. During her battle with brain cancer including long hospital stays and weeks without playing with her friends, her mom gave her a small silver frog in the hopes of cheering her up. Payton loved it and carried it around in her pocket always. She would tell everyone that it gave her the strength to fight her cancer.

Forever Frogs was started to honor Payton's life by three moms and Payton's best friend, Brooke. They share, "Every time you design and buy a bag, we will donate a portion of the proceeds to **The Payton Wright Foundation.** We are passionate about their mission to support pediatric brain cancer research, assist families who have a child with brain cancer and support cancer research and care organizations throughout the country. Raising awareness and raising funds are ways we can stomp out pediatric brain cancer, together.

We've lovingly placed a frog on every handmade bag to remind us of her. We not only celebrate Payton and her passion for life, but we celebrate American companies and American workers. All of our high-quality designer fabrics and handmade bags are produced in the U.S.A. We're honored to support American companies that help keep our communities thriving. Our hope is that Payton's frog and our dedication to keeping jobs in the U.S.A. will inspire you and become your symbol of strength throughout your life."

Patrick and Holly Wright saw how courageously their daughter fought, and they promised her that they would never stop fighting. The Payton Wright Foundation and Forever Frogs were created both in Payton's memory and with her fighting spirit, so that children with brain cancer will know that "it's gonna be a good day!" Their promise to Payton was that they would do whatever they could to help other families caring for a child with brain cancer.

Mission Statement

The Payton Wright Foundation is committed to raising awareness and funds for pediatric brain cancer research, helping families who have a child with brain cancer, and supporting organizations tied to cancer research and care.

THOUGHT TO PONDER:

Could you start a Foundation which celebrates someone you love? For more information on The Payton Wright Foundation, visit their website at www.paytonwright.org and to design and order a custom bag visit Forever Frogs at www.foreverfrogs.com.

When the great finals come, each one will be asked five questions:

First: What did you accomplish in the world with the power that God gave you?
Second: How did you help your neighbor and what did you do for those in need?
Third: What did you do to serve God?
Fourth: What did you leave in the world that was worthwhile when you came from it?
Last: What did you bring into this new world which will be of use here?

J. Stanley Durkee

Chapter Nine:

"Pass It Along Gifts"

thank the teacher who helped me
thank the pastor who helped the teacher
thank the child who helped the pastor
thank the mother who helped the child
thank the stranger who took a moment
thank those who benefit
no need to thank me

©Andrew Grossman 1999
Newton, CT

I FIRST BECAME especially aware of the joy of Pass-It-Along gifts when many years ago I received in the mail a little card that read, "The world is more special because you're in it," and on the back it read "Pass It On® cards," Argus Communications. The idea was to enjoy the card and then to pass it on to someone who had brightened your world. I not only have ordered thousands of these little cards to share with friends and audiences, but I have also created my own card that reads, "Thank you for CARE-ing!" I know that these small cards have touched many lives.

Sometimes it is difficult to "let go" of things which bring us pleasure, but what is so exciting to me is that it brings even more pleasure to share a treasure with someone else who will enjoy it. Lately, I have decided to think much more about giving gifts of possessions that are special to me and that

I know another person would enjoy instead of buying a "new" gift for them. How fun it is when someone admires something you have, to simply GIVE it to them! And somehow, as we pass these gifts along, we are also sharing a part of our spirit and love along with the gift.

The Little Brown Bear

By Barbara A. Glanz
Sarasota, Florida

Charity is twice blessed—it blesses the one who gives and the one who receives.

WHO WOULD EVER have thought that a small little brown bear could have such an impact on so many lives?

In 1999 when my husband Charlie was diagnosed with lung cancer and had to have part of a lung removed, he received a very special CARE Package from Cheryl Perlitz, a speaker friend of mine. Accompanying it was this note:

There are so many who will be with you both all the way through this journey, no matter where it leads and how rough and tough it gets. Hopefully that will make the path a little smoother for you.

I am sending you this little brown bear that was given to me the day after my husband Tom died by my childhood friend, Marjory. Marjory was given this little guy by a friend when she was recuperating from colon cancer surgery. When she finally knew she was "a survivor," Tom died, and it was time to pass him on to me.

Those cute little beady eyes watched over me and reminded me that I am loved. For four years I have had him sitting on the table next to the bed. So now I've finally "rounded

the bend", and I think he has another duty to perform. I'll miss him, but I know he will
be in the perfect home.

That little brown bear sat on the nightstand next to Charlie's bed, even on
the many days when he was in the hospital, until his unexpected death in
May of 2000. From that day on, I "adopted" the bear as my soul mate and
confidant as I worked through the loss of my husband and then a sub-
sequent move two years later that involved the loss of EVERYTHING that
was familiar in my life. He bore the brunt of many nights of agonizing tears
and aching loneliness, and he was always there waiting when I came back to
an otherwise empty home after my many travels and speaking engagements.
He truly was an anchor in my life as he had been for Marjory, Cheryl, and
Charlie.

Just before Christmas four and a half years since Charlie died, I began to
realize that I was finally nearly whole again. I had made some wonderful
friends in my new home and I truly felt as if I finally "belonged" here, I had
started dating and had met some wonderful men, and I found hope and joy
in my life again for the first time in the nearly six years since Charlie had
gotten sick. I knew it was time to share my little bear with someone else in
need.

I had been praying for several days about who needed the bear the most.
On Tuesday of that week I received a call from Jeff Fendley, a client of
mine who has become a precious friend. His dear wife, Caroline, died last
fall after an agonizing bone marrow transplant, leaving Jeff with two young
sons, including Daniel and Andre, whom they had just adopted from
Russia. Jeff has a very stressful fulltime job and no family in the area, so he
was just holding on by a thread these days and had had no time to even
grieve his wife. After that call, I KNEW that Jeff and his boys needed the
bear.

That night, amidst a lot of tears, I took several pictures of my angel bear,
packaged him up in a pretty gift bag, and the next day mailed him off to
my friend, Jeff. A part of me felt as if I were sending away my best friend,
and there were a few moments of panic, thinking, "What if something

happens and I need him again?" But then my new, stronger self took over, and I realized that this was a life marker moment for me: I no longer needed the constant reassurance that I was loved. I knew that in my heart, and that was enough. And best of all, in my healing, I could share the gift of caring with someone else who really needed a special little friend right now.

Who would ever have thought that a small little brown bear could have such an impact on so many lives? I wonder where his next home might be ...

THOUGHT TO PONDER:
Can you start a CARE-ing tradition like this with those you love?

"Caring Is Contagious" Cards

By Katherine Wahl
Bellmore, New York

Giving never moves in a straight line—it always moves in circles! It goes round ... and round ... and round.

Robert H. Schuller

ORIGINALLY, MY LITTLE yellow business card was entitled "A GIFT FOR KATHERINE." I designed it to pacify guests who were invited to my annual birthday party. My friends were quite uncomfortable attending without a gift in hand. Repeated attempts to assure them that the only gift I wanted was "the pleasure of their company" fell on deaf ears.

Many frustrating conversations ensued. Hence, I created my "gift card" as somewhat of a compromise. It was my attempt to promote spiritual gifts of the heart in lieu of materialistic ones. As Emerson once said, "We give of ourselves when we give gifts of the heart: love, kindness, joy, understanding, sympathy, tolerance, forgiveness." I wanted my cards to exemplify this sentiment.

I gave each invitee a "gift card" and asked them to follow the instructions on the back of the card when they felt the time was appropriate:

Perform an act of kindness

*Make someone smile * Give a compliment*
*Listen intently * Do a favor * Help a stranger*

Ask just one thing in return ... that the recipient
of your kindness do the same for someone else.

Pass it on. See how far it travels!

The responses were creative, spontaneous, and heartwarming. They exhibited true sparks of spiritual enlightenment on varied levels. They were as diverse in nature as we are as individuals.

- A 14 year old special education student of mine won $25 in a raffle and immediately donated it back to charity.
- A colleague joyously retells her experience of putting a quarter in the expired parking meter of a complete stranger.
- A neighbor began to volunteer regularly at a retirement home.
- A newlywed decided, he told me a week later, to wash the dishes for his new wife without being asked.

The list goes on … but it was after the original outpouring of this caring and sharing that I began to realize the card's unlimited potential for spiritual awareness in all of us. It was then that I changed the name of my card to "CARING IS CONTAGIOUS" and began distributing these cards wherever I went.

I continue to give out these cards to both friends and strangers. I send them with my monthly bills; I enclose them in letters. I leave them at phone booths or on bulletin boards. I pack them when going on vacation. It is wonderful to receive the feedback and trail the cards around the country. The idea gave birth to a website where people all over the world visit, sign the guestbook and request FREE Caring Cards.

I have received notes from Dave Thomas (the owner of Wendy's) as well as from the Olympic speed skater, Bonnie Blair. Jack Canfield (*Chicken Soup for the Soul*) has distributed my cards in New Zealand and the Fiji Islands and wrote to let me know. My last e-mail was from a gentleman from Tel Aviv … before that, a woman from Pennsylvania who found my card vacationing in Pompano Beach, Florida (I have never been in Pompano Beach!) I had a bride request 100 cards to distribute at her wedding. Another woman wrote and asked for cards to put on each of her Christmas gifts before she gave them out. A company in Delaware sends a "Caring is

Contagious" Card with each mail order it fills. Celebrity or everyday person, the thrill is the same for me … my message is getting out!

In this new age of enlightenment, my "card" suddenly presented itself as the perfect avenue to remind others to spread caring. It could be used, I thought, to awaken those of us who may have become somewhat complacent regarding our emotional and spiritual journeys. I continue to use my card as a grassroots movement. Its goal is to foster kindness and caring worldwide.

I am still amazed at the number of people who continue to ask why I distribute these cards. My reply is simple—My "Caring is Contagious" card acts as my personal motivator by connecting my spiritual path with my everyday life. In turn, It benefits others, so I benefit. It transcends barriers of all kinds (age, color, cultural differences, location). It gives my life purpose and direction … IT PUTS JOY IN MY JOURNEY!

The "Caring is Contagious" card is my personal reminder to be open to the endless opportunities to perform and promote caring acts. It reminds me to reach out to others, to keep my heart open, to be thankful, creative, and cognizant.

As I coalesce with others via my caring card I truly believe in and feel the contagious spirit with which its message is embraced. Scores of people have requested my cards to distribute where they live, work, and play. And so begins, what I hope is the never ending Contagious Cycle of Caring.

I encourage anyone who would like some of my cards (free of charge) or would like to comment or encourage, please contact me at:

giftsofjoy@aol.com or
Katherine, P.O. Box 3, Bellmore, NY, USA 11710.

It is always a thrill to hear from those all over the world who have been touched by my "CARING IS CONTAGIOUS" card.

THOUGHT TO PONDER:

What might you do to "pass on" something you believe in? And while you're thinking, write Katherine for some of her cards!

Share an Amish Friendship Cake

By Barbara A. Glanz
Sarasota, Florida

The miracle is this ... the more we share, the more we have.
Leonard Nimoy

THIS IS A special tradition in many parts of the country, especially because the starter keeps growing, so the tradition can go on and on. As you give part of your starter to other friends, theirs will continue to "grow" as well so that they can pass it on to other friends! A number of people all over the country have sent me versions of this recipe:

Amish Friendship Cake

Day 1: Put starter in bowl, stir, cover.

Day 2, 3, 4: Stir daily and re-cover tightly.

Day 5: Add 1 cup each of sugar, flour, and milk. Stir and cover tightly.

Day 6, 7, 8, 9: Stir daily and keep tightly covered.

Day 10: Add 1 cup each sugar, flour, milk. Always hand mix.

Take out 3 separate cups of starter, two to give away, and one to start all over again.

To the remaining starter in the bowl, add:

2/3 cups oil
1/2 tsp. Salt

1 cup sugar

2 tsp. Baking soda

2 tsp. Baking powder

3 eggs

2 cups flour

3 tsp. Cinnamon

1 cup applesauce

2 cups nuts

3/4 cups raisins

3/4 cups currants

3/4 cups dates

3/4 cups chopped apple

Grease and flour two loaf pans. Bake 50 minutes at 350 degrees.

THOUGHT TO PONDER:

You can start with a regular packaged sourdough starter if you want to start this tradition in your community. One caution—if you don't use the starter or give it away, it keeps growing and GROWING ... However, this becomes a constant reminder to <u>pass it on!</u>

A Gift for the Teacher

By John Blumberg
Naperville, Illinois

There are two ways of spreading light: to be the candle or the mirror that reflects it.

Edith Wharton

GIFTS ARE PROBABLY the most fun to give or receive when they are least expected. Such was the case when our niece began her very first year of teaching elementary school. Knowing that Sarah would be the perfect caring teacher, we wanted to celebrate her entrance into her new calling. We had fun visiting the nearby "teacher-supply" store to compile a package for her. We gathered stickers, pads and other materials that she could use to celebrate the accomplishments of her students. We knew that it would be the kind of gift that was just like her ... a gift that would keep on giving!

THOUGHT TO PONDER:
Do you have someone you know who needs encouragement in a new endeavor? As you encourage them, they will pass that spirit and joy on to others.

Tribute CDs
By Mike Hall
Denver, Colorado

Things will come in the most amazing, unexpected ways. Don't evaluate whether you need them or not; receive them with gratitude on behalf of those you will eventually give them to (or, more accurately, pass them along to).
John-Roger and Peter McWilliams,
We Give to Love

MY FATHER, BILL Hall, was hospitalized for serious neck and back surgery which proved to be more complicated than planned. The anticipated four-hour surgery turned into eleven hours. Dad seemed to be progressing following surgery until a heart attack and other respiratory problems occurred.

My brother John and I thought we might offer some additional help to Dad to recover from these setbacks. Dad was a graduate of The University of Kansas and a lifelong Jayhawk—he even wore Jayhawk boxer shorts! Dad also loved jazz. We called the University of Kansas bookstore to see if they had a CD of the Jayhawk Fight Song which goes, "Rock Chalk Jayhawk, KU."

John and I got a CD player and played the KU music and Dad's favorite jazz station to try to help him through his recovery. Unfortunately, Dad's condition worsened, and he passed away. However, John and I will always cherish the memories of dad's face lighting up in recognition of his beloved Jayhawk fight song and familiar jazz tunes.

Since Dad's passing, we have tried to find a way to keep his memory alive and we've finally found a unique way to remember him. We create resiliency CDs for friends or others who are in the midst of challenging life situations. We send a CD and a note to encourage the recipient to have faith and hang in there. This gift is a tribute to Dad and his legacy of unselfishness and determination when times were tough.

For anyone interested in the Tribute CDs, they are offered in the following themes:

* Sports (Boy's or Girl's Versions) entitled "Winners Go The Distance"
* Resiliency with no religious message
* Resiliency with a light Christian message
* Positive Parents Model
* American Pride (Great to reinforce pride and commitment to community)
* Team Sports (perfect for pregame listening to reinforce resiliency and sportsmanship)
* Coach's Thank You
* God Cried The Night The Savior Died (music based on the theme that

* There was a heavenly tribute to the Savior on Good Friday evening—arguably the most moving devotional music ever assembled)

Contact information:
Mike Hall
sahall16@yahoo.com<mailto:sahall16@yahoo.com>
303-770-5828

CDs are $2.50 each to cover mailing and expenses. This is a totally non-profit tribute to Bill Hall.

Here are the questions that will help Mike put together your tape.

1. What instrumental music would you choose to listen to after a challenging day?
2. What male and female vocalists inspire you?
3. What are your favorite sports?
4. Who are your political heroes?
5. Do you prefer a tape that is non-religious, light Christian or the "God Cried" version mentioned above? One side is reflective; the other is inspiring and upbeat.
6. Do you want the tape to encourage your personal resiliency?

THOUGHT TO PONDER:
Mike has blessed Charlie and me with several of his delightful customized tapes. Since I was a Jayhawker, too, many precious memories have been brought to mind by that fight song he recorded for his Dad!

The Gift of a Name

By Cathy Hamilton
Holland, Michigan

We receive from life what we give to it, and what we give to life we never lose.
                                                            Douglas M. Lawson

CATHY WROTE THIS to me about our daughter Erin's name:

Mike fell in love with the name "Erin" when you and your sweet daughters came to deliver a wedding gift to us just after Christmas in 1981. Erin was <u>precious</u>—holding a little chocolate Santa that was probably turning to mush but very politely not eating in front of us while we were talking. Eleven years later when our girls were born, he <u>knew</u> that one of them had to be "Erin." Thanks for that visit many years ago which resulted in our daughter getting the perfect name!

THOUGHT TO PONDER:

How thrilled our Erin was to hear this story! Do you have memories like this of ways someone has influenced your life or the lives of those you love that you can share with them? Do so NOW! It will be a gift that they will never forget.

The Friendship Bag

As told by Lucille Bauerle
Grand Junction, Colorado

A mother is not a person to lean on, but a person to make leaning unnecessary.

Dorothy Canfield Fisher

MY MOTHER, LUCILLE Bauerle, lived in a lovely retirement community in Grand Junction, Colorado, for several years after she could no longer live alone. Making the transition from a small town in Iowa where she had lived all her life was very difficult for her. In Harlan, Iowa, where I grew up, everyone knew her and loved to stop by for coffee, lunch, or dinner, especially since she was one of the best cooks in the world! She was very active in her church, the Literary Club, and she attended every single community event from the high school concerts and football games to church bazaars and local theatre productions.

In her new community she had to make all new friends, and transportation was difficult since she no longer had her car. However, she has found other ways to make a difference and keep active. One of the projects she was involved in was having different residents write their own versions of nursery rhymes, and then they printed them in a booklet for their children and grandchildren.

Another project was what she called a "Friendship Bag." She bought a package of pretty little cellophane baggies, filled them with the following contents, tied them with ribbon, attached the little card explaining what was in the bag, and passed them out all over the town. Each bag contained the following items:

LIFESAVERS: To remind you of the many times others need your help and you need theirs.

SWEET TARTS: To help you appreciate the difference in others.

BUTTERFINGERS: To remind you that everyone makes mistakes— remember to forgive and ask for forgiveness.

SNICKERS: To remind you to always smile, enjoy life, and friendship.

HUGS AND KISSES: To remind you that we all need hugs and kisses every single day.

She made many people happy as well as finding lots of new friends!

THOUGHT TO PONDER:
What a delightful idea to pass along to others in your school, neighborhood, or workplace!

NOTE: My mother has passed away since this story was written. However, her spirit lives on in all her friends, children, and grandchildren. She taught us all about the real meaning of Giving.

Chapter Ten:

"Practical Gifts"

This I can use.
And using, think of you.
This will stay
In my hands, in my days.

©Andrew Grossman 2000
Newton, CT

MY DEAR FRIEND, Karna Burkeen, is my most practical friend. When we first met and became friends, she informed me that she keeps a card file on each couple or friend in her life. On the card she lists your likes and dislikes, all the occasions you've been together, and what she served each time you came to her house. (It would be grievous to a practical person to duplicate meals!) We always laugh because the card for Charlie and me on food dislikes is the only one in the file which is blank—we like <u>everything</u>!

No one puts more thought into a gift than Karna. Her gifts are not only customized and personal, but above all they're <u>practical.</u> Knowing I love butterflies, for my birthday one year she gave me a large box filled with the following:

* A butterfly picture frame for a photo of our new grandson
* A large travel bag with butterflies for my frequent business travel

   * Two butterfly hooks and butterfly soaps for our new home in
      Sarasota, Florida.

One of her most practical gifts of all was something I had never seen before
or since. It looked like a flat sponge on a long plastic handle. When I called
her to ask what it was, she said since I lived alone on the beach with no one
to help me and loved to walk and swim, it was an applicator to put suntan
lotion on my back. I have thought of her with love every time I have used it
over the years—and it has probably saved me from skin cancer!

They all have a theme, and they're all practical!

Many of us were raised in households where there wasn't much extra
money, so gifts were always practical—things like mittens, new underwear,
and other things we needed. Now and then, we received a luxurious gift,
but most of the time that was not possible financially. It made it easy to buy
a gift for someone because we just thought about what they needed. And
often we even made the gift we gave.

I will never forget the first year I had enough money to buy my parents a
"really nice" Christmas gift, something they needed but also a bit extravagant. I had just gotten a job at age fourteen helping clean up in a local doctor's office. My little brothers and sister pitched in what they had saved
from their allowance, and together we bought my parents a pink and black
clock radio. How thrilled we were! (My mother just parted with that old
radio a few years ago. Even the most practical gifts can hold precious
memories!)

Today we have become a consumer society, often accumulating things
simply for the sake of having more rather than because we need them.
Consequently, gifts seem to have become more and more extravagant, and
it is often difficult to some up with an idea of what to give the person who
"has everything." Sometimes we forget that practical gifts—pragmatic,
usable, common sense gifts—may be the most valued of all. My 94-year-old
grandmother used to say, "Give me something I can use up and throw
away. I don't want any more 'stuff!'"

Sometimes we get so caught up in giving "special" gifts that we forget the practical things which help make one's life better in a pragmatic way. You'll read about some wonderfully practical gifts in this chapter. Perhaps it will cause you to re-examine your own gift giving. Think of the people with whom you regularly exchange gifts. What might be a new and different, practical, usable gift you could give them?

For the Children

By Rebecca Preston
Perth, Australia

Each gift contains within its sharing a special magic of its own.
Arthur C. Frantzreb

MY HUSBAND AND I were just approved to become foster carers. We did some short term respite care to start with, and we had our first placement—a ten year old boy for the weekend. We really enjoyed having him!

After visiting your website today (www.barbaraglanz.com), I got a great idea. I don't know why I didn't think of it sooner. I am going to do little CARE packages for the children who come to stay with us—perhaps a little box with some practical things like an amusing toothbrush, a small packet of tissues, and some fun things like a colouring book and crayons. It will be a special way for them to remember that someone cares about them.

THOUGHT TO PONDER:

It is such fun to give someone a CARE package. It makes them feel special and as if someone really does care about them to take the time to do something special just for them!

The Hurricane Kit

By Kathy Miller
Medford, New Jersey

Let him that desires to see others happy, make haste to give while his gift can be enjoyed, and remember that every moment of delay takes away something from the value of his benefaction.

Samuel Johnson

A FEW YEARS ago, my aunt and my grandmother, whom I'm very close to, moved to Florida from New Jersey. Ever since then, every fall, we have all had to live through hurricane season! From August until November many storms form in the Atlantic and often sweep across Florida. Every time we'd hear about another hurricane that might hit central Florida, the "up north" part of the family became very concerned. And we felt helpless, because all we could do was keep watching the weather on TV and keep trying to call down there to see if our loved ones were all right.

I was tired of feeling helpless and far away and wishing I could do something to help my aunt and my grandmother. Finally I had an idea—I made them a "hurricane kit." I assembled a bunch of things that they could use in an emergency, both things they'd need at home if the power went out or things they could use if they had to evacuate to a shelter.

I bought a mid-sized waterproof bag with several outside zipper pockets. The main section was filled with the larger items: one pocket contained food; one contained toiletries; and the third held "comfort items." Here are some of the things I packed in the main section of the bag: a first aid kit, a flashlight and batteries, a small portable radio with batteries, candles and waterproof matches, two plastic ponchos, two silver emergency blankets (they are only a few inches wide when packaged), a small bottle of water, and a small bottle of sports drink.

In the toiletries area I included a washcloth and soap in a plastic bag, toothbrushes and toothpaste, mini mouthwash, mini deodorant, a comb, and a mini hand cream. I even found a travel-sized tube of denture adhesive for my grandmother! In the snack pouch I put high-energy foods that would keep for months (and they know to replace them so they'll be fresh for every new hurricane season)—small packs of nuts, energy bars, and chocolate. In the "comfort" pouch I put a tiny Bible, a couple of family pictures, a deck of cards, a small notepad and pens, and a crossword puzzle book. These things, I thought, would help them pass the time while they were either stuck in a shelter or awaiting a rescue.

When I gave the kit to my family and explained everything, they absolutely loved it. They felt very cared for and said it would ease their minds in time of emergency to know that they were prepared. (In fact, the kit was such a hit that later I made a second one for my cousin and his family who live in a different Florida city.) During a few close calls that my relatives have had since then, they've told me that they've had the bag out, sitting by the door in case they got the signal to evacuate. Thankfully, they have not actually had to use it yet.

It's true that the waterproof bag, though small enough to carry, holds a lot of things, but it still was not too expensive to put together. I got many things at discount stores, especially in the travel-size toiletries section and the camping section (waterproof matches). I gathered things over time as I saw them and could afford them, until the kit was full.

Knowing that my family has these kits has eased my mind a lot. Now when I see a storm headed their way, I know that they are prepared for whatever may happen and that I've done all I can to help them, even though we live hundreds of miles apart.

THOUGHT TO PONDER:

What a life-saving gift this might be! What kind of kit might you put together for someone you love?

A Close Call

By Rita Emmett
Des Plains, Illinois

All worthwhile men have good thoughts, good ideas and good intentions—but precious few of them ever translate those into action.

John Hancock Field

WE HAD A terrifying thing happen last night. The smoke alarm woke us at about 3 am, and flames were roaring out of the vanity under the downstairs bathroom sink. Bruce put out the fire which was brave but dumb. Brave, because he had it out before the firemen arrived. Dumb, because the firemen said that the flames could have caused all the aerosol cans under the sink to explode like a bomb.

The cause was a can of Raid which had corroded around the bottom from some kind of moisture or a small water leak under the sink. Is that crazy? Doesn't everyone have a can of Raid someplace? They did not even call it "spontaneous combustion". They made a point that the corrosion on the bottom of the can (which looks like a little bit—not even a lot—of rust) had something to do with the can bursting into flames. There were no rags or papers or boxes, just mouthwash and a few other cans. The vanity was installed in December 1995 so the can was put there after that. (They asked, "Have the cans been there a long time?" Four years, at the most, to them did not seem like a particularly long time.)

We are mystified. Also, we are grateful to be alive. The firemen and police all made a big point that the smoke detector saved our lives, because the toxic fumes could have done us in long before any flames reached us. (The smoke detector was right outside the bathroom door).

There is very little damage. The vanity is scorched, the carpet is still wet (water from the bathroom got on it), and the white carpet looks as if a bunch of firemen tromped everywhere checking the fire and opening windows with their big ol' sooty boots (which they did, God bless them!)

Another mystery: We couldn't find our cat, Howard. The firemen threw open ALL doors and windows, and I was out searching for him, thinking he ran out. After everyone left (maybe about 4 am), we found him hiding behind the couch. This morning we realized he is scorched.

We rushed him to the vet, and and gratefully, he was fine, but his fur and his belly were scorched on both sides, plus his whiskers, were melted away, but there were no signs of burns to his face or body. It looks as if he somehow jumped through the flames, yet we think the flames were confined to inside the vanity. There was no way he could (or has ever) opened the vanity door. By the time we woke up, the flames were bursting out of the door, but they went up, not out. So we can't figure out what happened to Howie.

The firemen said we were very gracious during a crisis. I offered to make them coffee and they declined but told me that Bruce had just offered them each a can of pop. Everyday we thank God for blessing us with so much, especially our health. Last night, we held hands and sat on our bed and thanked God for our lives. When we think of the many ways this could have been worse, we know for sure this year we are having Happy Holidays.

THOUGHT TO PONDER:

Rita has given us all a gift in this story, I think. Make sure your smoke detectors are working and check your cans of Raid!

Switchboard.com

By Mike Wynne
Naperville, Illinois

It is one of the most beautiful compensations of this life that no man can sincerely try to help another without helping himself.

Ralph Waldo Emerson

MY VERY BEST friend in grammar school was Jimmy Finnan. However, we were separated in sixth grade when my parents moved our family to Latin America. For a few years, Jimmy and I managed to keep in touch sporadically. Eventually, we lost track of one another. Upon returning to the U.S.A. many years later, I tried by every means possible to find Jimmy. I even went to the last address where he had lived in Brooklyn, but no one there knew him or his family.

Last year, knowing my interest in finding my friend, my daughter suggested I try Switchboard.com on the internet as a locator. After a few tries, Jim's name popped up. I immediately telephoned but no one answered, so I wrote a letter including my phone number. While I was away on a trip to Europe, he called and left a message. As soon as I got back I called, and we had a joyful telephone reunion.

A few months later, we scheduled a meeting in the Miami airport; I was returning from a business trip to Latin America, and Jim was now living in Florida. We met for the first time in 56 years! It was wonderful. After all that time and so many things, good and bad, that had happened to each of us along the way, we were still the same people. And we owe it all to Switchboard.com!

THOUGHT TO PONDER:

Isn't technology amazing? Use this idea to find someone you have lost track of and share it with others.

A Hat for John

By Mike Hall
Colorado Springs, Colorado

It's not what you'd do with a million,
If riches should e'er be your lot;
But what are you doing at present
With a dollar and quarter you've got?

Unknown

I HAVE AN older brother named John whom I think the world of. John is my only living brother—we have lost three brothers over the years to illness and accident.

John likes wearing baseball caps. They hide his thinning hair on top and make him look younger than his age!

For his birthday, I invited John to lunch and presented him with a commemorative cap with the initials of our brothers and parents who live together in heaven. The cap will hopefully lift John's spirits and reinforce the fact that his family is with him always.

THOUGHT TO PONDER:
What a great way to give a gift that is practical yet still has special meaning.

Hoopla

By John Pearson
San Clemente, California

I never lose an opportunity of urging a practical beginning, however small, for it is wonderful how often in such matters the mustard-seed germinates and roots itself.

Florence Nightingale

AS A CEO, "fun" never came naturally to me. I always felt we had too much to do and too little time. ("No time to party today; the FedEx deadline is looming!") But one year at my professional association meeting, I attended a workshop by Barbara Glanz on "How to Put Fun into the Workplace." In one hour, I got a $10,000 idea!

One day, I announced that we'd provide lunch for our team of 11 in the conference room the following Wednesday. Everyone eagerly arrived on time, but instead of sandwiches in their brown bags, they found them bulging with candy.

"Oops," I bluffed, "the deli made an error. Well ... we'll have to go out for lunch." I took them to a great restaurant, where I had already made reservations. We ordered from the menu and had a relaxing meal. But that was just the start!

After dessert, I gave everyone a sealed envelope with these instructions: "In your envelope is cash that you *must* spend in the next 60 minutes at the mall next door. You must spend the money *only* on yourself. Buy whatever you'd like. Cash that you don't spend, you must return to me. We'll meet at exactly 2:30 p.m. by the fountain for 'Show and Tell.' If you're late, you owe me 50 bucks. Ready. Set. Go!"

Staff members leaped out of their chairs and ran through the mall. Each envelope contained $50 and not one person returned any money an hour later! (And before I left the mall, several shoppers asked if we had any openings at our organization!)

That day is still a vivid memory for team members—and the good will it created lasted a long, long time. It was the right time and the right event for the right team. They felt appreciated.

LEADERSHIP RULE OF THUMB #7: The amount of time and resources you spend on "Hoopla!" is directly proportional to the morale and spirit of your staff.

THOUGHT TO PONDER:
When you give an employee a gift that is uniquely for him or her and especially one that is fun and different, you are building trust, appreciation, and loyalty, and the practical result is that that employee will want to give you his or her best work. What about trying something like this with your family or a few good friends?

The Gift of a Piano
By Rosemary Aikens
Lansing, Michigan

Today is unique. Don't let its wonderful moments go by unnoticed and unused.

Pat Boone

WHEN I WORKED for Kelly Temporary Services in September 1997, I received the most precious gift I have ever been given. When I was a young child, my parents learned of my gift for music and had me take piano lessons. My music teacher was Blanche Miller, a very kind and affectionate woman who took an interest in young people and loved music. One day she told me that I would be great if I just kept up with my music. I played in the church as a young teenager, and we had a family team. The younger ones sang, and I played the piano. For many years, however, I have not had a piano, so I have not been able to use my gift.

That assignment in 1997 was one of the shortest assignments I have ever worked in the Michigan Housing Assistance, Section 8 Division; however, it was the most significant one I have ever had. <u>On my first day of this assignment</u> one of the staff members in the department came to my cubicle and showed me and the woman who was training me a list of things her sister wanted to sell or give away before they left to move to Arizona.

On the list was a **"FREE PIANO to a good home"** in bold black letters. I said, "I'd <u>love</u> to have the piano," not really thinking or believing I would truly get it. She said, "Do you think you can get someone to move it?" I said, "I am sure I can arrange to do that. I certainly would not expect you to give me a piano and move it, too!" We both laughed. She said she would call her sister right away and tell her she had a lady who would love to have the piano and not to give it to anyone else. I was overjoyed! The following Friday I was abruptly told the assignment in that office would end, but I had been there long enough for God to work a small miracle in my life.

After I had been told the piano was mine if I could have it moved, I immediately started calling movers. I finally talked to a mover who claimed he was an expert in moving pianos. I also had spoken with one or two professional piano movers, but they were too costly for me. The following Friday the movers met my great nephew and me at the couple's home to move the piano.

The couple was very happy to have someone who would appreciate and enjoy the piano. I reassured them that I would treasure such a precious gift. It's a 1920 upright, and I just love having it! Even though the "movers" turned out not to be very professional and they barely got it up the stairs, we finally got it into my apartment, and I immediately began playing my version of the Lord's Prayer by ear.

Before I received this wonderful blessing, I was looking through a Christmas magazine and saw an advertisement about learning to play gospel music by ear, something I had always wanted to do. When I saw the ad, I so wanted to order the book, but at the time, I didn't even have a piano. Now my dream has come true! I am overjoyed with the way God has blessed me spiritually through music. I did order the book, and I can now listen to a song on the gospel station, a tape, or TV and I can pick up the tune immediately. I spend every free moment playing my piano. My hope is that someday I can share my gift with many others.

THOUGHT TO PONDER:
Do you have something to give away that might become such a blessing to another?

A Special Birthday
By the Rhea Family
Waco, Texas

There is nothing to make you like other human beings so much as doing things for them.

Zora Neale Hurston

LESLIE RHEA SHARED with me that last year when her daughter, Jordan, was going to be ten years old, she told her Mom that she really didn't need anything and could she do something special for others for her birthday. She wanted to do something for children who were less fortunate. Since Leslie is involved with the Junior League of Waco, she suggested collecting food for a backpack program at Talitha Koum.

This is the invitation they sent for Jordan's party:

Jordan feels so blessed to have great friends like you that she does not want any gifts! She would like to ask that you bring an item to donate to the Talitha Koum Backpack Program. We have listed some items that are needed and a description of the program in case it is new to you. Please let me know if you have any questions.

The backpack program started at Talitha Koum in the Spring of 2008. Teachers were noticing how hungry the kids were on Mondays when they came back to school. They realized the children had not eaten all weekend except for the occasional bag of chips, candy bar or soda.

The Junior League of Waco's Talitha Koum committee, which meets with the Pre-K class once a month, decided to take action to address this need. A committee member would take six bags of food to the children every Friday. Food consisted of cereal bars, peanut butter crackers, juice and fresh fruit—anything that a child under five could open by himself or herself and eat. There were six children in this particular class, and the program proved to be an immediate success! Teachers and staff noticed that the children weren't starving when they returned on Mondays. This resulted in greater success for the children both socially and physically. At this point, the Junior League relied on donations from the membership and the committee budget for food supplies.

In the fall of 2008, Talitha Koum approached JLW about supplying food for all twenty-four of the children. League members worked diligently to find a solution, but it was not until Spring of 2009 that a sponsorship program was born to fund our project. JLW decided to offer sponsorships to the community to help feed the children every weekend for the entire year. For $186, a backpack was provided that each week was filled with pop-top dinners (such as mac-and-cheese, ravioli, soup, or spaghetti), cans of fruit, cereal bars, and pudding snacks. For the infant children, formula was provided instead of canned or prepackaged food.

Within two weeks of launching the sponsorship program, JLW had sponsors for all 24 children. This was so successful that they decided to seek sponsors for their siblings. There were 18 siblings who needed food on the weekends. As of May 2009, *ALL* 38 children were sponsored. Beginning June 1st 2009, they all received a backpack of food every Friday. As of 2010-2011 Junior League year Talitha Koum was currently at capacity with 40 kids needing backpacks.

To help this great project please bring one of the following items to the party. They don't mind if they are in "Sam's" quantity boxes or singles. They feed these kids 52 weeks a year so they are happy for any donations!!

Items Needed:
*Mac & Cheese individual cups
*Mandarin Orange fruit cups
*Assorted Variety fruit cups
*Snack pack pudding
*Cheese crackers
*Granola bars
*Chef Boyardee

THOUGHT TO PONDER:
On your birthday (or any other time of the year), what creative, practical ways might you give to others because you feel so blessed? I was awed that a ten-year-old child would recognize a sense of her blessings and want to share them with others when most children would want all the gifts for

themselves. These parents have certainly raised their children to be generous and loving, a gift that will last them for a lifetime!

<u>Chapter Eleven:</u>

"Romantic Gifts"

We have watched the fire at sunset, and the child of our making
take her first step.
We have felt the hornet's wings brush our lives, and were cured,
and grateful, cried.
The mountains have taught endurance, as the stream has stilled
our trembling duress.
I had travelled capitol to capitol, trail to trail, with no one to tell,
until you made it real:
The beauty of the world was contained in our first embrace,
the first and each again.
Each new link of our togetherness, each breath we share in a kiss
scents the air with our love.
If there is a border, and time continues beyond the finest hour,
let it give us more of each other,
Until we are a smooth stone that skims across the water, in the rhythm
Of the wave's caress.

©Andrew Grossman 2000
Newton, CT

MY HUSBAND OFTEN surprised me. He was not what I would consider
a true romantic, but as the years went by, I realized that he was romantic in
simple, homey ways. He loved to hold hands and touch. I must admit that
sometimes I was annoyed by this, especially in the middle of the night when

he couldn't sleep or in the middle of a movie or sermon to which I was intently listening. However, more and more, I have realized what a comfort and an anchor his touch was for me. I <u>knew,</u> without a doubt, that I was loved, and I so miss that touch today!

When we first met in the summer of 1964, he was my boss! He was managing Marina City restaurants for the Hilton Corporation, and I had a summer job as cashier and hostess in the coffee shop. I was twenty-one years old, a small town Iowa girl in the city for the first time, and I had just finished my junior year at the University of Kansas. Charlie was thirty-three, a very handsome, well-respected, high-powered manager who'd not only had a tryout with the Milwaukee Braves as a pitcher but who had also been a paratrooper, a plain clothes detective, and a night club manager, so I was immediately dazzled by this suave, experienced man-of-the-world!

In those days he was <u>very</u> romantic. Of course, we had to "date" in secret since the boss was not supposed to fraternize with any of the employees, so we always met at Gus's, a restaurant about a block away. On our first date, after a lovely dinner we drove to the Planetarium and then went wading in Lake Michigan. (He later told me that he had NEVER done that before!) Since our first date was on a Tuesday, we celebrated our "anniversary" every Tuesday from then on. Each week he took me to one of the most exclusive places in Chicago—the London House, Mr. Kelly's, the Showboat Sari-S, the Empire Room. What a fabulously romantic summer I had! However, the end of the story is that after we were married, he rarely took me to any of those places again … ;-)! Instead, we saved to buy a house.

I was sometimes envious of other women whose husbands brought them flowers, jewels, and chocolates and surprised them with spontaneous trips to islands or nights on the town. And then I think about the constancy of my dear husband—for thirty years of work he came directly home every single night, he never deceived me in any way, and he supported me in every endeavor I attempted over all our years of marriage. What could possibly be more romantic than that?

A Houseful of Flowers

By Barbara A. Glanz
Sarasota, Florida

Some people, no matter how old they get, never lose their beauty—they merely move it from their faces into their hearts.

Martin Buxbaum

THIS STORY HAS become a legend in my family. When my mother, Lucille Anderson, graduated from college, she was given a prized teaching position as the art teacher in Storm Lake, Iowa. As many of you may know, in small towns at the end of the summer they print all the pictures of the new teachers in the local paper, welcoming them to the community.

My father, Wayne Bauerle, was a successful, single young man working for Standard Oil in Storm Lake at the time. My father was a quiet man, but a very determined one, and when he did speak, you listened! He saw my mother's picture in the paper that August and decided then and there that he was going to marry her, so he devised a romantic strategy.

My mother was rooming with a widow lady at the time, so my father discovered her address, and every day <u>for the next two weeks,</u> he sent her a bouquet of flowers. Remember that at this point she had never even met him! Finally, her landlady called him and told him that if he sent any more flowers, he'd have to give her more vases. Mother said the house looked like a funeral parlor!

However, my Dad was pretty shrewd, I think, because he waited all that time to call to ask her for a date. How could anyone possibly turn him down after all those flowers?

The end of the story is that they were married, had four children, and were disgustingly romantic (or so we thought as teenagers!) until my father died. And my romantic father made sure that my mother had fresh flowers in our home every week of their marriage!

I often think how glad I am for all those first flowers—I might not have been here without them!

THOUGHT TO PONDER:
How long has it been since you sent someone you loved flowers?

A Skeleton for Life!

By Mike Wynne
Naperville, Illinois

Love is a priceless commodity. It's the only thing you can give away and still keep.

Unknown

I WAS A first year medical student and needed to buy a skeleton for my Anatomy studies. A friend who had just successfully finished his first year Anatomy course offered to sell me the skeleton he had used. He lived only a few blocks away, so I told him I would pass by his house to look at it. A few days later, I stopped by his house and rang the door bell. His very cute younger sister came to the door. One look at her, and I forgot about his skeleton; hers was much more interesting! That was the beginning of a life-long romance, as a few years later we were married. By the way, I did buy the skeleton and did pass first year Anatomy. Eventually, I decided I really didn't care for the medical profession and switched careers, but I did keep the girl. We've been married for over 40 years.

THOUGHT TO PONDER:
Is there a "skeleton" on your closet?

Prince Eugene

From *Small Miracles II*
Yitta Halberstam and Judith Leventhal

A bit of fragrance always clings to the hand that gives you roses.
Chinese Proverb

WHEN IT CAME to love, Mary Margaret Dereu was blessed. For thirty-four wonderful years she was married to her soul mate, Eugene. She had many pet names for him, but mostly she called him her "Prince."

Then, on October 24, 1995, Eugene unexpectedly passed away in his sleep. Mary was devastated. They were just three months shy of their thirty-fifth anniversary.

Days turned into weeks, which turned into months, and with the passing of time, a slow healing took place. But as Valentine's Day of the following year came around, Mary found herself inconsolable about Eugene's death. To distract herself, she took a drive downtown, ready to lose herself in the sights and sounds of the local market.

Once inside the market, Mary glanced at several booths, but nothing in particular caught her eye. Then, suddenly, she found herself beckoned by a row of camellia bushes in the corner of the marketplace. The flowers were majestic, in full bloom, pure white. They reminded her of the flowers at her wedding, and she purchased a bush without any hesitation.

At home, Mary chose a special place beside Eugene's favorite shade tree to plant her new shrub. While she covered the roots with earth, she kept repeating, "Happy Valentine's Day, Eugene … Happy Valentine's Day, my Prince."

Then, just as she leaned on one hand to stand up, a small white tag attached to the base of the plant happened to catch her eye. She might easily have overlooked it.

"They must name these bushes just as they name rosebushes," Mary thought, she turned the tag in her muddy fingers. She read the name and felt the sting of a tear. There, in black ink, was the name of the pure white flower: Prince Eugene.

Perhaps it was his kiss, blown from beyond.

THOUGHT TO PONDER:
Halberstam and Leventhal say, "Flowers are often the messengers of our emotions, hopes, and dreams. Through them we send and receive, in this world and beyond."

The Last Quarter

By Nancy Coey
Reprinted with permission from *Finding Gifts in Everyday Life*
Raleigh, North Carolina

Beauty is in the heart of the beholder.

Al Bernstein

HE'S IN THE family room, my husband of twenty-eight years, watching yet another football game. Well, maybe this one is not "yet another" game; this one is the play-offs. But it sure seems that they're all pretty special—or at least that's what I've been told over the years.

"We'll leave as soon as the game's over; this one's really important."

I resented both him and his dumb games in the early years. It sure seemed that he wasted an awful lot of time.

And when the kids were little, time was one thing I never had a chance to waste. Even if I had wanted to watch, there was always something that needed doing. ("I'll just start a load of laundry during the commercial.") But now with the boys grown, I can watch if I want to. And I'm surprised that without ever having tried—simply through years of osmosis—I not only know a bit about football, I actually sometimes even care about the outcome! Of course, hardly enough to watch an entire game, but enough to watch the last quarter …

So that leaves more than two hours of some of the most gorgeous free time on earth. Quality, loving, happy, companionable free time. He's in the family room, my husband of twenty eight years, watching every play. If it's cold, he's built a fire and its warmth and smell fill the house.

The sounds of the game also fill the house. Happy, Fall sounds. Sounds, I promise you, I would never hear if I were alone.

Companionship and contentment ooze out of every nook and corner, and I write or think or curl up with a fat novel.

And then, as the fourth quarter starts, I ask the question that I've more or less been asking for twenty-eight years, "Who's in blue?"

And he is as patient with this routine as he was when we were first married.

So, we watch football together, each in our own way. He, knowing and caring, intent on every play. Me, the last quarter only, with three quarters of my mind on something else.

And it is sooooo great!

© Nancy Coey, *Finding Gifts in Everyday Life*. Reprinted with Permission.

THOUGHT TO PONDER:

Do you watch "the last quarter" with your spouse or significant other? Sharing does not have to be a fulltime commitment. Just a little quality time can work wonders in a relationship!

The Anniversary Surprise

What is love? Love is when you care more about someone else than you care about yourself.

George Akers

AS TOLD BY a special friend:

My former husband and I had a tradition whereby we took turns surprising one another with the celebration venue on each wedding anniversary. It was as simple as planning and preparing a candlelit dinner at home, going to a new restaurant, or as involved as whisking the other away for an out-of town weekend retreat.

On our 5th anniversary, it was his turn. He surprised me with dinner at the Bel Air Hotel, the most secluded and arguably the most romantic hotel in Los Angeles. Being relatively new to the area, I had never been there. Dinner was absolutely superb, as we sat at a gorgeous table, gleaming with silver, crystal, and candlelight, while swans floated past us on a lagoon laden with water lilies.

After dinner, he invited me into the dark, cozy bar to hear the famed pianist who played there weave his musical magic spell. Soon he pulled out a beautiful anniversary card for me. As I opened it, I was stunned to see a key fall out of the card. Enclosed with a beautiful, loving inscription was a key to a room at the hotel for the night! I couldn't imagine what was happening ... I thought we'd only come for dinner!

He led me through a winding stone path, engulfed with lush plants and flowers to the most beautiful hotel room I'd ever seen. The suite included a stone fireplace, huge overstuffed bed, and most luxurious of all—an enormous marble bathroom and dressing area. As my head cleared, I thought ... how can I stay the night? ... I've brought nothing. Just then David opened the large closet in the dressing area. There hung my swimming suit, casual clothes for the next day, sandals—everything I would need. On the dressing table behind me, my cosmetics were neatly displayed. I was stunned that he could be so thoughtful! He had left work early to pack my things, checked in, and then came back home to pick me up!

As if this wasn't enough, as I looked back into the bedroom, I realized that the bed was covered with gifts for me—all beautifully wrapped. Well, if ever a woman was ready to melt—this was the moment. It was absolutely astonishing! I was overwhelmed with his thoughtful attention to detail and the fact that he had surprised me so thoroughly. I knew at that moment that he loved me deeply and had gone to extraordinary lengths to show me that this 5th anniversary—and each one that would follow—was a sublimely important day, and one that would never be taken for granted. He is, to me, the most loving and romantic husband in the world.

THOUGHT TO PONDER:

Wouldn't you LOVE a husband like that? Remember that you can do something similar for your loved one on a much less grand scale. It is the idea that counts!

Poems of Love

By Bob Bruce
Howie-in-the-Hills, Florida

If your life has been enriched by love, once or more than once … the memory of it … never leaves you.

Olivia De Havilland

BOB HAS A beautiful hobby of writing poetry whenever he is moved by a person or an event. He says, "I am enclosing a few photos with poems superimposed for you to read. The photographs are all original as are the poems. I try to match the topic to something that carries the mood of the poem. I do not use any photos that I have not taken. The name of the little notebook in which I keep them is called 'Notes from the Heart.'"

These are poems that Bob has written as a tribute to his wife:

A Note to my Queen

If I could change the world today
Right by my side you'd be.
I'd hang the moon ... pull down a star
To light your way to me.

The starlight glowing through your hair;
The moonlight in your eyes ...
Would generate a glow of love
And illuminate the skies.

My love for your just knows no end.
You're in my mind each day.
The thought of you here in my arms
Still guides me on my way.

I swear if I were made a king
To rule a kingdom wide,
'Tis you I'd choose to be my queen
To stand right by my side.

© 1997 Bob Bruce

Share my Moon

I'd love to share my day with you,
From Sunrise to Sunset.
Each moment filled with happiness
And joy you'd not forget.

I'd share with you my Sunrise.
We'd watch the glowing sky.
We'd simply sit, your hand in mine,
Together ... you and I.

And then we'd share the Daytime,
Enjoying many things.
We'd take a walk along a beach
Until your sweet heart sings.

We'd have a little picnic
And share a bite to eat.
I'd make some very special meal
And share with you this treat.

And then you'd share my Sunset.
Again … that golden glow.
I'd hold you close and share more love
Than you could ever know.

And then, as every other day,
This day would end too soon.
But I would feel true happiness
If you would share my Moon.

©1997 Bob Bruce

Inspiration

Each life needs inspiration
A reason to go on.
Something to give it meaning
Like the lyrics of a song.

To me, you've been my everything.
My love, my life, my dream.
You brighten every single day
Like a golden sunlight beam.

With you I've found such happiness:
Far more than words could say.

You've helped me through my darkest nights
And through each lengthy day.

The faith you've shown in me, my dear
Has helped me realize
The meaning of true, endless love
Is right before my eyes.

You've given me the strength to see
There's nothing I can't do
Except find words to tell you how
Much love I have for you.

© 2000 Bob Bruce

THOUGHT TO PONDER:
Have you ever written a poem to the one you love?

Tips for Romantic Gift-Giving

By Heidi Tyline King
"All Wrapped Up"

I think true love is never blind,
But rather brings an added light,
An inner vision quick to find
The beauties hid from common sight.

Phoebe Cary

IF YOU THINK successful gift giving requires a flair for the creative or hours spent navigating a gauntlet of perfume-wielding saleswomen, think again. "Gift-giving is not as hard as people think it is," says Marnie Lerner, cofounder of Star Treatment, a Los Angeles gift-buying company that specializes in gifts for Hollywood honchos. "To become a good gift giver, the first thing you have to do is know a person's personality. And you have to listen—people give hints all the time about gifts they would like to receive." Buy like a pro with these eight tips from professional gift buyers and personal shoppers.

* **Shoot straight for the heart.** "The best gifts have meaning behind them," says Kristine Dang, merchandising director for Red Envelopes Gifts Online, an online personal shopping service. "They evoke an emotion, a memory of a sweet moment or a special time. A ticket stub from the first movie you saw together tucked inside a small box is more special than diamonds to some women. She knows it came from your heart, and if it means something to you, it will mean something to her."

* **Know before you go.** Arm yourself with information about your lover before you shop. "Many men don't know their better half—the simple things like hobbies, sizes, likes, dislikes, and favorite colors," says Paul Buckter, director of At His Service, one of the personal shopping services offered at Bloomingdale's in New York. Other clues to consider: her birthstone, whether she is family-oriented or focused on career, and if she's independent or enjoys being pampered and taken care of. It is also helpful to remember what gifts were hits in the past.

* **Plan your presentation.** An unwrapped gift in a department store bag looks last-minute, no matter how much thought you put into it. "The gift wrap and packaging are a big part of giving a gift," says John Brantley, store director for Gump's in San Francisco. "No matter what the size and cost, we give each gift the same treatment. We want it to get and 'ooh' and an 'aah' when it's presented."

* **Use the available tools.** "We spend an exorbitant amount of time looking for ideas in our favorite stores and fashion magazines," says Lerner of Star Treatment. "The Internet is also a great tool for finding gifts." If you don't have time to shop around, look through magazines and listen to what people are talking about on television to help you keep up with the trends.

* **Imagine the reaction you want, then buy accordingly.** "Are you purchasing a small token to acknowledge a holiday or are you buying a gift to commemorate a major anniversary?" asks Brantley. In other words, if it's a monumental life event that you are remembering, think big. It doesn't have to be an expensive gift—only one that is loaded with sentiment.

* **Don't wait until the last minute.** If at all possible, avoid shopping the night before a big holiday. Otherwise, you'll only have leftovers to choose from. Instead, remind yourself several weeks before with a note in your calendar or taped to your desk. Keep a running list in the back of your date-book when you think of a good gift idea. And if you see something in March that would be perfect for your sweetheart's birthday in July, go ahead and buy it.

* **Remember who you are buying for.** "A man might love to play tennis, so he'll buy his girlfriend a really nice racket, forgetting she has two left feet," says Lerner. Forget about what *you* would like and focus on *her* interests.

* **And finally, avoid the pinnacle faux pas.** At the sage advice of Buckter, "If you're in doubt about size, always go with the smaller one," he warns. "And by all means, steer clear of buying a woman exercise equipment or a gym membership for a gift—unless she specifically asks for it!"

THOUGHT TO PONDER:
Has this helped give you a few new ideas?

The Gift of a Romantic Story

By Mike and Kirsten Goddard
Aurora, Illinois

Love without laughter can be grim and oppressive. Laughter without love can be derisive and venomous. Together they make for greatness of spirit.

Robert K. Greenleaf

ON WEDNESDAY, MAY 12, 1999, my boyfriend Mike had the biggest interview of his career—an interview with American Airlines to be a pilot. We had met two years prior, and our relationship was getting pretty serious. I knew things were heading in the right direction with us!

Mike had worked a long time towards this goal. As the day grew near, I helped him prepare for his interview. He kept telling me, "This was our big day." Little did I know what he really meant. I anxiously waited all day to hear about his interview. I couldn't wait to get home from work and hear how it went! When I walked in the door, I saw him sitting on the balcony enjoying a glass of wine with a big smile on his face. I joined him, and he told me all about it. It went great!

After the excitement died down a little bit, he handed me a story to read:

"The List"

A story of a little boy in his own words:

From the time I was little, I knew truths that seemed to elude others. I saw people getting divorced and giving up on a marriage they vowed to keep forever. I also knew the key to happiness isn't about things. It's not about a new baseball mitt or car, but about our relationships with family and friends, and I knew the place to start was with a wonderful wife. So, I started praying for the perfect wife.

As I grew older and learned more about what I might want in a wife, I began making a list of qualities I wanted her to have. Each night I closed my prayers by requesting to be blessed with a wonderful wife some day. I also knew I would have to prepare myself to be worthy of such a lifelong partner. I watched my father because he was one of the best and tried to emulate him. Sure it was only make believe, but I knew I would make a wonderful husband for my future wife.

After many years, I felt the time had come. I was confident that the Lord already had her picked out, and I would simply have to ask Him. As I waited to see Him, I watched God give equal time to every person in line. When I saw that He wasn't busy, I timidly approached my Lord. He turned toward me and finally noticed me nervously trembling with my list shaking in my hand. I could feel His warmth and love as He came near me.

"Lord," I said, "I am so grateful for all my blessings, and I know that I often ask for more than I deserve." He gave me His undivided attention, and I continued, "Remember my special request for a wonderful, caring, beautiful wife?" The Lord gave me a puzzled look. Frantically, I stretched out my arm so He could see my list a little better. He squinted and made a funny face as He looked at it.

I suddenly felt greedy, and I could feel my face beginning to turn red as I recalled some of the things I put on my list. "What man would be deserving of all of those wonderful qualities?" I thought. I began to doubt the plan that seemed so sure years ago. I remembered number thirteen was, "As beautiful as Your prettiest angel," and number six was, "A smile so warm it would light up the life of any who saw it, but mostly mine." My feelings of greed culminated with my last request, which stated, "In summation, Lord, I would like my wife to make me feel like every day is Christmas Eve."

The Lord looked very stoic. "My son ... this is quite a list," He said. "I remember all of your prayers, and I could provide you with a woman who satisfied all these requirements on your list, but I'm just not ..."

"What?!!" I thought to myself. Then He raised his mighty hand and called out in a thunderous voice. Immediately a mighty winged horse raced to Him out of the sky. He put His hands softly on the horse's head and whispered in its ear. The grand beast took a running start and lifted off. Everyone's attention was fixed on the sky in anticipation. As I struggled to see as far into the bright sky as I could, I detected a small speck, and I heard an excited murmur from those around me. They were all smiling, as if they knew something I didn't!

The horse came racing back, soaring gracefully with angels as escorts. He landed softly in front of us, and he was not alone. On his back was a vision so beautiful, she had to be an angel. Her smile radiated warmth and caring. Her hair flowed like the ocean, and her eyes spread happiness to all they gazed upon. The Lord took her hand and helped her down from the horse. She stepped back, smiling bashfully, and turned her attention towards me. I had butterflies in my stomach as I watched them come closer.

I could not take my eyes off her! The Lord looked at me with a mischievous half smile, like a father on Christmas morning who has saved the best gift for last. "My son," He said, "because you have prayed and believed in me, I would like you to meet my answer to your prayers. Her name is Kirsten."

I had no idea at first that he had written the story for me and was proposing. I didn't realize what it meant until I finished reading. I looked at him, and he was all teary eyed. He got down on one knee and asked me to marry him. Of course, I said, "YES!"

THOUGHT TO PONDER:

Have you ever considered writing a story for someone you loved? What a precious way to propose! Kirsten and Mike now have three beautiful children.

My Favorite Father's Day Gift

By Dick Bruso
Denver, Colorado

Love doesn't just sit there, like a stone, it has to be made, like bread; remade all the time, made new.

Ursula K. leGuin

A COUPLE OF years ago, shortly before Father's Day, Jenny, one of my four grown daughters asked me what I wanted for Father's Day, since "Dads are hard to buy for!" For once, I had an immediate answer. Earlier that month, my wife, Joann, and I had visited an upscale women's clothing store where my youngest daughter, Joy, was working as a sales associate. For the fun of it, my wife decided to try on some expensive outfits, including a beautiful brown and gold silk dress that looked absolutely fabulous on her.

Although I could see how much she liked it, we both realized it was a little more than we could afford. Thus, when my daughter asked me what I wanted for Father's Day, I suggested that all my daughters consider pooling their resources in order to buy "me" that dress for Father's Day. And that's exactly what they did!

When our family gathered together on Father's Day to celebrate, my four daughters (Julie-ann, Jackie, Jenny, and Joy) presented me with my gift, wrapped, of course, in a manly looking gift-box. When I opened it, much to my wife's surprise and delight, there was that special dress she so desired. Since then, I have had the pleasure on numerous occasions of seeing my lovely wife light up a room wearing my favorite Father's Day gift. What a blessing that gift has been—It has brought so much joy to all of us over the years!'

Dick and Joann in her new silk dress!

THOUGHT TO PONDER:
Have you ever asked for something for someone else on your special day?

Special Romantic Gift Ideas

Love is like the sea, it's a moving thing; but still it takes its shape from the shore it meets and it's different with every shore.

Zora Neale Hurston

KATHRYN L. ENGEL, a professor in the department of psychology at the University of Illinois at Chicago, says, "The best gift is something heartfelt that's private about the relationships. What I hear from happy couples is that what women remember most are personal or handmade gifts, like when a man wrote them poems."

John Gray, author of *Men Are from Mars, Women Are from Venus,* says, "It's not the price of the present that makes a woman happy, it's the time and attention you put into finding or creating the present, particularly if you don't have a lot of money."

For example, you can start by thinking about her hobbies, her tastes in everything from music to plants, her goals and even the difficult aspects of her life. Cook her dinner and dance with her in the living room if she is tired of cooking, give her a gift certificate for a spa day if she is particularly stressed, or buy her clothing or equipment for a hobby she loves. Use your own talents, too. Just notes with "promises" can be very special.

To be sure your gift isn't memorable in a negative sense, avoid these common pitfalls:

* Sending flowers or any other gift with a card that is signed for you by someone else.
* Asking your assistant to order the flowers, make the dinner reservations, or worse, pick out a gift for your wife or girlfriend.
* Giving an impersonal gift, like a new computer printer, no matter how much you think she needs it.
* Giving a gift that is more for you than for her, such as buying slinky lingerie for a woman who prefers flannel.

THOUGHT TO PONDER:

Have you ever made any of the "mistakes" mentioned? I will never forget when Charlie gave me an electric can opener and a sandwich grill for Christmas one year. The next year he got a shovel! ;-)

Chapter Twelve:

"Sharing our Wealth and Resources with Others"

So much.

So many.

I have felt the blessings fall as rain, and have blossomed.

Give away.

Given back.

Each handful of caring brings crowds of riches into my arms.

©Andrew Grossman 2000

Newton, CT

ONE OF MY favorite parables about giving in the Bible tells of how many people brought large sums of money to give to the poor, but the greatest gift of all came from a poor widow who gave her very last coin. The teaching: it is not the monetary value of what we give to others that is important. Rather, it is how willing we are to share our wealth and resources, whatever they may be.

In Biblical times as well as in many homes today, tithing is practiced— giving 10 % of our wealth to the church or other charities. Others decide each year how much of their money they will share with others, depending upon their income for that year. My Aunt Adah was a wonderful role model for this kind of family giving. When she had had an especially good year financially, she would surprise 17 different family members with a check. Since most of us were struggling young families, those checks always seemed to come at a time when we needed them the most—the washing machine had broken down, we had many extra medical bills, or the house needed a new roof. How very grateful we were for those unexpected gifts of sharing.

My belief is that we all have a responsibility as citizens of the world to share some of our wealth and resources with others. The more we are blessed with, the greater our responsibility. We can share our wealth in many ways:

* With family and friends who are in need.

  Our church has a "Fellowship Fund" which is specifically to help people in our community. Sometimes we may choose to anonymously help those we know who are in financial difficulty to help preserve their dignity. Many times I can remember my mother placing a box of groceries or clothing on the steps of someone's home without their knowing it. And at other times, we may gift loved ones by fulfilling a specific need they may have. I will never forget when we were buying our first little home and a relative sent us a check to help with the down payment. Although the amount of money was not huge, it was enough to help ease our monthly mortgage payments so we could afford to buy a sofa for the living room.

* With our communities.

  A hometown friend of mine has a passion for reading, so she has given a great deal of time and money to build or upgrade libraries in the communities in which she's lived. In *CARE Packages for the Home* I wrote about how the whole community of Harlan, Iowa, shared its resources, both financial and physical, to build a spectacular playground for the children of the town. Mary Schulz, a dear friend of mine from Downers Grove, Illinois, has become deeply involved in and organization called "Still Missed." She donates her time and resources to make tiny layettes for stillborn babies in her community. Since mothers cannot purchase baby clothes tiny enough for these little ones, Mary wants then to have the dignity of a precious outfit made with love to bury their babies in.

* With organizations whose mission is to help others.

As a family, we have chosen to support many organizations over the years, including our church. When our second son died, we decided to adopt a little boy from Colombia, in his memory, through Compassion International, and when that child was grown, we supported another young boy. Now I support children in Haiti as a gift to my grandchildren of the same ages. I donate a portion of all the royalties from the *CARE Packages* books, including this one, to the CARE organization which brings relief to hurting people worldwide. We also support Bread for the World to help the hungry around the world, the American Cancer Society and the American Heart Association since we have lost so many loved ones to these diseases, and Focus on the Family because we deeply believe in the value of family. I am also a member of the National Advisory Cabinet for Guideposts, the organization started by Dr. Norman Vincent Peale, and I serve on the National Board for Ken Blanchard's Lead Like Jesus ministry, both of whose missions I value and support.

It is important to find organizations whose mission resonates with you and your values, and then do everything you can to encourage and support them. And when you do this as a family, like the Cheerful Givers project you'll read about in this chapter, it has even more meaning. You are not only having fun together, but you are also teaching your children the important value of sharing your wealth and resources with others.

Cheerful Givers

By Robin Maynard
South Saint Paul, Minnesota

You must give some time to your fellow man. Even if it's a little thing, do something for those who have need of help, something for which you get no pay but the privilege of doing it. For remember, you don't live in a world all your own. Your brothers are here, too.

Albert Schweitzer

I FIRST MET Robin Maynard in Minneapolis when I was speaking there, and we connected immediately! When she told me the story of how she started "Cheerful Givers," I was humbled, enthralled, and deeply committed to help further her ministry. This is her story:

It is in giving that we receive

After years of sending checks to different charities, Kevin and I began to wonder if these contributions were really making a difference. The donation solicitations became more like additional bills and sending money to them no longer made me happy. Kevin and I decided to pray for a way to make a valuable contribution to our community. Within days of this request, I was made aware of a couple, Rick and Pat, who ran Trinity Mission food shelf out of their home. I called them and made an appointment to tour their home and food shelf myself.

One statement hit me like a lightning bolt: "Parents come here to get a boxed cake for their child's birthday gift, and if there are no cake mixes left, they find a box of their child's favorite cereal or can of vegetables to give them as a gift." I felt God touch my heart. He had led Kevin and me to something we could do for His people. On a Sunday evening I delivered our first twelve birthday bags to Trinity Mission. I prayed that each gift would reach the children in greatest need and bless their lives. Monday morning, God reaffirmed this ministry. I was at my full-time job when I received a call from Pat. She recounted this story that I will never forget:

Pat found a woman panic-stricken and on the verge of tears in front of an empty shelf where the boxed cake mixes had been. The mother explained that she had taken the bus to the food shelf, praying during the entire ride that there would be something here for her child's birthday, but now the shelf was empty. Pat told her not to cry—that she could give her something better. At that point, Pat brought out one of the newly-delivered birthday bags and said, "Look at these birthday bags that were just donated."

The parent was overwhelmed with joy as she held the gift bag with crayons, a coloring book and other small toys. She exclaimed, "I prayed and prayed, but I never dreamed that there would be something so beautiful."

Within hours, all of the bags were gone, prayers were answered, and more birthday gifts were needed. That was in 1993. We have been providing children's birthday gifts for low-income families ever since.

The purpose of Cheerful Givers is to provide birthday gifts to children ages 3-12 from families that are struggling financially. The gift is considered a gift to the parent to give to their child. So, the gifts are completely anonymous. The parent signs the gift tag or card. By remaining completely anonymous, we hope to help the parents as much as the child. It would be terribly difficult to be a parent faced with having to choose between food for the family or a birthday gift for their child! We wish that there was no poverty so families could afford to make their child's birthday special, but until that time, we will continue to provide children's birthday gifts for families.

After seeing the need and positive benefits to less fortunate families, we decided to create a charitable corporation to enable us to sustain and grow the program. We named the charity "Cheerful Givers" because through our prayer, God led us to a ministry that truly provides for His hurting children and teaches them to value birthdays as much as He does. Through God giving us this experience, we now feel great joy in giving with a "cheerful" heart—a feeling which we had lost.

What touched Robin's heart was to think that the only thing a mother would have to give her child would be a can of vegetables! So, she and her husband Kevin vowed to do something about that. They began asking organizations and individuals for donations of small items such as coloring books, crayons, small toys, bubbles, books, small games, and other items that a child would like. Then they began putting 6-8 items in a pretty bag with a gift card that the mother could write to her child. As their ministry grew, it began to take over their entire home and garage, and finally, they decided to incorporate as a non-profit organization and choose a Board of Directors. As you can see from the numbers below, schools, churches, scout troops, corporations, and many other groups have become involved, and 465,000 birthday bags have been given to otherwise totally bereft children.

When a professional group I belong to in Illinois wanted to do something different at their end-of-the-year picnic, I suggested that we make birthday bags for a shelter in the Chicago area. We asked each family to bring 25 of any item that a child would like. Depending upon their budget, we had everything from jump ropes, small books, packages of gum, toothbrushes, and puzzles to wonderful stuffed dinosaurs. 30 families made over 100 birthday bags to be distributed, and part of the joy was that the whole family, no matter what the ages of the children, could be involved in filling the bags. Not only did we have fun together, but we also felt good about helping someone else to have a special day. I highly recommend a project like this to your school, church, workplace, or interest group.

This is the information about Robin's ministry of giving, Cheerful Givers:

Mission: We provide toy-filled birthday gift bags to food shelves and shelters so that parents living in poverty can give their child a birthday gift.

*Food is essential; shelter and clothing are essential. Families that are having hard times work very hard to attain the essentials that everyone else has. The NEEDS are taken care of, but the WANTS are for "someday" down the road. Every day, even a Birthday or a Holiday, is the same day—a day with no money. People with so little long for just a little something extra to make them feel special. Every delivery of gift bags, is met with smiles and tears of joy. Our products are answered prayers to our clients, and we are determined to keep providing these special gifts for as long as they need them. **With the*** *help of generous contributors, we have provided more than 465,000 children in need with wonderful birthday gift bags.*

THOUGHT TO PONDER:

If you would like to organize a group to provide and assemble toy-filled birthday gift bags for less fortunate children in your own community, make a donation, or learn more about individual virtual volunteer opportunities, contact karen@cheerfulgivers.org or visit www.cheerfulgivers.org.

Little Miracles

By Brenda Howard, Sponsor and Compassion Volunteer
Reprinted with permission from "Compassion at Work," Fall 1999
issue, *Compassion International*

> *I will tell you the truth, whatever you did for one of the least of these brothers of mine, you did for me.*
>
> Jesus of Nazareth, Matthew 25:40

"THIS IS NOT the child I wanted." As I stared at the picture of a square-faced girl with dull eyes, that thought shocked me. Why was I—a person with a degree in occupational therapy, accustomed to working with disabled people—reacting so negatively to sponsoring a child with Down's syndrome?

For years, I had dreamed of visiting the child my family was sponsoring. But before I could make that dream a reality, she left the Compassion program. With a heavy heart, I held the picture of this girl, Aracely, sent to replace her.

As I prayed and wondered about my initial reaction to this child, an image came to mind of a young mother, abandoned by her husband, making a meager living by seasonal work and raising a daughter with an expensive, debilitating, and disheartening medical condition. My heart broke, and suddenly I understood my initial feelings. I was thinking of this little girl not with my therapist's mind, but with a mother's heart. Any time a child is born with a disability, parents grieve for the perfect child that might have been while adjusting to the reality of parenting one with a disability. I was grieving the loss of our previous child and learning to accept this new little girl with all her imperfections.

I met Aracely in March 1997 during a church mission trip to El Salvador. She was a sweet, shy 11-year-old. I was pleased to see that her basic needs were being met, and although she was unable to progress academically, she was capable of doing chores and playing with other children. During my visit, Aracely's mother was at work, but her grandmother was a gracious hostess who thanked me profusely for our family's help. I left after an emotional day, full of love and gratitude for this little girl and her family, but concerned about her possibilities for the future.

Throughout the past two years, I have seen some wonderful results of sponsorship in Aracely's life. Her grandmother wanted to teach the little girl to sew as a trade, and she asked me for a sewing machine. Someone in our church donated a used machine, and a friend delivered it to El Salvador. We later received pictures of Aracely, her mother, and Compassion workers with the machine. Also, a Compassion education fund was used to send Aracely to a special-needs school.

God enabled me to visit Aracely again in March 1999, this time with a group of Compassion volunteers. Gone was the awkwardness of our first meeting. Aracely greeted me with open arms. She chatted with me all day, carried my bags, and introduced me to her mother and new baby brother. She wore a dress sewn on the machine we had sent. Having attended the special-needs school for a year, she demonstrated progress in math, reading, and writing. She was also much more comfortable relating to peers and adults.

Through my family's relationship with Aracely, and through our becoming her advocate, God has worked miracles of provision and education in her life. But when the child I hadn't wanted became the girl I love as my own, God worked the grandest miracle of all.

THOUGHT TO PONDER:

Compassion International is an organization in Colorado Springs, Colorado, that provides a ministry to impoverished children worldwide by connecting each child with a sponsor. These sponsors,by sharing their financial and personal support, send a message that every child of poverty longs to hear: "You are precious, you are loved!" Right now, more than 20,000 children are waiting for a sponsor. What a wonderful family project it is to adopt a needy child! For more information, contact: Compassion International, www.compassion.com, 800-336-7676.

The Gift of Socks

By Steve Lipman
New York, New York
From *Small Miracles II* by Yitta Halberstam and Judith Leventhal

Man discovers his own wealth when God comes to ask gifts of him.
Rabin-Dranath Tagore

IN NEW YORK City, the police advise you not to take out your wallet when approached by a beggar—but you develop a sixth sense about these things. So I had no misgivings about the young black woman, shy and rail-thin and obviously homeless, her matted hair covered by a scarf, who approached me a few years ago in the nearly empty Times Square subway station while I was waiting for the train.

Could I give her some money for a meal?

I took a few dollars from my wallet. Then I noticed her feet. She was wearing threadbare sneakers and had no socks on. I asked her why. She had no money for socks, she explained as she turned to ask another commuter for spare change.

I had no more money to offer. But the vision of her sock-less feet accompanied me home. I rummaged through my dresser drawers for a few pairs of nearly new, thick socks and put them in a plastic bag.

I waited for the woman for the next several days in the same place, at the same time, but she never showed up. Unwilling to give up, unable to linger on the platform, I brought my little package up a flight of stairs to the woman who worked in the token booth. Though we had never spoken, we did have a smiling relationship. I usually traveled to and from Manhattan before the rush hour, and she knew my face.

I asked the clerk to open the booth's side door. I handed her the bag and an assignment: Please be on the lookout for a thin, black homeless woman who comes to the station in mid-afternoon and has no socks. And give her these socks.

My schedule kept me from that subway station for the next several weeks. When I finally went by her booth again, the clerk excitedly waved me over.

No, the young homeless woman had never showed up, but the clerk told me the day after I left the bag, two homeless men knocked on the booth's door and said their socks were wet. Their feet were cold. Did she have any dry socks?

She gave the men my package.

She had never seen those men before, she said. She had worked at that station for several years, and no one had ever asked for socks before.

"The Lord," she said, "sure works in mysterious ways."

THOUGHT TO PONDER:
When we choose to give to someone else, there is no limit to the good that can come from that selfless act.

Making Angels

About Frances Johnson, as told by her daughter
Denver, NC

The central purpose of each life should be to dilute the misery in the world.
Karl Menninger

FRANCES JOHNSON WAS blessed with a son who was developmentally disabled, Luther "Butch" Johnson. She first started making angel pins out of all sorts of materials when Butch was enrolled in Murdock School. Some time later that year, Butch lost his eyesight and finally died. That first year of making angels Frances earned $2500 which she gave to the Murdock School in memory of her son through her Eastern Star chapter.

After the first year she got so many requests that she continued to make the precious angel pins—out of wire, beads, metal pieces and any other materials she could find. That second year she made $11,000 on her angels! She donated the money that year to a burn center in Cincinnati where the daughter of the Grand Matron of her Easter Star chapter was hospitalized. The following year she donated the money from the angel pins to the

Greenville Shriner's unit for handicapped children where her husband was active.

When her church was being refurbished, people in the church sold Frances' angel pins, and they made enough money to redo the entire kitchen. Never has Frances ever advertised, and her daughter says she gives away almost as many pins as she sells. Frances says, "When you give one away, you can often sell a dozen!" What a beautiful mission she has to share her talent and resources!

THOUGHT TO PONDER:
What might you create using your God-given gifts to help other people?

A Life Lesson in Haiti

By Sondra Brunsting
Western Springs, Illinois

Mother Teresa on volunteers: *"I just ask them to come and love the people, to give their hands to serve them and their hearts to love them."*

"JUST HOW WAS your trip to Haiti?" I am asked repeatedly. I feel a bit awkward as I try to put into words an experience that my vocabulary inadequately describes. "It was wonderful," I begin, "one of the best experiences of my life." At this point, I often get a rather incredulous look from the one graciously asking of my travels, for Haiti rarely gets top billing as one of the most sought-after vacation spots.

How does one adequately convey the deeply moving experiences of two weeks observing God at work in the midst of poverty, filth, typhoid, malaria, Aids, hunger and significant lack of medical advancements, advancements that we in 21st century America have come to know and depend on?

I will be honest ... it is good to return to many of the conveniences of life that we have come to know and love. It is wonderful to turn on the faucet and brush your teeth without thinking twice about the contaminated water supply. Warm showers are wonderful ... although, I do believe I turn them a little cooler since my initiation to the 'cold shower' experience. I am grateful to find that I no longer have to use a flashlight to find my way to the bathroom in the middle of the night. I love not having to step cautiously to avoid the untimely demise of resident stink bugs, giant cockroaches, salamanders and tarantulas. Truly, I do believe you would have heard of _my_ demise had such a catastrophe occurred! Certainly, these cooler days are a welcome relief from the relentless tropical heat of the island of La Gonave, Haiti.

Nevertheless, I must be honest in telling you that there are aspects of my two-week experience that I desperately regret leaving behind as I return to the cushy life of upper middle class suburbia. To put it simply, when you remove all of the trappings of life as we know it—the materialism, the luxury, opportunity, entertainment, scientific/ medical advancement ... all of the 'stuff' that we spend so much time accumulating and maintaining—when you take away all but basic life essentials, you see God at work in a dramatically different way. In the basic environment of simple life, sustaining existence, one is limited, yes ... but for that very reason, one is so keenly aware of the limitations of man and the power of our almighty God.

We initiated this mission endeavor with the intent of giving the gift of ourselves to our brothers and sisters in Haiti that have so little of this world's material bounty. We ended up receiving the far greater gift of a significant life lesson that not one of us will ever forget; a lesson that abundance often clouds.

How fascinating to see how much simpler life can be with fewer choices. To my surprise, I found daily efforts simplified and time multiplied by the reduced demands of the maintenance of 'stuff.' There is time to read, to think, to ponder ... time to 'rest in Him'.

As a nurse, whose very life passion urges the provision of care and healing medical resources, I learned the inevitable frustration of limitation. In the town of Anse a Gallet on the island of La Gonave, life is hard and life expectancy tragically challenged by disease, lack of medical resources and poor nutrition. As visiting care providers; (physicians, nurses, instructors and students, all trained in some of the most up-to-date 'state of the art' medical techniques offered in the US,) we found ourselves dramatically limited and unable to provide some of the most basic medical care. There was an end to the options that we could offer, and we reached that point much sooner than we would have in the states. We much more quickly and repeatedly reached a point of saying, "We have done all we can do ... now it is in God's hands."

I wonder if we <u>ever</u> truly reach that point in the US. There is always another drug, another consultation, one more medical technique that may make the difference. Rarely do we step back and let God be God. Rarely do we have the privilege of experiencing the reality that God alone could have done it. There is always the temptation to dally in thoughts that human efforts made the difference—"but," we hasten to add, "we know, of course, that God was directing it all!"

Miracles were happening all around us, miracles we would have been oblivious to had we been caught in the tyranny of 'doing it ourselves'. Not only was God providing our group of 12 with daily demonstrations of His miraculous power in <u>providing basic need</u>, but He was also delighting us with 'our heart's desires'. Never before have I so vividly seen God at work, and I will be forever grateful for the gifts I personally received in the lessons that I take away from the experience.

We have been instructed, *"**Ask**, and it shall be given you ... **seek** and ye shall find ... **knock** and the door shall be open for you ..."* Have we become so focused on our own efforts that we have come to look at *asking, seeking* and *knocking* as cop-outs? Have we prevented, distorted, or at least complicated the comprehension of the 'miraculous' by making OUR efforts the focus.

Far too often, Lord, we think You need OUR help. Forgive us. Forgive us and help us to keep in perspective the delicate balance between responsible action and total abandon and trust in You. And may I never forget the lesson of the little town of Anse a Gallet on the island of La Gonave, Haiti ... one of the poorest places I have ever visited; one of the richest life experiences I have ever had.

"for it is in Giving that we Receive"

St. Francis of Assisi

THOUGHT TO PONDER:

Have you ever gone on a mission trip or donated your time to others? What gifts did you receive?

"Age with a Giggle"

Feel for others—in your pocket.

Charles H. Spurgeon

MY FRIEND, SHARYN Chapman, has written a delightful little book titled, "Age with a Giggle." In the introduction she writes:

This book has been written to assist all women who are searching for spiritual and emotional wisdom and a way to cope with aging. Women come in every size, shape, and color and, although we are paradoxically different, we are truly the same. Our experiences might change because of the zillion and twelve variables in our individual lives, but out issues, feelings, and desires remain constant. We are complex bodies of love and good deeds who very often shortchange ourselves ... This book is intended to encourage us all to forge ahead with grace and humor while making good life choices.

The most wonderful thing about Sherry's book, besides her delightful sense of humor and writing style, is that she is giving ALL the proceeds to charity. You can order a copy at Charitable Foundation, 1219 Sharswood Lane, Sarasota, FL 34242.

THOUGHT TO PONDER:

What talent or resource might you use to do good for others? Have you always wanted to write a book? Give a recital? Paint a picture? Then think about sharing the proceeds and making many people happy.

"25 Days of Christmas Kindness"

Leslie Rhea
Waco, Texas

Two phrases—"Will you help?" and "Yes, I will!"—comprise the most beautiful duet in American history.

David S. Ketchum

AS A WAY of sharing our blessings during Advent, we came up with ideas as a family of things we could do to help people in our community during the month of December. I made a calendar and wrote out one of the activities we decided to do on each day. I then put these strips of paper in our advent calendar, and the kids pulled the strip each morning to find out what our "Christmas Kindness" of the day would be.

Here is a list of some of the things we did:

1. Cooked a meal and delivered to Ryan's teacher and her family.
2. Bought toys and donated them to the Family Abuse Center.

3. Made Christmas snacks for the 40 college Young Life leaders that have Sunday night leadership at our house.

4. Bought a $50 gift card at Wal-Mart and gave it to the man in line behind us.

5. Bought the person in line behind us a meal at Sonic.

6. Donated toys to a local charities discount Toy Store.

7. Donated dog and cat food to a local "no kill" shelter.

8. Donated kids books to the school library.

9. Baked cookies and delivered them to friends.

10. Bought $5 gift cards and hid them in 3 different books at Barnes and Noble.

11. Put mittens and hats on the "Mitten Tree" at school to be donated.

12. Took donuts and coffee to the local fire station on Christmas Eve.

THOUGHT TO PONDER:

The Rhea family was accomplishing many things in their giving: sharing their own resources, teaching the children the joy of giving, blessing many others, and having fun as a family. What better use of our resources than this! And it was all done in the true spirit of Christmas.

Chapter Thirteen:

"Gifts of the Spirit"

On the forest path
above Blue Light Lake,
feeling the restlessness of the day,
hearing still the sounds of old conversations

A man sits by a rock
looking down on the lake;
he sketches the contours of the waves;
a sparrow flies into the sunlight ... silence

©Andrew Grossman 2000
Newton, CT

SPIRIT IS THE essence of who we are and what we believe in. When we give someone a gift of our spirit, it is sharing the very essence of our being. In college to receive my degree in English, I had to take a course called "19th Century British Writers." What I thought would be a very boring class ended up significantly impacting my life! I was introduced to John Ruskin, an architect and philosopher who wrote a great deal about spirit. In an old building, for example, he said we can "feel" the spirit of the many craftsmen who put months and even years of their lives into creating a place of beauty. Contrast those buildings with the sterile, quickly built high rises of today which have no spirit whatsoever.

Consequently, the best gift anyone can give me is something they have created. Anytime I receive a handmade gift, I feel as if the giver has given me a part of herself, a treasure beyond measure. Our home is filled with precious gifts of love from people who are dear in my life, so there is a warmth and radiance from their spirits which fills the rooms. From gifts of cross stitch, needlepoint, photography, painting, calligraphy, ceramics, silk flowers, pillows and afghans to friend's books, music CDs and videos, I feel constantly surrounded by love and caring.

While speaking in Valdez, Alaska, several years ago, I was privileged to meet two beautiful ladies, Jody Morgan, and Teri Rennie, who are quilters. How awed I was by the love they put into each work of art they create! These are truly gifts of the spirit. Another friend, Sharon Jakle from Illinois, knits what she calls "prayer scarves." The reason she calls them this is that she prays for the person she is making the scarf for the entire time she is knitting. I have been privileged to receive one of her scarves!

Another kind of gift of the spirit is when we reach out to others in caring and kindness, when we give them the gift of valuing them as human beings and perhaps doing just a little extra or going a bit out of our way to make their experience a better one. Sometimes gifts of the spirit come from the universe, or as Christians, we would say from the Holy Spirit. We cannot explain in rational, worldly terms how these gifts happened, but we know in our hearts that we were blessed by a force larger than our human understanding.

The stories in this chapter represent many different kinds of people—from a stranger in Chicago to a young daughter in Thailand, from a cabbie in London to a baker in Illinois, from a child in Africa to a businessman in Greece. Yet all have either given or received the blessing of a gift of the spirit.

Saving the Fish—
A Gift for the Immortal Soul

As told by Hanthip Amornsing
Phuket, Thailand

The thing which counts is the striving of the human soul to achieve spiritually
the best that it is capable of and to care unselfishly, not only for personal
good, but for the good of all those who toil with them upon the earth.

Eleanor Roosevelt

IN THE BUDDHIST tradition it is bad kharma to kill any living thing, so this is the story of how Hanthip, nicknamed "Jang," saved her father's soul by begging, buying, stealing, and giving away his catfish!

Somsak Amornsing, Jang's father, planned ahead for his retirement by building cement tanks in his backyard to raise catfish. When the fish were babies, Jang helped her father feed and care for them, but when she found out that the fish were being raised to be eaten, she immediately decided that she had to help both them and her father, so she devised a plan.

On her birthday, for a gift, she asked her father if she could take ten or twelve of the fish and release them in a national park so they could be free. Her father agreed to that, so Jang was happy. Then, whenever her friends had a birthday, Jang again asked to free a few fish (always taking a "few" more than her father had agreed to!) Often she would bring money home that she had earned and tell her father that her friends wanted to buy fish for their dinners. Then she would take the fish and again free them in the park.

Finally, one day when her father went out to check on his fish, he saw an amazing sight—there were no more fish! He decided that he couldn't run a business that way, so at last he gave up. Jang was delighted—she had saved his immortal soul AND the fish. Now when you go into their back yard, all you can see is dozens of empty cement fish tanks!

THOUGHT TO PONDER:
The wisdom of children is the greatest gift of all!

Seeing the Queen
By Bill and Darlene Willard
Portland, Oregon

If you have much, give of your wealth; if you have little, give of your heart.
Arab Proverb

EARLY ONE EVENING while vacationing in London, we wandered toward St. James's Palace to see Prince Charles' London home. That particular evening, there happened to be a reception and dinner for the Council of European Ministers taking place at St. James's. We positioned ourselves across the street so we could watch the arrivals of the well-known guests.

We were the only ones there until a friendly coach driver, who had driven a busload of dignitaries to the dinner, struck up a conversation with us. He informed us that the Queen was due to arrive momentarily and we might get a glimpse of her if we waited a little longer. After a while, when the Queen hadn't arrived, he spoke with someone familiar with the Queen's schedule and learned that she had already arrived via another entrance and would be leaving via that same entrance in about an hour. Just as it began to rain lightly, he told us we needed to go around to the opposite side of the palace. He was getting ready to move his coach to avoid a parking ticket and graciously offered to drive us around the palace to the appropriate spot, so he could point out where the Queen would exit. Eagerly, we accepted his kind offer.

Before disembarking from his bus, we offered him a tip to thank him for his extreme generosity and graciousness. He adamantly refused it, explaining, "Some people think money can buy anything, but I don't. Please put your money away. If you want to thank me, please do so by saying a prayer for someone in need." We will never forget his kindness. By the way, we did see the Queen and her mother. They gave us a slight smile and wave as they rode past in their cute "Queenmobile!"

THOUGHT TO PONDER:
This lovely gentleman created a very special memory for the Willards. Have you ever shown kindness to complete strangers? That is a gift in the truest sense!

The Pizza Party
By Antonette Addante
Chicago, Illinois

The most enthusiastic givers in life are the real lovers of life. They experience the soul—joy that comes from responding with the heart rather than the head.
Helen Steiner Rice

I HAVE RECENTLY become involved in an organization for Mentally Challenged Adults. In February of 1998, my former employer asked me to volunteer at a Fund Raising Event they held for the group. Since then, a group of us have dedicated one Tuesday per month to join these individuals and share good times through various activities.

From time to time, depending upon the activities, I would request certain donations from my parent's business since my dad owns a bakery. For example, for a Valentine's Day activity this year, we decorated cupcakes and had a Valentine's party. My dad supplied the frosted cupcakes and a variety of decorations.

During our last visit, the group decided to have a "Pizza Making Party". Once again, I approached my dad for all of the supplies. But what I did differently this time was to actually get my dad involved. Operating a bakery has left my dad with very little time to enjoy the meaningful things in life. So, I was determined to get him to experience the intrinsic gratification one feels from engaging in sharing, caring activities with others who need more joy in their lives.

The result was incredible! My dad had an experience he has never felt before. One of the staff members at AVENUES TO INDEPENDENCE, who joined us that evening, stated, "This is one of the best times they've ever had!" The AVENUES residents laughed and laughed and even learned how to make pizzas! My dad not only taught them about making pizzas, but he entertained them with the melodies of Italian music, a side to my father I have rarely seen before.

I share my story because it meant so much to me to see my dad happy instead of just always working—and he was making others happy, too. That is what CARE packages can do!

THOUGHT TO PONDER:

Antonette gave a CARE package to both the group and herself when she began spending time with them once a month. She also gave her dad a gift by inviting him to join them. Her dad gave a CARE package in the supplies he furnished, but the beautiful part of this story is that he gave a much more meaningful gift when he truly gave of himself, his talents, and his joy in life. And the gift came back to Antonette as she saw her father in a new light. EVERONE received a gift!

Gifts of the Spirit from Greece

By Dimitri Tsitos
Athens, Greece

The heart of the giver makes the gift dear and precious.
                                        Martin Luther

ONCE WHEN I was visiting another city to deliver a speech, even though I had earlier booked a very nice room, I discovered upon my arrival and to my deepest dismay that, according to the "hotel's Front Desk villain," they did not have my reservation. The room he gave me was noisy and beyond the limits of acceptance.

My first thought was to raise a hail and even verbally attack the people of the Front Desk and the Management. Then I decided otherwise.

I went down to the reception and, looking forlorn, I asked the receptionist, "Would you like to share a glass of whiskey and my miseries?"

He asked, "What happened?"

I answered, "She is going to give me hell's time all the night. And she is good at it. She did not like the room".

He reacted immediately, "Don't worry. I'll give you the suite at no extra charge. Don't worry".

"No, don't bother. It happens all the time. I can stand it".

"No way. This time you'll get a good night's sleep!"

Now I have my "friend" in that city. Just "re-framing" my anger gave me a life-time good friend and extraordinary service at that hotel.

***

Oftentimes I have the opportunity to attend the rehearsals of the Greek Byzantine chorus. The conductor, Mr. Lycourgos Angelopoulos, insists that his singers know exactly what they sing, in other words not just the notes but the inner meaning of the text. Then he asks his people not only to read the notes but to sing "with their souls." He says, "Notes are perfect for discipline; souls are for singing."

***

My most well-paid job ever was offered to me because five years ago I sat for a lunch with a desperate PhD—unemployed then—who had just returned from the States. That lunch, offered by my company, and the friendly discussion we had finally blossomed after four years. That person is now a General Manager in a very large company, and he always gives me first choice when he has a training need. Make friends when you don't need them!

THOUGHT TO PONDER:

The way we treat people, no matter who they are, can make a big difference in both our lives and theirs! Respecting them as human beings with a soul is the best gift we can give to anyone.

A Little Girl's Prayer

By Helen Roseveare, Doctor missionary
Zaire, Africa

If you want to lift yourself up, lift up someone else.

Booker T. Washington

ONE NIGHT I had worked hard to help a mother in the labor ward, but in spite of all we could do, she died, leaving us with a tiny premature baby and a crying two-year-old daughter. We knew we would have difficulty keeping the baby alive, as we had no incubator (we had no electricity to run an incubator) and no special feeding facilities.

Although we lived on the equator, nights were often chilly with treacherous drafts. One student midwife went for the box we had for such babies and the cotton wool the baby would be wrapped in. Another went to stoke up the fire and fill a hot water bottle. She came back shortly in distress to tell me that in filling the bottle, it had burst. Rubber perishes easily in tropical climates. "And it is our last hot water bottle!" she exclaimed.

Just like in the West it is no good crying over spilled milk, so in Central Africa it might be considered no good crying over burst water bottles! They do not grow on trees, and there are no drugstores down forest pathways. "All right," I said, "put the baby as near the fire as you safely can; sleep between the baby and the door to keep it free from drafts. Your job is to keep the baby warm."

The following noon, as I did most days, I went to have prayers with any of the orphanage children who chose to gather with me. I gave the youngsters various suggestions of things to pray about and told them about the tiny baby. I explained our problem about keeping the baby warm enough, mentioning the hot water bottle. The baby could so easily die if it got chills. I also told them of the two-year-old sister, crying because her mother had died.

During the prayer time, one ten-year-old girl, Ruth, prayed with the usual blunt conciseness of our African children. "Please, God," she prayed, "send us a water bottle. It'll be no good tomorrow, God, as the baby'll be dead, so please send it this afternoon." While I gasped inwardly at the audacity of the prayer, she added by way of corollary, "And while You are about it, would You please send a dolly for the little girl so she'll know You really love her?" As often with children's prayers, I was put on the spot. Could I honestly say, "Amen"? I just did not believe that God could do this. Oh, yes, I know that He can do everything. The Bible says so. But there are limits, aren't there? The only way God could answer this particular prayer would be by sending me a parcel from the homeland. I had been in Africa for almost four years at that time, and I had never, ever received a parcel from home; anyway, if anyone did send me a parcel, who would put in a hot water bottle? I lived on the equator!

Halfway through he afternoon, while I was teaching in the nurses' training school, a message was sent that there was a car at my front door. By the time I reached home, the car had gone, but there, on the verandah, was a large twenty-two pound parcel. I felt tears pricking my eyes. I could not open the parcel alone, so I sent for the orphanage children. Together we pulled off the string, carefully undoing each knot. We folded the paper, taking care not to tear it unduly. Excitement was mounting! Some thirty or forty pairs of eyes were focused on the large cardboard box.

From the top, I lifted out brightly colored, knitted jerseys. Eyes sparkled as I gave them out. Then there were the knitted bandages for the leprosy patients, and the children looked a little bored. Then came a box of mixed raisins and sultanas—that would make a nice batch of buns for the weekend. Then, as I put my hand in again, I felt the … could it really be? I grasped it and pulled it out—yes, a brand-new, rubber hot bottle!

I cried. I had not asked God to send it; I had not truly believed that He could. Ruth was in the front row of the children. She rushed forward, crying out, "If God has sent the bottle, He must have sent the dolly, too!" Rummaging down to the bottom of the box, she pulled out the small, beautifully dressed dolly. Her eyes shone! She had never doubted. Looking up at me, she asked: "Can I go over with you, Mummy, and give this dolly to that little girl, so she'll know that Jesus really loves her?"

That parcel had been on the way for five whole months. Packed up by my former Sunday school class, whose leader had heard and obeyed God's prompting to send a hot water bottle, even to the equator. And one of the girls had put in a dolly for an African child—five months before—in answer to the believing prayer of a ten-year-old to bring it "that afternoon."

"Before they call, I will answer!"—Isa. 65:24

THOUGHT TO PONDER:
I believe we have small miracles in our lives every single day. However, we will only see them if we look with our heavenly eyes. Listen to the messages of your heart and soul. Sometimes we are prompted to do things that make no sense at the time, but like the Sunday school class package, they are often for a higher purpose than we can even imagine.

Anything Is Possible

By Connie Krauth
Minneapolis, Minnesota

Kindness is loving people more than they deserve.

Joseph Joubert

THE GIFT OF knowing that anything is possible came to me from Paul McCartney on a Sunday afternoon, May 22, 1993.

I grew up in the 1960s in a small town in North Dakota, far from Liverpool, England. Since 1964, however, my dream had been to meet the Beatles. They gave me so much joy that I wanted to thank them personally, but it seemed to be an impossible dream. In the early days of their tremendous fame, there was not much chance of a meeting unless you had tight connections to the music world. And I certainly did not!

I did see them perform in 1965 and was so very thankful. It was the ultimate "high" for a sixteen year old girl, and that concert made a long lasting impression. Later, after their breakup, Paul and his new band, Wings, came to St. Paul in the summer of 1976. I was there, a little face in the crowd. I was as close as I could get. Then John was murdered in 1980, and the dream was shattered. One of the Beatles was gone, and it would never be the same. Still, I listened to their music and read about their climb to fame. And I learned just how they made their dreams come true.

By the summer of 1989, Ringo began to perform with his All Starr bands. He played at Riverfest, a music festival on Harriet Island in St.Paul and my passion to meet the remaining three came back full strength. Then Paul toured, and I traveled to Ames, Iowa, to see him perform. Paul and Ringo were still touring, and I still felt like a sixteen year old when they played and sang! They continued to draw large audiences, and my older face was in the crowd.

Again in 1993 Paul toured and, in fact, was scheduled for a performance in Minneapolis. But his venue, the Metrodome, was a horrid place for any band's sound system. I couldn't bear to have his words and piano chords bouncing from section 238 down to 103 and back up to the balcony in section 215. So a good friend in Long Beach invited me for a visit, and we attended Paul's concert in Anaheim, California. That was in April of 1993.

After returning home to Minneapolis, I saw a short TV clip describing Paul's routine on tour. He usually arrived at the stadium mid-afternoon to conduct a sound check, then would eat his dinner there, and continue to get ready for his 8 o'clock performance.

His show at the Metrodome was set for May 22. It would be Sunday, and that meant it would be quiet in downtown Minneapolis, easy to park my car, and well worth a chance of catching up with one of the Fab Four. From 1964 until this day in 1993 there had not been an opportunity to do something like this. So we knew we must take this chance. And so my sister, who had been with me at all the concerts and who shared my dream to meet the Beatles, drove with me to downtown Minneapolis.

It was a cool day with light rain. We were prepared with umbrellas and plastic gear to cover a few items that we hoped might get autographed. And, of course we had cameras. We parked behind the dome on the street and put enough quarters in the meter to keep us until 4:30 pm. We walked across the street to the Metrodome's back entrance. There was only one place that a car or truck could enter, and there we stood. One other person was there when we arrived, but more came later, and as we waited, we all got acquainted by sharing stories revolving around our love of the Beatles' music. It began to rain.

The week before, my sister called me to tell me she had one of those "very real" dreams. In her dream she saw Paul McCartney. She told me it was remarkable because he was so clear and real. A few nights later I had a dream. In my dream I saw Paul walking with a crowd of people following him. But for some reason, he singled me out in the crowded plaza and acknowledged me.

It was now 4 o'clock at the Metrodome's back entrance, and a limo was arriving. A few people got out of the long white car and walked through the entrance. They looked like business people; perhaps they were Paul's managers. I was very close. If he came in the same way, we'd be there.

But as the rain became heavier and I grew colder, some security men arrived. They asked us to move several yards back from the entrance. I was too far away to see Paul now. But what could we do? I fretted, but my sister convinced me this was still the best place to be. It really was as close as we could get.

Then, very swiftly, another limo arrived, and some hands waved at us through a partially open, smoked-glass window. As fast as it arrived, it escaped into the dome. Was it Paul McCartney's hand? We didn't know for sure. Perhaps he was tired and hurried, not interested in meeting us. Who would blame him? We were all drenched, and we must have been a sorry sight!

Most of the fans stayed in their places for the next few minutes. Then some started to leave. I was cold and soaked to the bone. It was 4:30, and the parking meter was spent. I convinced my sister to leave. As we moved toward the street, however, another fan encouraged us to stay for just a little while longer. I decided to put another quarter in the meter and come back.

My sister and I walked to the sidewalk to cross the street to the car, but we had to stop for a red light. I looked to the right and saw another limo on its way. It had to be Paul's! We were the only two fans on the corner. What could we do? I stared at the car, and as it slowly pulled directly in front of us, the window rolled down.

It was Paul! He waved and called to us. I hollered to him, "We love you. Thanks for the music."

It was as if time stood still. I can only compare it to watching the exaggerated tape of the Kennedy assassination. Every second was framed in my mind.

We were the only two on the corner. Once the limo turned the corner, it moved into the dome quickly. Had we remained in our original place, we would have missed him completely (as did most of our new acquaintances) because he was sitting on the other side of the car. I was in the exact place at the exact time all because of the parking meter, which most likely would never have been checked that Sunday afternoon. And to top it all off, he noticed us and took the time to roll his window down.

I screamed like a teenager and hugged my sister who had just gotten herself free from the security guard into whose arms she had fallen. I didn't realize until later that in my frenzied state I had thrown my umbrella up and behind me about five feet. It was just like "A Hard Day's Night," only 30 years later!

When we finally came to our senses, my sister revealed to me that she had taken a picture. But would it turn out? The sky was gray; it was raining; the car was moving; and she was excited.

And, yes, it did turn out! Better than we ever imagined—so very clear and real, just like in her dream. And just as in my dream, I talked to him, having his full attention for just a moment.

Well, that was just the beginning! I told my story to everyone who would listen. I wrote it and submitted it to the London Beatles Fan club magazine where it was published. Later I wrote a short book about what the Beatles meant to me and set up a mail order business selling books to fans around the world.

Through some of these new connections, I became aware of the Beatles' conventions. By attending these events, I met others associated with the Beatles. I eventually met Ringo's manager, David Fishoff and several of the players in his All Starr band, and through that connection I met Ringo in May of 1997. I stood face to face with Ringo Starr and told him I had loved him and his music for more than 30 years ... and he hugged me!

Later in November 1997 we attended Paul's US premier of "Standing Stone" (his classical work) which was performed at Carnegie Hall. I was in Row 5 near the stage and when the performance ended, he stood on stage right in front of me. I was spellbound, and once again, time stood magically still. Confetti came floating down from the ceiling to celebrate his work. But I was having my own celebration. I did it! Anything was possible! I was close, very close, and I had the happiest face in the crowd!

THOUGHT TO PONDER:

Have you ever been given the gift of a dream come true? Have you ever given that gift to anyone else?

This poem is about each of our "gifts of the spirit:"

Portrait of a Christian

Not only in the words you say,
Not only in your deeds confessed,
But in the most unconscious way
Is Christ expressed.

Is it a beatific smile?
A holy light upon your brow?
I know I felt His presence
When you laughed just now.

For me 'twas not the truth you taught;
To you so clear, to me so dim.
But when you came to me,
You brought a sense of Him.

And from your eyes He beckons me
And from your lips His love is shed,
'Til I lose sight of you
And see the Christ instead.

Author Unknown

Chapter Fourteen:

"Gifts of your Talents"

Her song glides from the radio
Her song patches the worn holes

Her old man in his pickup truck
Nuts and bolts flying at every bump

Remembering her singing on the porch
How we raised her and sent her forth

©Andrew Grossman 1999
Newton, CT

THE BIBLE TELLS us the parable of the talents: One person hid his talents. Another kept them only for himself. A third person used his talents to help others, and they multiplied many times over. Which one is true of you?

I have been taught that my talents are gifts, not gifts I deserve but gifts with which I have been blessed. Therefore, I have an obligation to use those talents to the best of my ability to make a difference in this world. When I was young, I was quite a talented pianist. From the earliest years of my playing, I can remember my mother taking me to the Baptist Memorial Home, the only long term care facility in our little town in Iowa, where I would play the piano for the residents. How they loved to hear a young person perform! I played at Sunday school, at church, and for many community gatherings over the years.

Besides helping others, there were also some great advantages to using my musical talent. All my girlfriends were especially jealous that I got to accompany all the boys' musical groups at the high school! I, of course, was the only girl, and when they had to travel to a contest or musical show, guess who got to go along on the bus?

Each of us is blessed with different talents, and none are more valuable or important then others. What is important, though, is how we use and develop them. Are you good at carpentry? If so, you can help repair things for older people or work with Habitat for Humanity. Are you good at baking? If so, you can share the fruits of your labor with anyone who needs cheering up. If you are an artist of any kind, you are creating a more beautiful world by sharing your talents. If you love older people or children or animals, you can find ways to add happiness and joy to a life. Even driving others or helping with errands is a special talent which you can share. Think about what you really enjoy doing and then ponder ways you can use that talent to give something back to the world.

The Gift of a Poem

By Bob Bruce
Howey-in-the-Hills, Florida

Give of the three things you have: time, talent, treasure.
Douglas M. Lawson

I WRITE A lot of poems for employees of our company and friends who have suffered a death in the family or who are celebrating a birth of a child or a wedding, or other special event. To me, it is a way of sending a little love to them in a different form. Many have been matted and framed, and several have found their way into a newsletter or similar publication, so I get to share in the pleasure of doing something nice for someone also.

The Gift of Love

To make a change in someone's life,
Just give a gift of love.
No greater gift could we receive
Than that from God above.

You needn't say romantic things
Or buy expensive gifts.
Just be a friend to one in need,
Then watch the life it lifts.

When we can touch another's life
Or brighten someone's day,
The joy that comes right back to us
Propels us on our way.

So when you try to find a gift
To show someone you care,
Just give some little gift of love;
A gift you both can share.

These are poems that Bob wrote when our first grandchild, Gavin William Glanz, was born. My son and daughter-in-law named him after our second child who had died and that meant the world to Charlie and me.

Gavin

For Gavin William Glanz
May 17, 1998

His name suggested memories

Of sadness from the past.
But Gavin brought a brand new love
Into the world at last.

He filled his mother's heart with joy;
His father's world with pride.
The love and caring they both shared
They simply could not hide.

He'll fill their lives with smiles and tears.
He'll put them to the test.
But, through it all, their love for him
Will always see the best.

And when he's grown ... become a man,
Their baby still he'll be.
Their love and pride will still shine through
For all the world to see.

A Springtime Gift

For Gavin William Glanz
May 17, 1998

Although the sun had not yet shone,
A golden glow was seen
It filled the corners of the room
And all things in between.

A loving couple had been blessed
With a bouncing baby boy.
And simple words could not be found
To demonstrate their joy.

Mom checked his fingers, one by one,
And then she checked his toes.

"He'll be a star," she told herself,
"No matter where he goes."

And Dad his joy could not conceal
Their Gavin ... here at last
His face aglow with father's love ...
His heart beat ... oh, so fast.

Then, as the sun began to rise,
It seemed much brighter, too.
How wonderful to start this day
With this family's dream come true.

THOUGHT TO PONDER:

My son, daughter-in-law and I, as well as Gavin someday, will always treasure this gift from Bob. In fact, my daughter-in-law has even had one of the poems framed. Bob has used his special talent to delight many people in his life. He has found the blessing that his gift of words can bring to others. Whether you write stories, poetry, lovely thoughts, or letters, your words can bring encouragement and joy to be read and reread for years. What talent might you share with others?

OTHER GIFTS OF POETRY:

The Pilot

By Jim Munroe
Sylacauga, Alabama

What you are is God's gift to you and what you do with what you are is your gift to God.

George Foster

AFTER MY HUSBAND died, Jim wrote this letter to me:

I wanted to tell you how saddened I was to hear about Charlie. I knew from previous newsletters that he had been sick. After I read the last newsletter and got to the last paragraph about your devotion, my mind whirled with thoughts. I wrote many of them down and enclosed you will find the finished work. It is my gift to you this Christmas.

I will never forget what you have done for me and the work that you continue to do for so many. Neither you nor I nor anyone but God knows why He placed these obstacles in your path. But I do know that He will never leave or forsake you, one of His children.

May the light that shines through you and warms our souls be rays of hope to the hopeless and a beacon of His love. My thoughts and prayers are with you.

Jim

Here is the poem he wrote for me:

He has been there all along with an unseen hand,

a strong and guiding force through uncharted lands.

When still water turns to rapids and darkness falls your way,

He moves you through the storm into the light of day.

The Pilot knows the danger of each bump that's in the road,

Just follow where He leads you, let him bear your load.

His hands are steady on the wheel, his eyes are open wide,

place your hand right next to his, stand closely by his side.

The Pilot sees the future, each challenge you will face,

and gives you peace and comfort and his abundant grace.

So when your path is foggy or the way seems so unclear,

REMEMBER

you're not without The Pilot if you don't know where to steer.

©2000 Jim Munroe *Rhymes4Life* All Rights Reserved.

THOUGHT TO PONDER:

I will always treasure this poem from Jim. He has decided to use his talent to start a new business to write original poems for people who would like to celebrate someone or something, so if you are not a poet yourself, you can still send someone a lovely poem. He just shared with me that he has recently written his 300th poem! You can see his website at

http://www.rhymes4life.com.

Poetry of the Spirit
By Judy Ballard Ellsworth
San Antonio, Texas

Use what talents you possess: the woods would be very silent if no birds sang there except those that sang best.

Henry Van Dyke

TEN YEARS AGO, my life changed dramatically due to a chronic health problem. During this time I lost my job, my independence, traveled through various stages of grief, and searched for ways to ease my chronic pain. I was homebound, and often, being in a body cast, could do no more than stay in my heavy braces in bed. However, I found that I could create poetry to express my feelings and often, my depression and despair.

Although my life seemed shattered, I found that writing poetry helped me regain some of my strength and confidence. In my mind, poetry was the one thing I was still successful doing! Although I had written high school poetry years ago, I had not written again until this time. The words would come to me quickly, and the poems were written in a few minutes. There was a kind of spirit working though me when I wrote.

My friend, Yolanda, who is a secretary, realized how therapeutic this activity was for me, and she was a true friend in her guidance and love. She would call me every day to see if I had written a poem that day and to tell me that she had typed up my last poem. She has a very strong personality, quite assertive and "motherly." Through all this time she kept a typed folder of all my poems so that I could feel as if I had accomplished something.

She would tell me that she was coming over, would bring us lunch, and pick up my new poem. If I hadn't written one that day, you can be sure I got right to it, knowing that I would be lectured if I hadn't produced one! She inspired me to write the poem "Angels on Earth," which I framed and gave to her as a "thank you" for her friendship and commitment. She was thrilled to receive it, saying that no one had ever given her such a beautiful gift. But, she was really the true giver of beauty and gifts!

My friends, family, church, and poetry were the keys to my mental health. Without my friends like Yolanda, who were always there for me, I doubt that I would have become "me" again. To show my love and appreciation, I continued to write poems for them and about them, had them framed, and presented them as gifts, using my gift of poetry that I had re-discovered in that difficult time of my life.

Giving and receiving is such a powerful part of our lives. Today I am living a rich, fulfilling life and no longer suffer from chronic pain. However, I still write poems!

April 8, 1989
Angels on Earth

There are some angels on earth
Without wings
Mortal beings
They are there when you need them.
Yolanda is one
She can't be outdone
In her tireless
Determination to
Minister to those in need—
Not for greed or
To win God's favor,
But because it is best for the other.
Like a mother—
She persists,
Insists
That you not lose faith
In yourself or God.
She takes over
When you can't go on.
Arranging, organizing
So you won't fall,
Gives you a call
On schedule, without fail
God, send some more Yolandas in Your mail.
No wings, halo or robe.
Like Job, never doubting Your will.
Showing strength in adversity
I believe you put angels on earth
To give us a glimpse
Of heaven and all it's worth.
Thank you, God

Christmas, 1989
My Faithful Friend

Always, when I've needed
Help or aid of some
Kind,
You've said, "I don't
Mind."
And, often, you say,
"I will pray
For you."
And I know it's true.
You are one of few
Real Christians.
My life has been so
Enriched and enlightened.
And often, I face
Burdens, unfrightened,
Because you have been
There,
And always will be.
You've helped me see
God.
Thank you,
My faithful friend.

January 22, 1989
Barbara

Barbara, glides in the room
Slight lovely, fair—
Erases the gloom.
Ready with a quip,
Fast of lip.

Spreads her cheer
Such a dear, dear
Friend.
One watches negatives around her.
Life for her, is born with content
Heaven-sent
Forward—bent
She gives her best,
Or more.
She pulls you up
Without you even knowing,
A gentle spirit, soaring—
Christ like, all knowing.
Barbara—glowing.

May 19, 1989
My Poet Friend

You are so kind.
Hope you don't mind
My dependency on you
To get me through
Tough times.
What rhymes
With times,
My poet friend?
Ties that bind—
Hard to find
These days.
Time often frays
Friendships.
But mine for you
Has become stronger.
I don't know how much longer

You'll hang on.
But thank you,
My poet friend
For your encouragement
To keep writing
And for your precious time
When it becomes mine.

August 8, 1989
Louise

Today we said good-by.
It's been such a high
To know you ...
Work with you,
Share and care with you.
You're more a friend
Than a boss ...
A great loss,
Now.
How hard it will be
Not to see
Your lovely smile,
Your radiant style,
Exuding confidence.
A Christian model,
Living as He would
Want us to.
Compassionate, kind ...
Sees the good
In people.
You lift them up
And fill their cup.
So many people want

A part of you
And you always have
More to give.
Oh, that we could live
Like you,
Louise.

December 6
Affirmation

A favorite friend visited
Today.
How she lifts me!
She gifts me
With her giving ...
Makes time for me
In her living,
Because she wants to ...
Not out of guilt
Or pity.
She said I say
What is in my
Heart.
As I search for
Healing,
My reaching out
Has given others
Affirmation
Of their goodness
And need to serve.

THOUGHT TO PONDER:

What a precious gift Judy found through her pain! Have you ever tried writing poetry? Or just a note or letter to someone? I have a friend named Carol Myers whose gift is writing notes of encouragement to those who are suffering. I have saved some of her notes for years, rereading them many times to help me through difficult times.

The Mentor

By Kay Hudson
Indianhead Park, Illinois

We must not only give what we have; we must also give what we are.

Desiree Joseph Mercier

MY STORY BEGINS when I moved to Washington, D.C., to put my life back together. I had recently been divorced, my eating was out of control, I was having other family problems, and I knew I needed a fresh start. Of course, moving to a new city meant dealing with a new job. So during this time, I was trying to understand my new job responsibilities, deal with an eating addiction, and make a new life all at once.

A major component of my new job was writing and editing technical material. My BS degree in mathematics did not prepare me to write. I was literally terrified of sitting with my blank legal pad in front of me (before the days of PCs!), waiting for inspiration. Meanwhile I began to attend 12-step meetings for my eating addiction during my lunch break. When it was my turn to speak, I told of my fear of writing and feeling like I was failing at my job.

At the end of the meeting, a very distinguished, well-dressed, and very kind man approached me. He happened to be an engineer—and technical writer—working for the Commissioner of one of the most technical Agencies in Washington. He told me he had been where I was and would help me! He gave me his office number and told me to call him first thing every morning, and he would coach me through the day. What a gift! I felt saved.

Day after day, I called him for instructions. Sometimes they were as simple as "get to work on time" and "don't leave early." Sometimes he helped me edit my work. But most importantly, he was at the other end of the telephone every day. This went on for two years.

Today, I live in a different city. I am recognized as being a good writer and editor. My co-workers often ask me to edit their work and help them write a variety of documents. Additionally, I seldom act on my eating addiction and have lost quite a bit of weight.

Ed was my mentor and my angel during the most difficult time of my life. I will always credit him with saving my career.

Epilogue

One of the major components of the 12-step programs is making amends when we have done something wrong or simply wiping the slate clean. When attending a conference in another city, I quite unexpectedly encountered my manager from the old agency. I told her how much I appreciated her working with me during those difficult days and that I knew in many ways I had not pulled my weight in the office, but she had worked with my strengths and saved my career. She was very gracious and told me how happy she was that I was doing so well in my new agency and in my life.

I then flew home, and that night the daughter we had been praying for, our only child, was conceived.

THOUGHT TO PONDER:

Have you ever been a mentor to someone? What a life-changing gift that gift of encouragement can be! My idea of Heaven is that we will see all the people we have touched in some way that we knew nothing about. Pick someone in your life right now and decide to be a mentor to them. Have you had mentors in your life who have shared their skills and talents with you? Thank them in a concrete way this very week.

The Magic of Massage Therapy

About Muriel Hattori
Ponte Vedra, Florida

It is only in the giving of oneself to others that we truly live.

Ethel Percy Andrus

RIC DEVERE IS a tall, handsome, soft-spoken fifteen year old who was born with a rare liver disease called Crigler-Najjar.

For years, Ric has tried to live as normal a life as possible by interacting with friends and participating in sports, for which he has a table lined with trophies. As he has grown older, however, it has become more difficult explaining to others why his eyes and skin color are often yellow. There have also been many occasions where he has found himself tiring easily, causing him to sleep much of the day away. Needless to say, this has affected his attendance and performance at school. Other students and faculty who have not been aware of his condition have made comments and hurtful remarks which this very sensitive young man has taken to heart and in turn, Ric has become even more introverted.

Ric's family has attempted to educate the public about this disease, but it has been an arduous, uphill battle with no support groups around in which to share or vent. With only fifty known cases of Crigler-Najjar in the United States, the family is very alone and isolated at times with only a handful of people who understand what they are experiencing.

Needless to say, young Ric has suffered in silence, withdrawing into his world of computers and sports. However, Ric has become an avid Jacksonville Jaguars football fan and also loves to watch golf on television.

One day, Katie, Ric's Mother, was contacted by Muriel Hattori, a nationally recognized massage therapist, who is known for her spirit and community service. Muriel, whose clientele reads like a "Who's Who" of the sports and entertainment world, volunteered to give Ric a series of treatments in an effort to relieve both muscle and emotional pain. Ric was ecstatic and found it difficult to control his enthusiasm, knowing that these were the same hands which had touched and massaged some of his sports idols such as football players Jimmy Smith, Keenan McCardell, and Jerry Rice, and golfers Freddy Couples and Seve Ballestreros. This thought kept Ric smiling for days, knowing that he now had something in common with his idols and a great new friend in Muriel!

Ric not only looks and feels better, but now looks forward to his next massage, just to hear who else has joined in his exclusive "Hands-on Club."

Once again the Power of Touch has done wonders, healing not only physically, but also emotionally. Muriel has used her special talent to help many people over the years, but she is most proud of the impact her hands have had on the life of one brave young man. Why hasn't everyone discovered the magic of massage therapy?

THOUGHT TO PONDER:
Whatever your special talent may be, use it, like Muriel, to make this world a better place.

Sunday Morning Gift from the Heart

Christopher House
Chicago, Illinois

He gives nothing who does not give himself.

French Proverb

SEVEN BOYS, AGED 10 to 12, gave a gift from the heart to homeless people in their area. At Christopher House, a North Side social service agency, a homeless man had just eaten pancakes, sausage, eggs, strawberries, and "about six cups of coffee," all courtesy of a group of young boys.

The youths, part of Christopher House's weekly after-school Business Baking Club for children of low-income families, decided to spend the $215 they had raised over the year baking and selling brownies on a home-cooked brunch for some of Chicago's street people. Though they could have done many other things with the money they had earned, like going to a ballgame or having a party, they decided to do something that they felt would help others.

One of them said, "We could have just made this for ourselves. But we did this 'cause it was nice and friendly, and it wasn't us just making pigs of ourselves."

Lauren Mitchell, owner of the mail-order business, Aunt Maimee's Brownies, came up with the idea to form a club to teach children how to bake the brownies—and at the same time become entrepreneurs.

Each week, in the Christopher House kitchen in the 2500 block of North Greenview Avenue, the boys baked brownies and then sold them at the front door to other children, the staff and parents for 25 cents, 75 cents or more, depending on the size of the brownie and, at times, the size of the customer's wallet.

Recording their profits in a ledger after reimbursing Mitchell for the ingredients and pocketing $1 each in commissions for a day's selling, they proved to be astute businessmen, as well as bakers.

On a Sunday morning, the boys set up a buffet table in the gym and prepared and served pancakes, hash browns, sausage, cereal, plums, strawberries, orange juice, milk, chocolate chip cookies and brownies. As a result of their idea, other members of the community got involved, too. Brown bag lunches, were given to the guests, beauticians gave free haircuts, and others even donated clean socks and t-shirts.

A man who identified himself only as Henry and said he lived at the Lincoln-Belmont YMCA said the youngsters, "did a real good job." "I ain't had no decent food for quite a while," he said. "This came just in time."

THOUGHT TO PONDER:
This is a priceless gift that was given by children who had many other choices. What a life-changing lesson they are learning through their generosity! Have you taught your children the joy of giving? This idea could be used by any group of young people to help others and to learn what true giving really is.

Who? Me??
By Kim Mooney
Canton, Georgia

You give but little when you give of your possessions. It is when you give of yourself that you truly give.

Kahlil Gibran

DONNA MCDONALD IS a friend of mine and my mentor (although I don't know if she realizes the last part). She came into my life one day when I attended an in-home kitchen show where she was the consultant. We spoke only briefly when I placed my order, and then I left.

A few weeks later, I called her and asked her to come to my home to tell me more about her business. You see, I'd left the corporate world to be a stay-at-home mom five years before. I ran an in-home daycare for four other children, besides having three of my own (ages 1-1/2, 6 and 8), and I also home-schooled my oldest two. I knew in the fall I was going to lose the majority of my income from daycare to the start of kindergarten, and I wondered if there was any way I could use my love of cooking and kitchen gadgets to earn some extra money to replace the lost income.

I had one major concern. I had a "Grand Canyon" size fear of speaking in front of people. In high school, the teacher would stand at the door and hold my hall pass so that I could "exit stage left" after a book report in front of the class! Now, being a bit more mature, I didn't think I'd still be that bad, but, I still avoided those situations in the same way I tried to avoid being within spitting distance of poison ivy!

I explained all this to Donna and that I'd never seen myself in "sales", but nonetheless, I was desperate for some adult interaction. I could not "sell" but maybe, just maybe, I could "teach" people about the benefits of these kitchen tools to enhance what they had at home. What I didn't realize at the time was that I'd just SOLD myself on a way to get into this business! Donna was very patient with me, answered all my questions, and addressed my fears in a very understanding, but encouraging way. We shook hands when she left that day, and I'd entered a new phase in my life.

That was over four years ago. She has become, since that time, someone I hold very near to my heart. In all my life, I have never known anyone who has ever led me so beyond my self-imposed "limits". She has never given me any reason to see myself in a negative way, and when I have referred to myself negatively, she has been adamant in making me see the positive side. My "I don't see how I can" … gives way to her "Of course you can! You've done … already! You'd be great at …!" Or she'd call to ask me to participate in … and I'd say, "Who? Me?" thinking she'd lost her mind to think that I could do such a thing. And she'd say, "Well, of course, you!" She's just seen so many things in me that I'd never even thought to look for. Her latest request was that I be one of three presenters in a workshop for consultants getting ready to promote to director. "Who, me??"

Today, I've stood in front of as many as 35 people at a time and presented my business at over 415 kitchen shows—rooms full of people I didn't know. And I've never needed a hall pass! I once encouraged myself by saying, "Well, I know more about my product and business than anyone else in the room."

A few months ago, I stood in front of a room full of about 30 other consultants and did a great training demo. Three days ago, a guest at one of my kitchen shows told me that she taught public speaking and that when I mentioned to the group how afraid I "used" to be of speaking in front of strangers and how this business had helped me put that fear behind me, she just wanted me to know that she thought I did an excellent presentation and spoke very well. Two days ago I gave that same presentation to a room full of other consultants on making a transition from consultant to director of consultants. "Who, me??"

On the way home from that presentation I told my husband, who had accompanied me, that I'd learned that evening that Donna had been in an accident earlier that day while horseback riding. She was being kept in the hospital overnight for a concussion she'd received and had been unable to attend. She was going to be fine, but when I told him about it, I cried. The lump in my throat was nearly choking me! He asked why I was so upset, since it wasn't terribly serious and she was going to be okay. It actually took me a minute to swallow down that lump enough to be able to tell him.

That evening, I'd made that presentation because of Donna. Without her encouragement and support over the last four years, I'd have never believed in myself enough to consider doing such a thing. I was thinking, just before I started to speak, that next year I could very possibly be doing the same thing in front of over 100 women at a conference workshop—and that I know I could do it. I believe in myself because Donna has taught me to. She has given me a chance to build my self-esteem and encouraged me to recognize my God-given talents. Now I am learning to help others to do the same.

I don't shake Donna's hand anymore. I hug her tight, and the next time I see her, I'll just flat out tell her how much I love her and that she's a very special part of my life, and I don't care if there is a room full of people who will probably see me cry! "Who? ME!!!"

(This is how Kim ended the stories she sent me—another gift!)

Okay, now reliving all of this, I've used up half a dozen Kleenex! I need to call and see how Donna's doing, and I need to e-mail Rebecca and see how her week has been and how that new grandson of hers is coming along.

But, before I do, I want to thank you, too, Barbara. The first time I e-mailed you, as I said, I didn't expect to hear back. My thoughts were that you were a famous speaker and author and would probably be just too busy to respond. I wasn't thinking this in a bad way, just being realistic, I thought, considering your schedule and the fact that you probably get so many e-mails and correspondence from so many, that I might just be one of hundreds.

You, too, have touched my life in a very wonderful way! Your prayers and responses have touched my heart. I know how precious your hours and minutes are, and I am truly grateful that you have shared some of them with me. I hope that my stories will be useful to you. I know there are probably many others that are far more compelling but just sharing these with you has cemented them even further in my heart as life changing, blessed events for me. Thank you for letting me share them, as your books have shared so many other's stories with me.

May the good Lord bless you and yours for the gifts you bring to so many.

Love,
Kim Mooney

THOUGHT TO PONDER:
How precious that Kim has now become an encourager herself because of
Donna's kindness, caring, and belief in her! As we share our talents, one of
the greatest joys is seeing them passed along.

The Gift of Encouragement

By Jodi Enger
Chicago, Illinois

*What shall I do with my life? How much am I willing to give of myself, of
my time, of my love?*

Eleanor Roosevelt

I WOULD LIKE to share what I did for a friend of mine to encourage him
to use his talents. My friend is an artist by hobby, but he has not been
inspired to pick up a brush and paint for quite some time. One day we were
having a conversation, and the subject of painting came up. He suggested
that he would like to switch from watercolors to acrylics, and he really
should go out and get some supplies and start up again.

I never heard anything more, and I occasionally asked if he had done anything with his painting, usually getting a "no" response. So, one day I
stopped into an art store and picked up a set of new acrylic brushes and
gave them to him as a gift with the following card:

"I hope that these brushes will inspire you to paint again.
Your Friend and Encourager, Jodi."

It really meant a lot to me to give a gift like that because I think it is the greatest feeling in the world to know that, hopefully, you made someone feel special, cared for, and inspired to be the best they can be.

THOUGHT TO PONDER:
Do you have a friend or family member whose talent needs encouraging? Why not give them a new tool to whet their appetite and get their creative juices flowing again!

Helping Others in a Time of Grief

As shared by Mary Schulz
Downers Grove, IL

Each citizen should plan his part in the community according to his individual gifts.

Plato

ROSIE ROOSE, WHO was a nurse at Hinsdale Hospital, knew about the hospital's "Still Missed" Parent Support Group, but when she had a miscarriage herself, she truly began to understand its importance in helping those suffering the devastating loss of a baby.

As a result, she studied to become a grief counselor to help parents who lose a baby from miscarriage, ectopic pregnancy, stillbirth or neonatal death. The goal of "Still Missed" is to bring these people together and help them cope with their grief under the guidance of hospital staff members. One of the things she learned that other grief groups were doing was providing gown sets—gowns, bonnets and blankets, often trimmed with lace and ribbons—to give to grieving parents who had lost their baby so that they would have something in which to bury the child. She began to search for volunteers willing to create the very tiny burial and memento garments that would symbolize sympathy from caring adults.

"I saw the notice in the news bulletin of the First United Methodist Church of Downers Grove, and it interested me," said Mary Schulz, a former high school English teacher. "The idea may have bothered some people, but I could understand the need, especially since my dear friend, Barbara Glanz, had lost her newborn son. (Mary was my student teacher at Lyons Township High School many years ago and one of the dearest persons I have ever known.) Frankly, I really just responded to Rosie, whom I knew through the church. She is such a passionate, dedicated, gung-ho person, I was eager to help her."

Mary began creating "Still Missed" gown sets a number of years ago, often with the help of her daughter, Emily, now a mother herself; her son, Brian, a recent college graduate and about to become a father for the first time; and her husband, David. Later she talked a number of her friends and church members into joining her once a month to do their special sewing. Each sewing bee member had a specialty, some stitching and some adding the trim and pressing. Gowns were created in four different sizes, ranging from small, for a 16-week fetus, to large, for a full-term baby.

"We like to use flannels and knits, soft, comforting fabrics with delicate patterns," Schulz said. "For baptismal gowns, we use silk. We've done close to 100 sets in a year." All the fabrics are either donated by individuals or through a special "Still Missed" fund.

The babies are bathed, then dressed in the furnished garments for baptism, a short, memorial service, photographs and burial, according to the parents' wishes. An angel pin is attached to each outfit. They also offer the parents a duplicate set for a keepsake. All of these mementos are important to parents in the grieving process, to help them say "goodbye."

A grieving parent shared with them, "It is people like all of you who make each day here on earth a truly blessed event. While Danny was only with us three days, the memory of him in one of your tiny gowns will be with us forever. All your hard work and time is truly appreciated."

"It's a privilege to be a part of this program, to help others during their time of grief in whatever small way we can," Schulz said.

In addition to free monthly meetings with grief counselors and occasional speakers, Hinsdale Hospital's "Still Missed" Parent Support Group provides a newsletter and a Memorial Garden. Call 630-856-4497 for more information.

THOUGHT TO PONDER:
Although difficult to think about, this precious gift to a hurting parent is such a blessing, especially when the world often discounts the grief if a child has not lived long. People they don't even know show that they care! No matter what our God-given talents may be, we can always find special ways to use those talents to help others.

The Gift of a Cartoon

About Winston Hall
Bellevue, Washington

But it makes more sense to work at what you do best. If you do, you will be happier and you will make more of an impact.

MY FRIEND, WINSTON Hall, possesses a very special talent—drawing cartoons. Whenever he is inspired by someone, he sends them an original

cartoon. After I had spoken at the Pacific Northwest Chapter of the
National Speaker's Association, Winston sent me these precious cartoons:

I have had them framed, and they now hang in my office. What a unique way to say "thank you!"

Winston also customizes cartoons for companies and individuals. You may reach him at Winston@tunerphotography.com.

THOUGHT TO PONDER:

Have you ever tried cartooning? No matter what your talent, you can find unique ways to share it to bring joy to others.

Chapter Fifteen:

"Treasure Gifts (Keepsakes)"

We sat there, the four children of the great man,
in the manufactured light, as the voice droned on.
The hour was for lawyers, not for grieving or
wandering through the memories of my father's face.

We sat there until the business was brought to an end.
My mother leaned forward with father's emerald fountain pen.
She signed the last document, and scanned all the lists.
She put the pen in my hand, saying, He wanted you to have this.

©Andrew Grossman 2000
Newton, CT

HAVE YOU EVER received a gift that was someone else's treasure? Or that became a special treasure to you? When I was nine years old, my beautiful, courageous Aunt Gretchen died of cancer at age 23. The entire family was devastated, especially my grandmother and grandfather. Because I was the oldest grandchild, I became very close to them, in many ways, I think, filling some of the huge void left by the loss of their youngest child.

I remember that I thought Gretchen was a princess, and I wanted to be around her whenever I could. She was Homecoming Queen at her high school, always the most popular one in the room with her gorgeous figure and long, dark, curly hair. I was always a bit on the "chunky" side, so

Gretchen was my idol! One of her possessions which I had admired for years was a sterling silver charm bracelet, overflowing with charms, all of which had a special story. She wore it every day and often let me look at it and told me stories about each charm.

When I was twelve years old, my grandmother gave me that charm bracelet as her special "grown-up" gift to me. I know now how difficult that was for her to give away because it was the last small vestige of Gretchen which she had kept. However, to me it was the best gift I had ever received because I knew how special it had been to Gretchen. I wore it for many years and always felt it was a symbol of my guardian angel, Gretchen.

When our first daughter was born, guess what I named her? Gretchen, of course! And when she turned twelve years old, I passed the treasured charm bracelet on to her along with all the stories I could remember about each one of the charms. She rarely wears it because it has long since gone out of style, but it is lovingly kept in her special "treasure box" as a memory of her namesake.

What treasure do you have that you could pass on to someone else?

I have always loved dolls. When our children were little, I taught English as a Second Language part time at Argonne National Laboratory. My students were well-educated scientists from all over the world who had come to Argonne for six months to a year to do research. I always made it a point to invite them to our home at least once while they were in the US, and many of them became good friends. When they left to return to their countries, they would often ask if they could send me something from their native land. I began asking if they would send me a small doll for my collection. (At first, I really didn't have a collection, but I felt I could begin one now that I had the excuse of having a daughter!)

Over the years I have received nearly 150 dolls from students, traveling friends, and family members. When I visit a new country or part of the US, I always try to find a doll that represents that area to add to my collection. So, every doll I have represents someone I care about or a special place I have been. My collection is one of my most precious possessions, and I

have written down the stories of each of the dolls. I have decided that
someday I would like to have each of my children, family members, and
special friends pick two or three dolls that they admire from my collection
as a memory of the precious relationship we shared. I hope they will treasure my treasures and someday pass them on to someone they love.

The Compass

By Dawn Duty
Bensenville, Illinois

The excellence of a gift lies in its appropriateness rather than in its value.
Charles Dudley Warner

IN 1988 MY and husband and I were blessed to become foster parents to eight and nine year old half sisters. They had been pretty badly abused and had lived in foster homes for over three years. The older daughter was always afraid of getting lost. I would have to go the same way every time I went somewhere so that she would know how to get home again. It was always very important that I never change the route.

We were very fortunate in 1991 to be able to adopt the sisters. About the time of the older one's sixteenth birthday, there was a Grisham movie, "The Client," about a boy who saw a murder, so he hired a woman attorney to represent him. She always wore an old compass around her neck, and when asked about it, she said her father had given it to her so she would never lose her way. In the end the boy and his Mom go into hiding, and the attorney gives the boy the compass.

That triggered an idea for me. For my daughter's sixteenth birthday, I gave her a copy of the movie and a small gold antique compass hung on a gold chain. Now, as she grows up, she can <u>always</u> find her way back home!

THOUGHT TO PONDER:
What might be a treasure gift for someone you love?

The Doll Mender

By Eileen McDargh
Dana Point, California

Give whatever you give with pride. Gratitude for your support is not measured by the size of the gift but truly by its significance as measured by you.

Francis C. Pray

THE BEST PRESENT I've ever received was unwrapping a box at Christmas from my sister. On the cover it said, "Welcome home, Sally Walker and Bridesell." I pondered those words. Why, those were two of my favorite dolls when I was a child ... more than forty years ago! And inside ... yes ... Susan had found them at my Mom's. She kept them all these many years until she finally found a doll mender. Sally Walker was cleaned, and her moldy eyes sparkled. Bridesell, a virginal doll before the age of Barbie, with only a bride's dress to her name, had her hair back AND the second dress EVER in her life. What a gift!

It prompted me to write a poem:

The People Menders

Somewhere beneath bald spot and hand caked with dirt
A little boy lived, afraid and quite hurt
And under the tweed with patch on the arm
Once lurked boyish laughter and urchin street charm
Away from the perfume and dress with a frill
Stalked dreams and the music of a shy tiny girl
The leather briefcase with engraved name plate
Hid the pain of teen years with no one to date

And seated so straight in the CEO chair
In school they said "Stupid"; he remembered and dared
And high on a stage, performing for all
loomed a past of rejection she felt in school halls

We carry inside the pains of our past
We walk today shadowed by memories held fast
To think ourselves new and rise to new heights
We embrace what once was and let go of the night
More quickly it comes if our hands will extend
To celebrate others who also must mend

There are menders for dolls and pastors for souls
But where is the healer who can make people whole?

For the body and mind and the spirit within
Are the substance of life and the world we live in.
What would it take to heal, patch and sew
To soothe and calm, add balm to the soul?
Perhaps mending selves is done in two parts
We mend self and others when we open our hearts.

THOUGHT TO PONDER:

Because I love dolls, Eileen's story really touched my heart. I think dolls, for many of us, remind us of those precious years of innocence and joy when we could imagine all kinds of roles in life, especially that of the perfect mother. Are there special toys in your life or the lives of someone in your family that you could have mended? And, as Eileen says, as we open our hearts to the deepest needs of those around us, we also mend ourselves.

The Two Bears

As told by Bonnie Gordon
Gordon Lodge, Baileys Harbor, Wisconsin

Not what we give, but what we share, for the gift without the giver is bare.

James Russell Lowell

ONE DAY WHEN Bonnie had gone into town, she saw two precious bears at a Hallmark store. She had been missing her good friend, and so she decided to buy the bears and create a special treasure for both of them. She wrote a story about the two special bears:

They were cousins from Czechoslovakia who came over to America on a boat. After a long, long trip, they finally arrived together in Chicago. One of them was sent to the northern bay of Wisconsin to work at Gordon Lodge, but there was only enough work for one bear. The other little bear had no place to stay and was very lonesome and afraid of losing touch with his dear cousin when he had to stay behind in Chicago.

Bonnie wrapped up one of the bears with a copy of the story and a note, asking her friend if the second little bear could stay at her place so the cousins would always know how to find one another.

What a precious representation of their friendship those bears became since Bonnie's friend was in Chicago and Bonnie in Wisconsin! Bonnie told her she was keeping the other little bear to watch through the window over all the children in the swimming pool at the lodge to keep them safe—and to remind her of her dear friend so far away.

THOUGHT TO PONDER:

Do you have a dear friend who is far away? What creative gift might you give them as a constant reminder of your precious friendship?

The Last Perfect Gift

By M. Kay duPont, CSP, CPDT
Atlanta, Georgia

All you have shall some day be given; therefore, give now that the season of giving may be yours and not your inheritor's.

Kahlil Gibran

MY MOTHER, MY only parent, and my lifelong best friend, became ill in early August. I was traveling, and they told me not to come home those first few days. When they decided to operate, I hurried back to find a much sicker person than I had left. They told me that, due to her deteriorating condition and the instability of her heart and liver, she probably would not pull through. I kissed her and told her goodbye.

The operation was successful, but it seems that when one thing breaks down, they all begin to break down. She was so highly sedated after the operation that they didn't see the stroke immediately. Luckily, I was there to make them take her off the heavily sedating medicine so she could be treated for the things that really were going wrong at that point, but by that time she had lost her speech and the use of her left limbs.

She worked hard to regain her speech, practicing regularly, and using me as her interpreter. And, since the stitches that went all the way up the side of her leg were healing fairly well, they transferred her to a rehab center to help regain the use of her limbs.

I was working at a client site that week and would go by in the early morning to feed her breakfast and then go by after work to feed her dinner and visit, but I wasn't there all day to protect her. Within three days, she was in a coma from over-medication. When I realized they were lying to me about her lethargy, I called an ambulance, and we went back to the hospital. The doctors told me she'd probably not come out of the coma.

I called the funeral home, made the arrangements, and spent 12-14 hours a day at her side, talking to her, touching her face, telling her I loved her. On the third day, when I was getting ready to go home, I said loudly, "Mother!" And, in the grumpy way she'd answer when I used to annoy her as a child, she said, "What??!!" And we were alive once again, although not back to reality for a week or so. All she remembered was "her daughter" stroking her cheeks.

When she had recovered her thought processes, she asked about her jewelry, and I told her it was safe and sound at my house. She was particularly concerned about a diamond ring in the shape of a target—a large round diamond in the middle, surrounded by dozens of baguettes. I knew that particular ring meant as much to Mother as any other piece of jewelry she had, and it meant almost as much to me. It was the most beautiful and unusual ring I had ever seen. If Mother had told me I had to give away everything she owned except one thing, I would have chosen that ring, with no time for meditation. And my feelings became stronger every year for the decades that she wore it.

Since she had asked about her ring in the hospital, I went home that night and cleaned it up. The next day I wore it in—a perfect fit, a perfect look. It reminded me of the way things used to be, it recalled her youth and vibrancy, and I hoped it would show her that her jewelry was safe and would continue to be loved. By then, I knew she would never live outside a care facility and would never wear the rings again. When she saw it the next morning, she said, "That's nice. You can wear it, but be very careful. Don't let anything happen to it."

"I won't, Mother, I promise. You wore it for 40 years and nothing happened to it. I won't let anything happen to it either. I just wanted you to know that it's being loved."

Three months later, I was exhausted and operating on love alone. We had been through another short coma, hours of rehab that lead to nothing but frustration, and nights of prayers and tears. I was at the hospital from 7 AM to feed her breakfast until around 8 PM after I fed her dinner and made sure she got to see *Wheel of Fortune*. I was emotionally empty during the day and emotionally overwrought at night. I was supervising all her medicine, food, and care; fighting for her dignity; trying to close up her apartment, store her furniture and sell her car; and struggling to keep a positive attitude for her as well as not drive my husband out of the house. I was so totally focused on keeping her safe that I was barely aware of my own movements.

Then it happened. I lost her ring. As many times as I went over that day in my head, I only had three clear memories: Taking off the ring to put cream on her legs and telling myself that it was stupid to take it off and lay it down in a hospital; talking to a friend on the phone; and visiting the security station about a parking pass. However, no matter how hard I tried, I couldn't see my hands in any of those scenes. I even asked a psychotherapist friend to hypnotize me back to that day, but I still couldn't see my hands.

So I began to pray, and I began to ask others to pray for me. I wanted to share this horrible secret with my best friend, but Mother had enough on her mind and soul without hearing that. But what losing her ring did to me was devastating. I began to doubt my own ability to make decisions about her welfare, my own capability as a caretaker. If she couldn't trust me with her *ring*, how could she trust me with her *life*? And how would she ever forgive me? So I withdrew. I stopped being fully there for her, stopped talking to her from my heart, stopped being her best friend. Not intentionally, of course, but I see it clearly now.

A month later, she was gone, and I had lost the most wonderful mother a child could ever hope for. Soon I began to change my prayers. As I asked for Mother's forgiveness for my lack of soul in the last days (which became so obvious the moment it was too late to change), I also asked her to help me recover the ring. Since she now knew perfectly well that it was gone, and she now knew how much it had upset me, maybe she still loved me enough to help it somehow get returned. I had dreams of a package in the mail, a COD delivery with no return address, a call from hospital security about an anonymous gift with my name on it.

One of my dear friends, Barbara, who believes in angels and has a direct pipeline to Heaven, kept telling me that the ring was safe. And my other direct-line friend was busy praying to Sister Elizabeth Deceased, who is renowned for finding lost items (that's another story in itself). And I was, too. And of course to God. But I was also praying to Mother. One day close to Christmas, about three months after I lost the ring, Barbara told me that she still believed the ring was safe and that she envisioned it wedged tightly somewhere and surrounded by red. I laughed and said, "Yes, the woman who's wearing it has on a red dress!" But I prayed to Mother for guidance with this new information.

On the morning of December 21st, I woke up and knew of one place I had not looked. I waited for my husband to leave because I knew he would tell me it wasn't possible and probably grumble about my asking him to move the furniture again for such a futile attempt. When he was gone, I moved the end table next to the recliner sofa that weighs about 200 pounds, took out the pillows and bedspreads that had been stuffed behind the sofa to keep the new kitten out, moved the sofa away from the wall, and stuck a strong flashlight as far back as I could get it. I had looked under there before, of course, through the tiny slit in the sofa's front, but this time a sparkle caught my eye. "Don't get excited," I told myself, "it's probably just tinfoil."

But it *wasn't* just tinfoil. In the very center of the sofa's length, wedged against the wall where no one could have possibly put it, was Mother's ring—lying on our *red* carpet.

Mother loved Christmas as much as any person I've ever known, and she would buy dozens of presents for my husband and me every year, as we did for her. There were only three of us, but we had enough gifts for a huge family, and she loved every one of them. In the last few years, she bought mostly through the mail, and we put up her tree, but she never stopped loving the spirit of it all. And for fifty years, no matter how tight money was or what she had to sacrifice, there had always been something very special under her tree just for me—the perfect gift. And this year was no exception.

THOUGHT TO PONDER:
What is the most perfect gift you've ever received?

A T-Shirt Tradition

By Maria Marino
North York, Ontario

Giving presents is a talent; to know what a person wants, to know when and how to get it, to give it lovingly, and well.

Lady Pamela Wyndham Glenconner

WITH MY LATEST nephew celebrating his first birthday, I was reminded of the traditional T-Shirt I've been designing for my little ones over the years. I collect photos all year long, and then I make a collage complete with personal caption and press it on a t-shirt. Voila! They have an instant keepsake for years to come.

THOUGHT TO PONDER:
What a fun gift to make for those you love!

Remembering the Touch of Love

By Sue Rusch
Bloomington, Minnesota

If my hands are fully occupied in holding on to something, I can neither give nor receive.

Dorothee Solle

I MISS MY mom when I least expect it. It's not that we spent that much time together, or that our relationship was especially close. It's just that there's something very special about a mother. My mother was a woman before her time, juggling career and family long before it was fashionable. The stressful lifestyle of being a successful and independent woman, yet a wife, mother and homemaker, took its toll. She died at the tender age of 53, just months after my first son (her first grandchild) came into the world. Unfortunately, she died just as she was starting to experience the joys of new life.

I remember the day before her sudden death like it was yesterday. In the middle of her business day, she called to see if she could stop out for a visit over lunch. It had been a few weeks since we had spoken or seen each other. I wondered what in the world was going on with her that she would carve two hours out of her busy day to drive thirty minutes from the office to see her grandson. She laughed with him as she spooned pureed peas into his smiling mouth. It was clear that she cherished the pleasure of tucking him in for his afternoon nap. Before she scurried back to the office, she sat down for a moment and told me how much she loved him. She laid her hand on my knee and said, "You're a good mom ... I'm proud of you." I remember the touch of her hand ... it was rare from a woman so uncomfortable with sharing her emotions.

I have chosen not to put framed pictures of her on the mantle, even though my photo albums are filled with snapshots. The photographs I have of my mother remind me of her sadness. The lines in her face reflect the choices she made as she struggled to find balance in her life.

Yet she will never be forgotten. I feel her presence in a special way at the most unpredictable of moments, and <u>always</u> when I use a special clear glass platter. It's an ordinary plate to anyone else but special to me because it was the last gift I ever received from my mom. On the underside of the platter is the fine texture of a simple oak leaf:

It was my son's eighteenth birthday, and I felt a certain sadness. As I decorated his cake and placed it on the special glass plate, I missed my mother. I realized that she had never experienced the joy of watching my son blow out birthday candles. I had missed having a mother in my life as I raised my three sons, and today, as I felt a mother's pride, I remembered that day she came to the house and said, "You're a good mom ... I'm proud of you." On a day of joy, I felt sadness.

As I cleaned up the dishes after the birthday lunch, I ran my fingers across the textured oak leaf on the bottom of my special glass plate. In a strange way, I felt her touch. On my way to the china cabinet to put away the plate, the doorbell rang. The mail carrier stood at my door with a small parcel and a stack of Christmas cards. The parcel was lovingly hand-addressed, and I could see that it was from my Aunt Shirley. This little package delivered the joy that comes with a specially chosen gift from the heart. I hadn't even opened it, yet I felt a lump in my throat. I thought to myself, "This must be what it feels like to get a package from your Mom." How wonderful to be reminded that you're loved! How sweet of Aunt Shirley to think of me, especially when she's busy with children and grandchildren of her own. I made myself a cup of tea and sat down at the kitchen table to open the carefully sealed package, lovingly marked "Open Carefully."

Inside the box, I was able to see that significant thought went into sending this package. Its contents were wrapped in rolls of tape and newspaper, and again wrapped in tissue paper. I was curious ... Aunt Shirley and I hadn't talked for months and weren't in the habit of exchanging birthday or Christmas gifts. As I carefully tore open the tissue paper, I found the gift: an old photograph of my mother at the age of eighteen, in a beautiful antique frame. Her eyes pierced me as I looked into them. It was as if she was saying,

"I'm here … I'm watching you … I'm proud of you." Tears *filled my eyes as I ran my fingers across the textured border of the frame.*

The timing of a gift is often God's way of connecting us with each other. This special gift from my Aunt Shirley will never be forgotten.

I've placed the photograph on my desk in my home-based office. Each day, as I balance work and family, I see her smiling face. This photograph, over 50 years old, connects me to my mom at a happier time of her life. Her eyes seem to say, "I'm with you … and today, I am at peace." I feel her presence and I remember her touch.

© Sue Rusch, December, 1999. All Rights Reserved.

THOUGHT TO PONDER:
Is there a picture in your life that has special meaning for you? Do you have pictures that may bring joy to others? Why not send them off today?

Sharing a Treasure

By Nancy Coey
Raleigh, North Carolina
Reprinted with permission from *Finding Gifts in Everyday Life*

A gift is a precious stone in the eyes of him that hath it.

Proverbs 17:8

WE'RE A FEW weeks into a Fundamentals of Speech course and a gentle, shy nineteen year old gets up to give her first speech. She is very nervous, and we all look down, wanting not to scare her. The room is quiet. We're not expecting very much, just hoping she'll get through it and not cry.

She starts to speak, and we are spellbound. She tells of working as a bus driver while in high school, of being assigned to a bad neighborhood, of kids who give her trouble from the first day.

In particular the worst one, a boy of about ten.

One winter day, there's a patch of ice on the road, and she needs to back up to get a running start. She can't see out of the rear window and asks for help: "Is it clear?" The boy says, "Yes. You can go." She backs up … and into a three-foot ditch. A tow truck must be called; the principal arrives; she almost loses a job she badly needs.

But that's the low point; with each passing month, things improve. Finally, it's the last day of school. The boy is busy on the bus, going from seat to seat, but she overlooks it because he's been good for so long.

When they arrive at school, the kids are excited and all crowd around her. They know that today is also her birthday. The boy has gotten her a card, and everyone has signed it, and they are very proud as she opens it.

It is a *used* birthday card. The boy's name has been scratched out.

She has brought it with her to our speech class, and she holds it up for us to see. And we clap until our hands hurt.

We all know that we are seeing more than a card.

© Nancy Coey. *Finding Gifts in Everyday Life*. All Rights Reserved.

THOUGHT TO PONDER:

What treasures have you saved over the years? Have you ever shared them with others?

A Grandma's Treasure Gift

Anonymous

The joy of giving is as often overlooked as the giving of joy.

David Barton

A GRANDMOTHER SHARED this story with her grandchildren:

"I am like a penny, a very bright one. Remember, my darling children, I'll always turn up. Whenever you find a penny anywhere in the years to come, you pick it up and say, 'There's Grandma!'

"Here's a penny, take it. It is the first of many. In time you will have a thousand reminders that I'm telling you how much you are loved."

THOUGHT TO PONDER:
Many of us throw away pennies because we see them as having little value. What a beautiful way to add special value to something so common and at the same time create a lasting memory!

The Gift of Quilts

by Shannon Johnston
Oceanside, California

One of the deepest secrets of life is that all that is really worth doing is what we do for others.

Lewis Carroll

IN 1997 ON a trip to New York, my husband Ken and I went to an off-Broadway theater to see a play. In the lobby, enshrined in a large glass case was a quilt made from many t-shirts. The shirt fronts of various shapes, sizes and colors had been sewn together in a haphazard fashion. Some overlapped, none were straight up. I was taken by the idea and didn't forget it.

So, in 1998 when I was helping my son Andrew to unpack during a move, I noticed a huge stack of his t-shirts. I asked him why he had so many, and he told me that he had been collecting them over the years from concerts he had attended and couldn't bear to throw them out. Clearly, many would no longer fit him, as they had been purchased when he was a young lad. Having seen the t-shirt quilt in New York, I said with some confidence, "Well, if you'll cut out the printed parts, I'll take them home and make you a quilt." Little did I know what I was in for!

First of all, they were many different shapes, colors, sizes and patterns. Thinking I could simply sew them together as I had seen in New York, I set about doing so. It was clear that I either didn't know how to do it, or I was lacking some information because it didn't work, and I had to rip out all the connections I had made.

Finally, after asking lots of quilters (who had no ideas, either), I devised a plan. I measured the width and length of each piece, both for the size of the pattern, and for the size of the available material in total (I did not want to cut less than the pattern size itself, nor could I go wider or longer than the actual full size). Each piece was given a letter, and the sizes were put into the computer. After about 4 hours of sorting, and arranging, the pattern began to emerge.

When Andy was in Florida, he had selected a backing for the quilt that was comprised of white musical notes on a black background. Because the black material bled during the wash, it was washed in vinegar, then in salt until it no longer bled. This produced material that was slightly faded, giving the backing an older look just like the front (serendipity!).

One extra complexity was that Andy had a favorite shirt from a group called "Genesis." He loved the whole shirt—front and back. We decided that the shirt should be split at the sides, opened up and the whole shirt would become the centerpiece. That meant the front of the shirt pattern faced one way, and the back another. Andy liked the idea of having half of the shirts face with the front of the Genesis shirt, the rest with the back. After much struggling, sorting sizes, trimming and using the floor to lay out what would end up a queen-size quilt (he had 35 pieces), it came together.

I have a habit of giving my quilts names. During the time I was figuring out what to do and how to do it, the quilt became known as "The Quilt From Hell"—that was its working title. However, toward the end I thought the name "Blood, Sweat, and Tears" was appropriate, and found an old album with a beautiful LP cover. I scanned that, printed it on a piece of t-shirt material, and hand stitched it to the back.

This process took up the better part of the year, so that on my next visit I was able to watch him open the box and see the finished quilt for the first time. It was certainly worth all the blood, sweat, and tears when I saw his face. It didn't turn out to be a gift for him at all. I knew that what I had been doing all along was a gift for me, to myself, and that seeing his joy at having all his old t-shirts in one place, was wonderful. The only downside is that he lives in Los Angeles, and the weather is really never quite cold enough to require a quilt of such weight (t-shirt material weighs a lot). So, it will no doubt become more of a decorator piece than a useful cover.

A Second Quilt

After Andy's quilt was done, my older son Eric liked it and thought he would like one, too. On a trip to LA, I packed up his collection of shirts and brought them to Sarasota, where they sat for almost two years. Some of his shirts were from concerts, others were simply reminders of his life growing up—the Spaghetti Bowl where he worked for so many years, his love of his Apple Macintosh computer, a Guitar Shop, and so on.

This spring I thought it would be a good idea to get started. I stacked the shirts in my office, wondering where to start. His, too, varied in size from pre-high school, to fairly recent good-sized adult shirts. They stayed on my couch for some time, while I considered what to do.

The Digital Camera

I got the bright idea to take photos of each shirt with my digital camera, so I could manipulate the images on my computer. I put a cork board on a wall, in order to pin up each of the shirts. I attached the camera to a tripod so that each shirt would be the same distance from the lens. Once having all the images (front, back, and sleeves where there were designs), I downloaded them into my Macintosh G4 computer and began working with them in a program called Canvas.

Early Efforts

Having given each of the pieces a name (Genesis tour, Apple, Guitar Player, etc.), the first thing I did was to print small copies as individual pieces that I could lay out like a puzzle, and move around, in order to see what went well together. Not only did they blow around any time the air conditioning was on, but handling pieces of various widths and lengths didn't seem to work this way. So, I started to arrange them in my computer into columns using the Excel program, columns that would produce a finished quilt 110 inches by 110 inches. Once they were in columns, then each piece could also be numbered (column A, piece 1; column A, piece 2), such as A1, A2 etc. The names and numbers were put into an Excel spreadsheet, and I could then sort them by width or length, and still be able to get them back to the first sequence.

Ask Eric

With Andy's quilt, all the pieces were sewn to each other. I asked Eric if he would like to have it that way, or if he would prefer to have frames around the pieces. Because I had taken all the pictures, I was able to send him an example of each, and he chose the frames.

Creating the Columns

The key to creating the king size he wanted was to create columns that were all 110 inches long, and the total of the column widths added up to 110 as well (figuring in the frames and also allowing for seams). I started with the "probable width" for each piece, sorted them on Excel into sequence so that those of a similar width were together, and fiddled around until I found that seven columns would work best.

Sewing the Columns

Since the column length was an estimate, now it was time to measure every last quarter-inch. I measured each of the pieces in the proposed column, added them up, along with the extra frames, and minus the seams, and fooled around with individual lengths until the column added up to 110.

Then on to the next column. When I was satisfied that it would work, I began to sew the pieces into columns.

I called Eric for help

When I got to column E, I didn't like the combination of small leftover pieces that were required to increase the length to match the other columns. Eric and I conferred and we decided to print a copy of a picture of his Steinberger GL2T guitar on a small piece of t-shirt material and use it to complete a trio that included two pieces from a shirt that represented a frisbee club he belonged to in Minnesota when he lived there. With some relief I knew I could go forward with the remaining columns.

Naming the Quilt

One of the last things to do is to give an "official" title to the quilt. Ideas had been brewing, as I thought about some sort of musical title. In the end, though, it was the red Apple shirt piece that gave me the idea of calling it "The Apple of My Eye" and putting the Macintosh apple logo in the center of an eye.

T-Shirts

Having a photographic copy of the quilt was a real advantage. Now it occurred to me that it might be useful for something else. At first I considered using a copy of it to make a pillow. Then Ken suggested it be placed on a t-shirt front. What a great idea—a t-shirt of many t-shirts! I created Andy's shirt from a photo of the finished quilt; Eric's was a copy of the computer-generated model. So, there you have it. A finished quilt for each, and a copy on t-shirts to wear around town.

I won't get to see Eric open his birthday package with the quilt in it. Instead, I have included a throw-away camera so Andy can take pictures of

Eric's reaction. Again, the making of this second quilt gave me so much pleasure, that it is truly more of a gift for me, than for him.

Note: If anyone wants to contact me with questions about making a t-shirt quilt, I would be happy to help. I have made enough mistakes to help someone else avoid some problems. Contact shanshan1936@gmail.com.

THOUGHT TO PONDER:

What lucky young men Andy and Eric are! What other ideas might this story trigger for making a memory quilt for someone you love?

Chapter Sixteen:

"The Gift of Values"

Father, the hands you taught to swim, fish, swing a bat,
The hands of the child and of the man
I hold out to you.

Mother, the child you kept safe, helped to stand, stood beside,
The heart of the child and of the man
Holds love for you.

©Andrew Grossman 2000
Newton, CT

VALUES ARE THE very foundation upon which we build our lives, our deepest fundamental beliefs. Most of our values are unconsciously formed in early childhood, and as we mature and grow and experience more of life, we may decide to change or adopt new values. However, most of our core values are those which we have learned at a young age.

Because I grew up in a very small town in Iowa, I was raised with certain values and beliefs for which I'm deeply grateful:

* People are more important than things.
* Judge someone not by his or her educational level, status in the community, or material possessions, but by what he/she is on the inside, the person's character.
* Trust people and believe they will do the right thing.

* Look for the good in everyone and every experience.
* Learn continuously.
* Honor God in everything that you do.
* Marriage and family are forever.
* Live a life of service to others.
* Always do and be your best.

These values and beliefs were priceless gifts given to me by my parents, grandparents, teachers, neighbors, and friends. They are the foundation of who I am and how I live my life, and they determine my daily actions such as how I choose to use the gifts of time and material resources.

What are your core values? Who in your life or what life experiences helped you to form these values? Have you ever thanked them for these gifts?

My father blessed me with the value of lifelong learning. Even though he wasn't a college graduate, he was a very well-educated man because he read constantly and was always learning. I was terribly impressed as a child because he always seemed to know the answer to every question we asked. Years later, he sheepishly admitted that if he didn't know the answer, he simply made it up! The amazing thing is that I now know he was usually right.

He also gave me the gift of the importance of family. We knew, without question, that we were the most important thing in his life. When I was a junior at the University of Kansas, I received one of the university's highest honors—I was tapped for Mortar Board, a prestigious women's honorary open to only about 35 college juniors each year. It was a "secret" for several weeks, and then the announcement was made at an all-university convocation followed by an honorary dinner for the new members and their parents at the chancellor's home. Because my mother was in the hospital with pneumonia, I knew my parents couldn't come, so even though I was thrilled with receiving the honor, I was pretty "down in the dumps" and feeling very lonely that day.

Early that afternoon I heard my buzzer code in the sorority house, indicating that I had a phone call or guest. As I came down the stairs, there in the front hall was my Dad! He had driven six long hours all by himself to be able to be there to help me celebrate. I will never forget the feeling of love I felt from him that day. He had always been there at every performance, event, celebration, and honor I'd ever participated in in the past, but the self-sacrifice and total surprise of his being there for me that day is a gift I'll never forget. I hope I can always be there for my family in the same way.

My grandfather and my mother gave me the precious value of serving others. My grandfather was a dentist, and because as youngsters we heard people refer to him as "Doc," we thought that was his name. Thus, throughout his life, thanks to us, everyone called him "Docky." He was short, a bit stocky, and my favorite memory of him is with a cigar in his mouth. All his professional life, he volunteered his time and skills to help others. For years, he donated all the dental work for the county home residents, the children at two children's homes, and the nuns in all the little country towns around us (and we weren't even Catholic!). He always extended unlimited credit to farmers and others who were having hard times, and he never sent bills or collection notices. He gave hundreds of hours and a great deal of money to beautify the town cemetery when his daughter died at a young age, and when I was thirteen years old, he was named "Man of the Year" in Harlan, and I got to go to the awards banquet!

Because of his influence, my mother taught us from an early age to give to others and especially to value older people. At least once a month, we would take homemade cookies or dozens of little dishes of Dairy Queen ice cream or holiday treats of some kind to the residents of the Baptist Memorial Home. We'd pass out the goodies, I'd play the piano for them, and we'd listen over and over to their stories. My mother did much of her good work, like my grandfather, "in secret," leaving a plant or a plate of goodies on someone's porch or sending an anonymous card with a check when someone was in financial need. She was always a letter writer, and I credit her, too, for the gift of learning the value of thank you notes and the joy of the written word. As I write this book on giving, I am deeply grateful to my mother for her constant model of generosity and love.

You will read in this chapter about many gifts of values. As you read, think about who has influenced your values and what values you may have passed on to others through your life and example.

My Father's Gift

By Lynn Durham
Hampton, New Hampshire

How can we expect our children to know and experience the joy of giving unless we teach them that the greater pleasure in life lies in the art of giving rather than receiving.

James Cash Penney

THEY SAY THAT people die as they live. Such was the case in my father's life and death. Both were gentle, peaceful, dignified and with grace. He had a rough last two years—open-heart surgery, diagnosis of diabetes, and then prostate cancer that was found already in his bones.

I remember when he had a section of back removed and replaced with metal rods because of the growth of the tumor and the severe pain and prognosis of paralysis. He had valiantly attempted to regain all his pre-op activities. He was 6'4" and around 220 pounds most of his life. He began his decline in the spring, first needing a walker, then using a chair to get around, then sitting up, then resting in bed. He weighed less than 100 pounds when he was still able to stand.

It is painful to watch someone so well-loved prepare to leave you behind. I believe in miracles, so prayer for a cure is where my energy went. But there are all kinds of miracles.

He was wise to the end, even when his physical strength did not allow him to sit up. I remember my niece going to the funeral of a family member of one of her high school friends. Grandpa told her how proud he was of her, that it was important when someone is sorrowing to go to them and share in their sorrow. He also told her if she knew someone who was celebrating, to go to them and share their joy.

Even when he was unable to eat and in constant pain, he was always "fantastic." I can still see his face light up when a couple came and shared the news that they were expecting a baby. Days before he died, he was genuinely so "glad to hear."

Shortly before he died, he said some words that we had to ask him to repeat. They were barely audible because of his lack of strength. I put my ear close to his lips and heard, "I am content." My cousin was there and explained that it is the title of a Lutheran hymn (Dad was Lutheran; I am Catholic). We later used that hymn at the funeral.

But as I have reconsidered those events, I don't believe it had anything to do with that hymn. He had shared with us that the two most important things in life were your faith and your family. He was strong in his faith. He had told my mother she was a wonderful wife and they had had wonderful children. He had told us that he loved us. I feel it was an attesting to the all rightness of all, as Julian of Norwich had said,

"All will be well,
And all will be well,
And all manner of things will be well."

I believe in the anonymous quote I saw: "Death is not putting out the light, it is extinguishing the candle because the dawn has come." And it gives me peace.

In your life, what thoughts do you hold onto? It is easy to have faith when everything seems right in your world. When the crises or challenges come along, it is then more obviously the journey of your soul. That is the time to go deeper, praying for spiritual knowledge. "Then the peace of God that surpasses all understanding will guard your hearts and minds in Christ Jesus." Philippians 4:7.

I, too, am content.

THOUGHT TO PONDER:
Are you content, no matter what the circumstances in your life may be today?

Hope
By Tom Maher
New York, New York

The greatest gift I ever had came from God. I call him Dad.
                                                    Anonymous

Dear Rob, Jeff, Nicole, and Beth,

A father plays many roles. Each one important, some more than others. I feel compelled to assume the role of mentor and coach as each of you progress with your lives at a pace that makes breakneck to be dismally slow in comparison. It is curious to see how technology has moved this process into the 21ˢᵗ century. At one time fathers shared their knowledge by the lights of candles and fireplaces—that was then. I find myself sitting at an electronic keyboard typing words that will be sent at the speed of light across the country through a myriad of servers and networks to land on your respective PC's via e-mail. An icon, or flashing light or an audible "You've Got Mail," will announce my arrival.

Methods of delivery have changed to be sure, however the messages remain the same, as does my fervent hope that the marks you leave on the world will be notable and reward-ing. Ours is a family that has melded into existence, and I am ever so grateful that this has occurred. I love each of you so much for your uniqueness and special talents and abil-ities and for the fact that you allow me to be a part of your lives.

I have many hopes for you and your future. They may differ from what the world has proffered as desirable, but then the messages being put forth may not have advanced with the positive impact of other technologies. Some things cannot be improved on. Things like Personal Vision, Integrity, Purity of Purpose, Love and other values and principles re-main timeless. These are the noble pursuits, and only the noble pursue them. The curious thing about nobility is that it can spring from all walks of life and has little to do with social stature, money, position, or fame. Some of the most outwardly inconspicuous people exude the characteristics exemplified by a noble existence. It flows from those who choose to find it within themselves. So choose wisely! Set your sights on things of true value! Be proud of these traits, for what the world deems valuable is so transient that it is virtually worthless.

In the end, when I measure myself and my life, it will be based not on how much I have materially, but rather how I'll be remembered as a husband, father, neighbor, and friend. I'll reflect on the lives I've touched and the impact I've had on people, hoping that it will be positive. Remember this:

> *Whenever you interact with another person, you will leave that person better for the experience or worse as a result of it, because when there is interaction between two human beings there is no neutral contact.*

The choice is always yours!

THOUGHT TO PONDER:

Have you ever given your children the gift of your values in words they can save forever?

Grandma's Last Lesson

By Rosita Perez
Gainesville, Florida

I resolved that because I had no ancestry myself, I would leave a record of which my children would be proud, and which might encourage them to still higher effort.

Booker T. Washington

THE IRONY OF this gift I was given is that at the time, I neither considered it a gift nor wanted any part of it!

My mother-in-law, whose only son I married 42 years ago, was 94 and dying. The lung cancer had brought about renal failure, and it was unbelievable to me, the closest woman in her life for so many years, to see her deterioration. Days and weeks became months as Grandma was made comfortable with the help of Hospice as we took care of her at home. And then I began to notice a pattern that was amazing. **In the midst of Death, there was Life all around**: the seventh great-grandchild who would bounce in the swing in the doorway ... and how Grandma's eyes would light up when she saw the great grandchildren in their Halloween costumes.

Since we come from a Cuban family, food has always been very important to her, so it seemed strange to be serving her Jell-o and puddings with a house full of food for which she showed total disinterest. Actually, my three daughters and I commented that not spending so much time on food allowed us precious time to look through old photo albums and identify relatives that were now faded memories, brought to life by her recollections of better times.

We began to relate to her in totally different ways than we had for a lifetime. She was no longer the expert problem-solver or recipe maven. (By the way, after she died, we tried making the more common dishes we had become accustomed to, and none tasted the same. Obviously, there was a secret ingredient she took with her: love, time, and great care. And above all, experience!)

She was a feisty old woman who looked twenty years younger than her calendar age. I remember shopping in the mall when she was in her eighties and saying to her, "I can't walk another step. I'm tired."

She said, "You sit here and I'll be back. I still need to find a pair of shoes." So the 80 year old went while the 50 year old sat waiting on the bench! And when she returned empty-handed, I expressed surprise she had not been successful. She said, disgustedly, "All the styles they showed me were for OLD women! Ugly shoes!" That pretty much sums up her adaptation to aging.

In her last days, because she was on morphine and slept a lot, she was confused. One day her son came into the room, and she proceeded to address him as "Ramon" (her husband's name). I attempted to shed light on the matter by explaining that Ramon had died 33 years before and this man in front of her was her son, Raymond. She continued to speak to "Ramon" in Spanish, and the entire thrust of her conversation had to do with her great concern for "their baby who was cold and needed to be covered, and she was worried the baby had not been fed." No amount of explanation sufficed to quiet her concern.

Finally, hours later, one of our daughters, now in her thirties and the mother of two, came into the room, smiling and saying, "Abuelita (Grandma)! The baby is fine. We fed him and covered him and he is asleep." She smiled contentedly and slept peacefully the rest of the day.

The next morning, her son Raymond approached uneasily. He was not sure if she would be lucid. So he asked her quizzically, "Who am I?"

She reared back, dug her chin into her chest, and glared, "Who are you? If YOU don't know who you are, Raymond, how do you expect ME to know???"

And so it was, that in a room where Death was approaching, our family had the richest, most joyous laugh we had had in many months. Abuelita had taught us a lesson about making assumptions. And long after her ashes were buried at the cemetery next to her husband's remains, we sometimes smile and remember her spunk—right up to the last minutes of her life!

THOUGHT TO PONDER:
What life lessons are you teaching your family?

Coming of Age Gifts

Enlisting the Entire Family: "It is a rare and a high privilege to be in a position to help people understand the difference that they can make, not only in their own lives but in the lives of others by simply giving of themselves."

Helen Boosalis

EACH OF MY three children was blessed to receive a "coming of age" gift from our dear friends, Ken and Shannon Johnston, then of Lutz, Florida. Each of their interpretations of that treasured experience follow.

Garrett's story:

The Gift of Respect
By Garrett Glanz
Redmond, Washington

Each time a man stands up for an ideal, or acts to improve the lot of others,
or strikes out against injustice, he sends forth a tiny ripple of hope.

Robert F. Kennedy

THE SUMMER FOLLOWING my 16th birthday, our good family friends, Ken and Shannon Johnston, invited me to spend a week with them in Florida. They presented the trip as a coming of age gift and offered to pay all my expenses. In previous visits with the Johnstons, I had discovered that despite my age, they treated me like a true adult. They valued my thoughts and opinions, allowing me to make my own decisions. For a teenager struggling to establish a personal identity, this level of respect was unusual and appealing. I was understandably thrilled to spend a week away from home in the guise of an adult.

When I arrived in Tampa, Ken informed me that I would be able to plan my schedule for the week by choosing among a variety of exciting activities: flying lessons, scuba lessons, trips to Disney World or Busch Gardens, or any other adventures that I could dream up. He also indicated that I could choose to spend part of the week simply talking with him about various subjects including his current book project, religious philosophies, and life in general. I had immense respect for both Ken and Shannon, based largely on the respect that they had shown me. I felt that spending time with Ken would be the most rewarding option.

We started the week with Ken teaching me how to drive a stick shift car. The main reason for these lessons was to enable me to use the manual transmission Toyota that would be transportation for the week (my own car!). But Ken was also helping me develop an important life skill; you never know when you may need to drive a stick automobile. Many years later I'd meet my future wife, Ashley, who would own a sporty little car with a manual transmission!

I spent the rest of the week alternating between rap sessions with Ken and trips to the beach, Disney World, and the go-cart track. I learned a lot as Ken shared his experiences and general approach to life with me. While I don't recall many of our specific conversations, I remember a couple of main themes that have become important in my life:

* Accept other people for who they are and enjoy getting to know them and what makes them different.
* Allow yourself to be who you are and make an effort to get to know yourself so that you can enjoy what makes you different.
* While you should accept who you are, you should always strive to improve yourself.

Ken and Shannon played an important role in my adolescence. Having adult friends who offered guidance rather than specific directions was rare. I knew that they respected me, and as a result, I was more open to their input. I still consider them good friends and important advisors. I deeply value the special gift given to me by the Johnstons, and it is my goal to return this gift to a young person in the future.

Gretchen's Story:

Anything Is Possible

By Gretchen Glanz Gawlik
Portland, Oregon

There's a great joy in my giving. It's thrilling. It's exhilarating. It's important to be a part of sharing. It is my love. It is my joy.

W. Clement Stone

ONE OF THE most memorable gifts I have ever been given happened when I turned 16. We have some special family friends, who decided that when my brother, sister and I each turned 16, they would give us a vacation we would never forget. Their only requirement was that we had to be 16, we had to be able to drive, and we had to wrack our brains to come up with a list of things we had always wanted to do or learn or see. They wanted this to be a trip full of new experiences and challenges.

My 16th birthday was on June 29, and I was itching to go to visit them in Florida as soon I could. I got to bring a friend with me who was just as excited as I was. The first thing we did when we got to Tampa was to sit down with Ken and come up with a list of things we had always wanted to do ... no matter how crazy, dangerous, or extravagant they seemed.

At first I was a little tentative in what I was listing, but with Ken's encouragement soon I got into the spirit of the exercise and was throwing out ideas like scuba diving, jumping out of an airplane, flying an airplane, going to Disney World, driving on the highway with my two week old license, and, being the typical 16 year old girl ... driving to Daytona Beach by ourselves with no adults. According to Ken and Shan, there was no limit to what we could do.

We had a lot of fun sitting at the kitchen table coming up with that list. Then came the part where we narrowed it down and got to pick and choose what we would do each day. We ended up with a list of activities that I will never forget:

Day 1—We got to drive all by ourselves in their two week old Lincoln Continental to Disney World in Orlando. (I had never even driven on the highway before!) I got a pair of Mickey Mouse ears with my name on the back, which I still have.

Day 2—We took a scuba diving lesson for the whole afternoon at a small lake somewhere near Tampa.

Day 3—We drove by ourselves again (only my second time on the highway!) to the then-new MGM Grand amusement park near Disney World.

Day 4—We got to take flying lessons at a small airfield nearby. We actually got to fly the plane. I have pictures of me in the headset holding the controls. My mom was very nervous about that!

Day 5—We drove by ourselves to Daytona Beach from Tampa, which is about a 3 hour drive. We rented jet skis on the beach and spent the day there.

Day 6—We wanted our last day to be one where we just relaxed by their pool working on our tan.

All in all, it was by far the best vacation I could have ever hoped to have. It also taught me a valuable lesson: There are no limits to what you can do if you put your mind to it. (It also helps if you have supportive friends who help foot the costs!) If you had asked me before the trip if I thought I would do any of these things, I would have told you that you were crazy. But because of our family friends, I was able to see that anything is possible.

Thanks, Shannon and Ken.

Erin's story:

The Gift of Acceptance
By Erin Glanz
Portland, Oregon

We insure our valuables; let us insure our values with generous gifts of caring.
Arthur C. Frantzreb

ONE OF THE greatest gifts that I have ever received in my life came at a time when I really didn't deserve anything but punishment!

In my adolescent years, I became a master at causing trouble. To hear the word "no" was all the motivation I needed to do just the opposite! Right after my sixteenth birthday when I had just gotten kicked out of boarding school for taking an unauthorized trip to New York City, some dear family friends told me that they were still planning on continuing their legacy of a sixteenth birthday trip to spend time with them.

I was given two options: I could either bring a friend along to Florida for a week or I could go alone with them and choose any place that I wanted to see. I decided to take the second option. I chose to have them accompany me to New York City, since all I had seen of it the first time was the airport and the police station!

Since I was interested in acting and performing, they sent me information on all the theater events, and I was able to choose five Broadway shows to see in seven days. I was also required to read Stephen Covey's *The Seven Habits of Highly Effective People* and be prepared to discuss each chapter. We scheduled book discussions right into the week's plans. In these discussions, we came up with several "maps" of the course of my life according to different interests, goals, and dreams I had. We then broke these unattainable goals down into steps that could be taken now, in a month, and in five years. It soon became clear to me that anything is attainable. What once overwhelmed me suddenly looked possible! They opened my eyes to the infinite possibilities my life had in store.

At a time when everyone else in my life was struggling to maintain any patience at all for me and my antics, Ken and Shannon looked past all that and taught me the value of believing in myself and the value of respecting myself. I COULD take charge of my own life. They treated me with an extraordinary amount of respect and made it clear that they were also learning from our discussions. They challenged me. Although I loved seeing all the plays and eating dinner at fancy restaurants, the vacation was not just about fun—this time with them became a "growth spurt" for my life, getting me ready to start thinking and acting like an adult.

Ken and Shan were among the few people who did not judge me for my troublemaking. They saw past that and focused on the good in me, teaching me another important life lesson in how to treat other people. The Johnstons gave me an unbelievable gift in this trip and taught me some unforgettable lessons. My life has never been the same.

THOUGHT TO PONDER:
The gift the Johnstons gave my children was life-changing for them, not just because of the special things they got to do, but more importantly because these two adults whom they so admired and loved gave them a whole week of their time and attention. They made them feel special and important. Is there a child in your life who needs some of your time?

The Gift of Values for Children

By Steve Nedvidek, Chick-fil-A, Inc.
Atlanta, Georgia

All that I am or hope to be I owe to my angel mother.
Abraham Lincoln

IT IS THE goal of Chick-fil-A Kid's Meals to provide parents and kids a fun and interactive opportunity for education or character development. That is all we do. We do not do Power Rangers, Pokemon, Beanie Babies, or movie tie-ins like the rest of the industry. We do lots of books, audio cassettes and other fun mediums that can deliver our message.

For the 1999 holiday season, we featured a Veggie Tales book promotion. In 2000 and beyond, we will be featuring other items like Focus on the Family audiotapes, DK Eyewitness Classic books, Stephen Covey's *7 Habits of Highly Effective Family* books (written just for kids) as well as a special 50th anniversary tribute to C. S. Lewis' writing of *The Lion, the Witch, and the Wardrobe*.

We also have featured items that are branded with "Adventures from the Book of Virtues" which is an animated PBS show that we sponsor, plastic models of the planets with suction cups so children can learn about our solar system, and many interactive ideas and games for family discussions.

Parents are beginning to understand our strategy and as a result, they are becoming more and more loyal to us. This has become a great by-product of our mission to make a difference in children's lives by sharing our values.

THOUGHT TO PONDER:
It is amazing that a retail food establishment is sharing its values in such a concrete way. Does your organization share its values with its customers?

The Listener

By Andrew Grossman
Newton, CT

If I may, I wish to speak tonight of one who is absent,
One who is unknown in this room, where you honor me.
If she were to sit among you, you would perhaps not notice her.
She was not a forward person or particularly eloquent in speech.
Her clothes were plain. She spent little money on herself and her appearance.

If you became curious about her, how she seemed out of place
Sitting with her hands quietly in her lap among the professionals,
You might have the fortunate impulse to engage her in conversation.
You might even confide in her your aspirations, your unrequited dreams,
Your hopes for the future, because she somehow inspired such openness.

And she would look fully into your eyes then, and listen.
You could almost see your words absorbed by her small body,

Made manifest in the clarity of her wondrous spiritual certainty
As she touched your arm lightly, and said, You can do it. I believe in you.
You would know an infinitesimal part of the gratitude I feel as her son.

<u>Chapter Seventeen:</u>

"The Gift of Words"

THE GIFT OF WORDS

The empty subway car
Filled with strangers.

The noise of scraping wheels,
The noise of the steel wind.

How will tonight be better
Than what tore me last night?

In the ocean of city
One diminishing island.

She spoke. One does not speak.
She spoke. She used the word 'hope.'

"I hope you have a wonderful evening."
Amazing chutzpah, to 'hope' for me.

Then to step off at her stop
And to walk down the platform.

"I hope you have a wonderful evening"
Amazing ... seven words ... from a stranger

©Andrew Grossman 2000
Newton, CT

I BELIEVE IN the power of words! I was an English major, so I have studied words for many years. One of the greatest gifts I was ever given was a love of reading. The picture I will always carry of my Dad was seeing him every evening sitting in his easy chair, reading a book. In fact, he read a book a night. By the time I was twelve, he had read nearly everything in the library in Harlan, Iowa, and when new books came in, they called him, and he would stop by on his way home, pick them up, read them that night, and return them the next day. For many years I wondered if he was <u>really</u> reading them or just skimming, so one summer I decided to do some detective work. I would get to the library first, read the new books, and then wait until my Dad had read them, too. Then I would quiz him on the contents. Guess what—he always knew the right answers!

I decided even before I was blessed to become a mother that I wanted to pass on the and the love of reading to my children. So, as soon as I knew I was pregnant, I began reading aloud to the baby every day. In those days, we did not know that the baby could hear our voice in the womb, but today that is a proven fact. Each day I read aloud to them whatever I was reading until they were born. After their birth, I set aside 30 minutes each day until they were teenagers to read aloud to them. When they were infants, I read poetry and Shakespeare. As they grew older, I began to read them stories. When they were reading well themselves, we often read a book aloud together as a family in the evenings or at the dinner table. As a result, all my children love books and possess extraordinary verbal skills.

I also value the written word as a gift we can give to others. We had two non-negotiables in our home as the children were growing up. One was that they had to take piano lessons from age 7 to age 12, and the other related to thank you notes. When they received a gift, they could open it, but it did not become "theirs" until they had written a thank you note. When they were little, they could scribble a "pretend" note, draw a picture, or tell me what to write for them. As they grew older, they learned how to write a gracious note themselves. To this day, my children write thank you notes, a gift I chose to give to them that they are passing along to others.

Words can make such a difference in our lives, especially words of comfort, wisdom, or appreciation. We "hear" them in our inner minds over and over through the years, and when the words are written, we have the added gift of being able to read them again and again. When my husband was hospitalized with pneumonia in the midst of his long struggle with lung cancer, I had been spending 10-12 hours a day at the hospital. Already worn out from the stress of the holidays and my deep concern for his condition, I arrived home very late one night extremely down and discouraged and found this message on my fax machine:

Barbara Glanz *is a quality author, speaker, consultant, president, and wife! A* ***Professional*** *who always speaks from her heart, radiates good cheer, and makes life happier wherever she meets it and is always of good humor, vision and faith in serving others.*

(Thanks for making a difference even when you don't know it!)

Although you do not know me, I do know you through your friends and reading your inspirational book CARE Packages for the Workplace. I just want you to know that others whom you have not met yet in person love you and are thinking of you and Charlie. May God teach you and remind you to NOW be on the receiving line of others as you have been there for so many. May His love for you still shine in trying moments and the darkest of times, as you will always be a friend of mine. Enjoy life and all the life you bring to others. Just know that others care and we are praying and thinking of you.

Love, thoughts and prayers, Curt L. Hansen

What a precious gift of words! I had no idea who Curt Hansen was, but his message encouraged and uplifted me to be able to go through another day. No matter what our talent with words or our educational level, we can all give the everlasting gift of a kind word!

The Gift of a Teacher

By Nancy Provenzano
Oak Park, Illinois

Kind words do not cost much. They never blister the tongue or lips. Mental trouble was never known to arise from such quarters. Though they do not cost much, yet they accomplish much. They make other people good-natured. They also produce their own image on men's souls, and a beautiful image it is.

Pascal

THIS WAS A letter my husband received from one of my former students. It was a precious gift to both of us:

Dear Charlie,

Your wife has given me too much homework again!

I don't know if I'll be able to write a story about "a gift of love" by November 15th; I'm so busy doing the mundane dishes, laundry, etc. But I do know that you, Charlie, gave me a gift of love. You shared Barb with me and so many other students, even to the point that you got involved.

I believe in more than a teacup now, Charlie. Your home, wife, and your support of her have made the world a better place for me. Thank you for helping a troubled teenager.

I hope the Thanksgiving season and our Lord's birthday are the best ever for you, Charlie. And thank you for helping me when I was so young and angry.

Sincerely,
Nancy Wrablik Provenzano
Oak Park, Illinois

THOUGHT TO PONDER:

Was there a special teacher in your life who had an impact on you when you were growing up? What a gift it is to thank someone dear to that person for sharing them with you!

The Gift of Encouragement and Hope

From Beth, Katie, and Krista Munkres
Grand Junction, Colorado

Kind words can be short and easy to speak, but their echoes are truly endless.
Mother Teresa

DURING CHARLIE'S STRUGGLE with lung cancer, my sister and my nieces sent this poem to him on a beautiful plaque. As we read these precious words every day on our kitchen table, they brought great comfort and peace.

What Cancer Cannot Do

Cancer is so limited.
It cannot cripple love.
It cannot shatter hope.
It can't erode faith.
It can't eat away peace.
It can't destroy confidence.
It can't kill friendship.
It can't shut out memories.
It can't silence courage.
It can't invade the soul.
It can't lessen eternal life.

It cannot quench the spirit.
It cannot lesson the power
of the resurrection.

©Gibb McKee

THOUGHT TO PONDER:
Share precious thoughts, ideas, poems, and stories that have been
meaningful to you with those who are in pain. Sometimes we think
everyone has already heard or read something, yet those might be the very
words that get them through one more day.

What Might Have Been ...

By Mark Redd, Pastor
From: *The Matter of Fax*, Clay Road Baptist Church
Houston, Texas

Though I speak with the tongues of men and of angels, and have not charity,
I am become as sounding brass or a tinkling cymbal.

I Corinthians 13:13

DAN BURDAN IS the Education Minister as well as one of the elders at a
church in Mansfield, Texas. His older son, Evan, is a Youth Minister in another congregation in Topeka, Kansas. Dan's touching letter below to his
son is a powerful reminder of the impact each of us might have on those
with whom we come in contact, whether they be students, co-workers, or
even casual acquaintances. All of us, from time to time, second-guess our
past actions. Today, Dan is reflecting on some things he could have done
differently.

From: Dan Burden
To: Evan Burdan

Evan, I don't think I ever told you about the fourth member of my little gang that I ran around with as a teenager. Of course, you know Paul Berry and Gary Bailey. Paul is a deacon at Pleasant Ridge, Gary is a fire fighter and a member of the Church in Burleson. The fourth member of our gang was really quiet. He was a loner. He didn't come to the youth functions very often. His parents had a pretty rocky marriage. His father was mean as I remember him. The youth group was over at his house a lot, visiting his sister (Priscilla) who was dying of Muscular Dystrophy.

When our preacher, Wendell Winkler, started his "Preacher Boys" class, all four of us were involved. Wendell took us "on tour" of area congregations where we preached, led singing, read Scriptures, etc. Our picture was made and published in the Firm Foundation. We joked about the way our number four guy looked. Even Wendell remarked how he looked more like a preacher than the rest of us. He stood posed for the picture with a Bible in hand, held close to his chest, and sports coat unbuttoned. I lost track of "#4" over the years. I knew he joined the Navy for a while. His oppressive father died about three months ago. Funeral was at Pleasant Ridge. I saw the obituary in the paper and told myself to go, after all ... I haven't seen Larry in a long time. Maybe I could be of comfort to him since I know what it's like to lose a father ... but I did not go.

Larry, too, is dead now. He took a gun to the Wedgewood Baptist Church youth rally last night, killed seven people, and then killed himself. I should have gone to see him at his father's funeral.

Love, Dad

THOUGHT TO PONDER:

We can never know the impact we might have had as we look back on experiences in life. This letter from a father to a son had a profound effect. As we share in words our learnings and especially our failings, we give the gift of teaching in the midst of our pain.

A Gift for Jody

By Pam Randolph about her little sister
Tampa, Florida

In prayer it is better to have a heart without words than words without a heart.

John Bunyan

THIS WAS A letter I received from someone I had never known. However, it touched my heart, and I sent Jody a card and one of my books. So did hundreds of other people throughout the world, thanks to a loving sister's creativity and caring. As of this writing, Jody's cancer is in remission.

To Someone With a Heart:

Please help me if you can. I'm trying to help my sister who has metasticized breast cancer. My sister is not someone who has the opportunity to have access to a computer in her home; therefore, she doesn't have the opportunity to communicate with the outside world like most of us do. In fact, she is a very shy, gentle person who would have a difficult time even striking up a conversation with a nice stranger. She has a wonderfully supportive husband, but he's trying to do all he can to make a living and take care of her at the same time. They are ALL ALONE in their fight against her cancer in this huge world.

Today, she is in Charleston, South Carolina, having her weekly chemo treatment at her Oncologist's office. Her dear husband, Michael, has to drive her 60 miles into Charleston every Thursday while taking time off from his job to get her to her treatment from their small town in South Carolina.

All I'm asking of you, if you read this letter somewhere out there, is would you PLEASE send her a little encouraging word, prayer, note or even a little card to let her know that there ARE PEOPLE OUT THERE IN THIS WORLD WHO

CARE AND WHO HAVE COMPASSION, and even though she is someone you have never met, you still care! Please help me help her ... please.

Please do this from your heart. Please help me help my sister. I love her, and she needs to know the world loves her too ...

Sincerely,
Pam, Her Little Sister

THOUGHT TO PONDER:

Pam sent these letters to people worldwide, and Jody received replies from many famous people, including the President of the United States. Have you ever loved someone so much that you have asked others for help? Perhaps you can write and send a letter like Pam that will bring support and cheer to someone who is lonely and hurting.

Carly Elizabeth—Our Runaway Angel

By Jill Bayer
Bradenton, Florida

Mothers work, not upon canvas that shall perish, nor marble that crumbles into dust, but upon mind, upon spirit, which is to last forever, and which is to bear, for good or evil, throughout its duration, the impress of a mother's plastic hand.

George Washington

AT ONLY SIX years old, our daughter is filled with abundant faith and gratitude. She is constantly coming up with great insights. She asked me this week, "Mommy, what do you think happens when you die?"

Feeling intellectual, I gave her a well-educated, scientific, rational answer. "Well, honey … lots of people think all different things. Some people believe … others believe …"

She considered all my suggestions and gave them a moment of very intense thought. She made me feel a great sense of pride when she responded, "Mommy, I think we become angels in heaven and watch over the people we love, even boys too!!!"

This shouldn't have surprised me, for this is exactly what I told her when her grandma died last year. We even close each night with a "Special prayer for Grandma Bayer, who is up in heaven and smiling down on us". Of course, this is what she'd believe for I remind her of it each bedtime.

I looked at her and said, "You know, Carly, I think you are absolutely right. That's what I believe, too!"

She waited a moment and then with those huge sparkling brown eyes, she looked at me and said, "Well, mommy, when all those other people get to heaven, they'll find out they are wrong."

The greatest thing about being a parent is that you are given opportunities each and every day to both give and receive these little "care packages". They always come from the heart and certainly touch your soul.

THOUGHT TO PONDER:

Have your child's words ever given you special comfort? Have you written them down so that you will always remember their wisdom? In the Bible it says we must become like a little child to enter the gates of heaven. In simple wisdom and faith children often grasp the essence of things deeply profound.

Lessons from a Seed:
A Sponsor's Legacy of Letters

By Janet Root, Compassion Sponsor
Reprinted with permission from "Compassion at
Work," Fall 1999 issue, *Compassion International*

*If someone were to pay you ten cents for every kind word you ever spoke and
collect five cents for every unkind word, would you be rich or poor?*

FIFTEEN YEARS AGO June Bianchi was at a low point. Despite June's
new faith in Christ and a recent remarriage, her only child, whom she'd
raised for years as a single parent, decided to go live with his father. "In the
zealousness of my faith, I had been an unwise parent to Justin," she admits,
her eyes filling with tears.

Despondent over the broken relationship with her son, June prayed, "Lord,
allow me to touch one child for Christ." That same day, she turned on the
TV and heard about Compassion International for the first time. Within
two months, June and her husband, George, were the sponsors of 103
children.

Deeply grateful for this opportunity to touch so many children for Christ,
June made a commitment to encourage and disciple each child through
letters.

"I don't have many talents, and it's a struggle for me to write," says June,
when asked about this extraordinary undertaking. "But children in
developing countries often live without opportunities for encouragement—
letters are so important to them. Many have just one parent, who works
maybe 12 hours a day—who can't provide emotional and spiritual support.
For a stranger to reach out through letters is significant."

June didn't understand just how significant her letters were until she and George visited their sponsored children in the Dominican Republic for the first time. Early in her sponsorship experience, June sent a tiny mustard seed to each child to illustrate the little bit of faith needed to "move mountains" (Mathew 17:20). During the Bianchis' visit several years later, June discovered that every child either still had that mustard seed or had tried to plant it! And not only that, June says, "Each of the children showed me the special place where they kept my letters! I suppose it's conviction," June says, describing how she finds the time and the motivation to maintain regular correspondence with so many children. "When I read the Bible, I see that while Paul was away, he would write and encourage the people he ministered to. I also know my letters are probably the only ones the children will receive in their whole lives."

Ruben Toreros, like most of the couple's formerly sponsored children, still keeps June's letters. "Those letters are the pillar upon which my emotional and spiritual life is built," he says emphatically. This vibrant, energetic 24-year-old, who grew up in extreme poverty, says that if it hadn't been for the Bianchis' intervention, "I'd be a criminal today." Instead, Ruben is a certified referee for the Dominican Republic's National Basketball Association. He is also a loving husband and the proud father of two little ones.

Like Ruben, many of the Bianchis' formerly sponsored children are now beginning their own families and careers, but it is their personal relationship with Christ that confirms to June that her prayer of 15 years ago has been answered. "The many dozens of letters I've received from the children telling me that they've accepted Christ," she says, "knowing they have the best foundation—a biblical foundation—that is the whole point of this ministry."

Today, the Bianchi family includes 114 sponsored and formerly sponsored children, as well as the healed relationship between June and her son.

The legacy of one woman's faith has moved mountains indeed. June says, "After six visits and nearly 2,500 handwritten letters to our children,

George and I are proud to report that we have personally seen the excellent return on just 80 cents a day invested in the life of a child."

THOUGHT TO PONDER:

Compassion International is a wonderful organization that lets you sponsor a child in your country of choice. You can reach them in Colorado Springs, CO, 800-336-7676, www.compasssion.com. We never know when the gift of a simple letter may have a profound impact on someone's life.

The Letter of Appreciation

By Margie and Dan Kruk
Carol Stream, Illinois

Getters generally don't get happiness; givers get it. You simply give to others a bit of yourself—a thoughtful act, a helpful idea, a word of appreciation, a lift over a rough spot, a sense of understanding, a timely suggestion. You take something out of your mind, garnished in kindness out of your heart, and put it into the other fellow's mind and heart.

Charles H. Burr

A LETTER TO thank a wonderful teacher is a CARE package. In this series of letters you will see the lesson Margie and Dan learned of just how important that CARE package can be in someone's life.

This is their original letter to the Superintendent of Schools in their district:

Dear Dr. Gmitro:

It is not often that you hear about something good that has happened; however, this past year our daughter, Betsy, has had something wonderful happen to her. She had Mrs. Sherrill as her First Grade teacher at Western Trails. Mrs. Sherrill is an excellent example of what teaching is all about. She always found time to call us and let us know when things were going great with Betsy and when things were needing improvement. She gave our daughter a feeling of accomplishment and always encouraged her to stretch to the limit. She gave her guidance, self-esteem and most importantly, a love of learning.

Mrs. Sherrill's creativity never ceased to amaze us! She would send post cards to our house, with words of encouragement for Betsy. It seemed Mrs. Sherrill has a sixth sense knowing just what to do at the right time.

Betsy loves going to Western Trails! Often at night during bedtime stories, she would want to read to us. We would chuckle to ourselves as she read because she would imitate Mrs. Sherrill and we were her class. It gave us an insight on what a joy it was like to be in Mrs Sherrill's class.

I would like to thank you for recruiting Mrs. Sherrill. She truly is an excellent teacher and you should be extremely proud to have her as part of Community Consolidated School District 93 and most importantly part of Western Trails.

Sincerely,
Margie and Dan Kruk

Sometime later this is the handwritten note they received from Mrs. Sherrill:

Dear Margie and Dan,

I don't think I can find the words to express how touched I was by your letter to Dr. Gmitro. I love what I do, thanks to students like Betsy and parents like you.

I received a letter from Dr. Pagels (Director of Personnel) on Saturday acknowledging his receipt of your letter and thanking me for a great year.

No one has ever done something like this for me. I will never forget it.

Gratefully,
Christine Sherrill

One year later, she sent them the following letter:

Dear Margie, Dan, and Betsy,

I want to thank you for all the great Pampered Chef goodies, but I mostly want to thank you for something much more valuable to me.

This past year has not been easy for me. I have had to spend a tremendous amount of time outside of school planning, researching, attending meetings and mostly just thinking about my students. Every once in awhile, a teacher finds herself spending more time trying to solve problems for her students than the time she spends actually teaching. This can cause her to contemplate if it is the right career. Sometimes I become overwhelmed when I think of all that my students need and what I can actually give.

At several times throughout this year, I have questioned my career plans and each time I have pulled out the letter you wrote last year. It's amazing that just a few words can provide such a source of strength. I've always treasured the letters I've received from parents and students more than anything material. It's these letters and thoughts from people like you that remind me of why I am a teacher. Believe it or not, I keep my letters in a drawer of my nightstand, so at the end of a draining day, I can be revitalized for the next one. I would like to thank you for being such wonderful people who value and appreciate education and for the most valuable gift—your thoughts.

Fondly,
Christine Sherrill

THOUGHT TO PONDER:

The gift of encouragement that the Kruks gave to Mrs.Sherrill through a simple letter was one that made a huge difference in her life and ultimately in the lives of all the children she will one day be there to teach. Is there someone, especially a teacher, to whom you can give the CARE package of an encouraging letter?

The Power of Handwritten Notes

By Barbara Wingfield
Rushylvania, Ohio

Appreciative words are the most powerful force for good on earth.
George W. Crane

BEING FAR FROM those you love is never easy—especially when it is Mom away from her children. Several years ago a work-study program provided me with the wonderful opportunity to travel to South America for three weeks. The down side was leaving behind my husband and children, who were then ages 16, 12, and 10. I knew that phone calls would be rare, and connections would sometimes make it difficult to hear one another.

To bridge the connection between the children and me, I gave each child an envelope of special handwritten notes, one of which they could read each day. Some of the notes focused on school activities, wishing them luck on the day of a big game or telling them to have fun at a school dance. Other days, I would share what was planned on my schedule and where I might be visiting. Also included were my feelings of love and my gratitude for their support as I experienced the culture of a different land.

Rebecca, my youngest child (now 30), shared with me, "I couldn't wait to get home from school and read my special note. It was the best part of my day!" I realize now more than ever what an impact this had on my daughter's life. Recently her boyfriend, Adam, was gone for two weeks with the Air Force National Guard Unit for their summer training camp. Packed in his duffel bag was an envelope filled with daily love notes from my daughter to brighten each day. Once again notes pulled from an envelope were the best part of a loved one's day.

My heart swelled with pride as I realized that she had learned at an early age the power of written notes and how they can bridge distance between people who love each other. The value of the written word on paper—to be able to hold, read, and reread—is priceless. My daughter had experienced the gift of long-distance love notes and has passed it on.

THOUGHT TO PONDER:
Whose day could you brighten with a love note? Take a moment to pass it on.

A Mother's Gift of Words

By Ellen Warner
Boca Raton, Florida

A kind word to one in trouble is often like a switch in a railroad track ... an inch between wreck and smooth sailing.

Henry Ward Beecher

WHEN MY MOTHER died, I was completely devastated. My advocate, the person that loved me more than I loved myself, was well on Sunday night, and Monday morning she was gone. No time for good byes. Just gone.

Of course, that was the good news and the bad news. While it was more difficult for our family to adjust to her loss, she did not suffer, and I am so grateful for that.

My mom was very special. While she had a terrible childhood, she would wake my brother and me every morning with, "Good morning. This is the best day of the rest of your life!" She loved us no matter what we did or said, and I knew I could always count on her.

My mother was my teacher, the person I respected most on the planet, and an incredible spirit. The loss I felt with her passing was so profound that I went in to a very deep depression. I lost part of myself, and while I still feel that loss today, five years later, I did find an unexpected gift from my mother.

About two months after my mother died, I was going through her papers and found a notebook in which she kept inspirational messages. In the back of it I found a note to me. Here is the message:

"You must reach out for life, Ellen. Grab it with both hands. Live it to the fullest. Because before you know it, years will have slipped, and you'll be middle-aged, and then old, and it will be too late. Far, far too late.

"And another thing. Don't sacrifice yourself for others—you might end up being alone if you do, and believe me, loneliness is the most terrifying thing."

This gift from my mother repeatedly reminds me to live my life fully, to love and give to others, and to take care of myself as well. What a precious gift of life she gave to me, even in her death!

THOUGHT TO PONDER:
Have you given those you love the gift of your words to last long after you're gone?

Texas Communications Professor is a Class Act

By Dale Dauten
Lancaster, PA

There is a need for someone against which our characters can measure themselves. Without a ruler, you won't make the crooked straight.

Seneca

SEEMS LIKE EVERYONE who talks to Beverly Chiodo ends up crying. I heard about Chiodo from a neighbor, over coffee and a box of Kleenex, and I couldn't wait to get on the phone to her.

She's Dr. Chiodo (it's Italian, and pronounced SHY-doe), a professor of communications at Southwest Texas State, and she requires her students to name and write about a hero in their lives. The effect is that the class ends up thinking about and discussing what it takes to be admirable, a question that just isn't asked in our society.

"What does it take to get rich?" is asked. "Popular? Sexy? Successful?" Yes. "Admirable?" No.

And then Chiodo takes what each student has written, turns it into a letter and sends it to the hero. Often those letters are a surprise—"I've always admired my grandfather but I never knew how to tell him"—and many of them end up being framed.

Admiration is a deeply emotional experience. The heroes are moved to tears at the unexpected realization that someone has noticed and cared, and then write back, whereupon the students rush to their professor, insist on reading aloud the response but can't get through it without breaking down.

The students experience rapport on a new level—liquid communication.

So does all this Kleenex belong in a college course? Oh, yes.

While many students now learn PowerPoint, most learn neither the power nor the point of communication.

When I spoke to Chiodo, she said, in a charming drawl that recalls Molly Ivins or Ann Richardson (What is it about Texas that produces these warm, engaging, philosophical women?), "Character is the foundation to accomplishment—if you have diligence and determination, you'll succeed."

She told me of a student who said, "I had an ROTC instructor who told me, 'Paul, you're an honest man.' Ever since then, I find that I am incapable of being dishonest."

Chiodo herself tells of a friend once saying to her, "You are a woman of determination." That little sentence still echoes in Chiodo's head, and every time she is struggling, she refuses to give up, knowing that to do so would violate a decade-old statement of faith in her.

And that's the power of praising character—it gets in amongst a person's self-image and self-worth. It becomes you, in both meanings of that expression.

And the best way to communicate about character, Chiodo insists, is in writing. That way you can reflect upon the praise.

She told me of the time she was asked to give the commencement address at her university.

It was her first time speaking outside the classroom, and she was nervous: "The president was on my right, the vice president on my left, my dean and my chairman behind me, and Daddy in the front row. But it came off just fine.

"It went so well that when it was over, the president leaned over and gave me the most wonderful compliment, and I thought, 'I can hardly wait to tell

Daddy what he said.' The only problem was that by the time I'd talked to all the other people on the dais, and got to talk to Daddy, I'd forgotten what the president had said. To this day, I don't remember."

When you put praise in writing, it's a memorial—to show to visitors and to revisit yourself.

Chiodo has started a new exercise in which students discuss character traits with parents and friends and write a report about values—their own and their family's. Students have found these reports useful when it comes time for job interviews, leaving them able to comfortably discuss character issues instead of mere job skills.

One student told Chiodo that his father made copies of his report and sent it to three employers, and all three responded with versions of "I want to meet the young man who wrote that report."

I can't think of a better topic for a job interview than "Tell me about the people you admire."

I recently met the mayor of a town in Ireland, who told me of an Irish supermarket chain where all the employees wear miniature boomerangs on their lapels. The goal is to remind everyone that "whatever you send out comes back to you."

No wonder Beverly Chiodo is a hero.

THOUGHT TO PONDER:
Beverly Chiodo has given her students an awareness and love for the power and gift of words. Tell someone about the people YOU admire. Have you ever written about your hero—and then sent him or her that writing? You will be giving that person an irreplaceable gift.

The Butterfly

By Lisa Johnston
Tampa, Florida, about her mother, Nancy Boerman,
in Ridgway, Colorado

Wise sayings often fall on barren ground; but a kind word is never thrown away.

Sir Arthur Helps

IN THE SUMMER of 1982, shortly before I left for college, my Mom and I spent an afternoon talking about her family. This was a special time for me, as she rarely spoke of her childhood, and it gave me great insight as to how she became the special woman she is today.

As the afternoon came to a close, she gave me something which will always remind me of our time together that day. It was a stained glass butterfly, no more than four inches high with blue and green glass. Maybe it's not the prettiest butterfly ever made, but it is certainly the most loved—because along with the gift, my Mom gave me a wish.

She wished for me the freedom to do anything, go anywhere, and be whatever I wanted to be. She said, "Like the butterfly, I want you to spread your wings and fly."

Those words of encouragement were deeply important to me at age eighteen. Now that I'm thirty-six and a mother myself, I know how difficult it must have been for her to send her youngest child out into the world on her own. But she raised me to take care of myself and then gave me the freedom to find my own path.

Thanks, Mom, for the butterfly and for the words that made a difference in my life!

THOUGHT TO PONDER:

Is there a concrete symbol that expresses your feelings and wishes and wisdom for someone? Give them that gift. Like your words, it will last a lifetime and be a constant reminder of your love and encouragement.

The Postcard Connection

By Rita Emmett
Des Plaines, Illinois

Whoever gives a small coin to a poor man has six blessings bestowed upon him, but he who speaks a kind word to him obtains eleven blessings.

Talmud

LIKE MANY PROFESSIONAL women, I'm on the road for business trips a great deal and never seem to have as much time as I'd like to spend with our seven grandchildren. So I send them little "care packages" in the form of postcards.

I've set up my database so that all I have to do is push a button and a set of labels with all seven names and addresses pops out. When I arrive at my destination, one of the first things I do is find some great postcards, and it takes just seconds to put on the labels.

For the bigger guys, ten year old Kenny and seven year old Mike, I might put some educational fact such as, "This is almost the biggest state in the United States. Do you know the name of the one state that is bigger?" and for the little ones I might find a picture of a chipmunk or a riverboat or a choo-choo train and write a simple message about whatever is in the photo.

Or I'll let them know I'm thinking about the important things in their lives. "Can't wait to hear about your swim lessons" or "I'll pray that you do well on your test this week." Sometimes I'll send them all something silly. "I was on top of this mountain and saw Pokeman" or "Would you believe I sneaked onto this rocket ship and went to Jupiter and back??"

It seems that it doesn't matter WHAT I write, children of all ages love receiving their very own mail. Several of the children have saved all the postcards they've received and sometimes the cards generate discussions. They'll ask me how a certain town was or did I really sneak on to a rocket ship or they'll tell me that when I was in New York, they saw a show about New York and it showed that very same thing that was on my postcard. It's a fun, easy way to have an extra connection with each of them and just a simple way to let them know somebody cares a whole bunch about them.

THOUGHT TO PONDER:
This idea will work for many different relationships besides just those of a traditional family. Whether a trip is for business or pleasure, the more ways you can find to share it with people whom you care for in your life, the closer you will all be and the more you will learn and grow together.

Create a "Word Picture"
By Heather Hopkins
Richmond, BC, Canada

Good words cost nothing, but are worth much.

IF YOU WANT to create a special gift for someone, make a list of words that describe that person well. Go to www.wordle.net and enter those words, including the person's name, in the "create" section. Then hit the GO button. The result will be a beautiful collage to print and give to them. Play with fonts and colours to get the look just right. The more duplication of words, the larger each will appear.

THOUGHT TO PONDER:
I tried this and made a collage for my youngest daughter. It was fun, and she was thrilled. What a wonderful birthday card to give someone!

A Thank You Letter
By Kevin Engle
Chantilly, Virginia

Too many of us hear without heeding, read without responding, confess without changing, profess without practicing, worship without witnessing, and seek without sharing.

William Arthur Ward

THIS IS A letter that Kevin Engle wrote to the people who had helped his mother:

Sometimes the words "thank you" just don't seem to be enough. This is one of those times.

In the early morning hours of June 20th, my mother's long battle with lung cancer came to an end. For anyone who knew her, Cecelia Engle was certainly no heavyweight, but she sure fought like one, longer and harder than anyone thought she possibly could.

Because my brother and his family live in NC and my wife and I are in VA, we couldn't be there as often as we would have liked to help my dad take care of her. But the good news is that they were not alone. Friends, neighbors, relatives and church members came to the rescue. Whether it was a tray of lasagna or a pot of homemade soup, an offer to sit with my mother while my dad went to church or the grocery store, a visit to the house to chat, or a call or letter to offer some words of encouragement, each act of kindness was greatly appreciated.

When you watch the evening news or read the paper, you're overwhelmed with stories of rape, murder and all of the other unpleasant things that go on in the world each day. It's not often you hear about the good things that people do. The Engle family knows firsthand how supportive and caring people can be. When I think about everything you did for us, I can only shake my head in amazement. My only regret is that we didn't get to know how nice you are both sooner and under better circumstances.

I wanted to say a few words about my mother at the funeral but knew I wouldn't be able to. As you read these words, I hope they'll bring a smile to your face as they do mine.

-If there's a Bob Evans restaurant in heaven, I'm sure my mother is already a regular, eating grilled cheese sandwiches on rye.

-I don't know what type of houses angels live in, but I'll bet Cecelia Engle is already active in the real estate market and more than likely has opened up another branch office for Howard Hanna.

-I doubt that heaven is a dirty place, but with my mother around, you can be sure things are spotless.

From the bottom of our hearts, thanks again for everything. You've been great.

THOUGHT TO PONDER:

Is there someone in your life who needs a letter of thanks?

<u>Chapter Eighteen:</u>

"Gifting the Giver"

GIFTING THE GIVER

Dear Brian: When you went away,
I was heartbroken, the scenes
Of our togetherness played in my mind,
Each delightful memory brought tears,
Tears and bitterness at what I had lost,
But worst of all, I thought,
Were your parting words—"Our best future,
As individuals, as fixtures in each other's life,
Is to recognize that we are best friends"—
And the mockery they made of my feelings.
I cried many nights over those words.
I cursed fate and the stars and the wet pillow.
This morning I woke after a long dream of you.
I reached for the phone to tell you the details
Of walking through a garden, sharing the beauty.
I realized you would be at the other end.
You had not gone away, I had gone.
I had withdrawn the best part of my self,
Which along with the not-so-good,
Is what I have shared with you
And wish to share again.
Please accept my dearest friendship. Love. Anita

©Andrew Grossman 2000
Newton, CT

THE BIBLE SAYS, "It is more blessed to give than to receive." But that is very difficult for many of us, particularly those of us who are born givers! My friend, John Blumberg, puts it this way:

Giving the gift of Receiving

We have so often heard that "it is better to give than receive". And what a joy it is to give! But sometimes we get so focused on giving that we forget how to receive. So often we may have a feeling that we need to pay the giver back, or simply say, "Oh, you shouldn't have done that". Receiving sometimes takes a dose of humility. The truth is that in receiving we actually give! We give joy to the giver. The next time someone gives you a gift, just be ready to give them one of the greatest gifts of all ... receive it!

We are giving a precious gift when we complete the circle and let others know what their gift has meant to us. I received just such a blessing this week. A dear new friend, Sue Rusch whose story "Love Heals" you will read in Chapter Six, called to tell me an amazing addition to her story of being hit by a car when she came out of the grocery store. (It was a miracle that she wasn't killed in that freak accident.)

She said, "Barbara, I just want you to know that I was wearing the angel pin you gave me on my coat when I was hit, and I am <u>convinced</u> that is why I wasn't hurt more badly. Just know that even though you didn't know about the accident until now, you've been with me in spirit all the way through." What a precious gift she gave to me in that phone call!

I, too, try to remember to gift my givers. Tonight I will write a note to Dr. Lester Hoffman, who recently sent me a book called *The Positive Power of Prayer*. When my husband was in the hospital at the Moffitt Cancer Center in Tampa, Florida, we spent several hours reading that book aloud, and it was a great comfort to both of us in a very difficult, lonely time. I hope Lester will be blessed by my note as we have been blessed by his gift.

Think about ways you might bless some of the givers who have impacted your life.

Therapy Recovers a Lost Voice

From "Success Stories"
JFK Johnson Rehabilitation Institute
Edison, New Jersey

The quality of mercy is not strained,
It droppeth as the gentle rain from heaven
Upon the place beneath: it is twice blessed;
It blesseth him that gives and him that takes.

Shakespeare

AS A MARKETING guru for an international corporation, Joe Tischio acquired a reputation for knowing just the right words to sway decision makers. It was one of life's cruelest ironies when a laryngectomy left him without a voice.

A diagnosis of squamous cell carcinoma mandated surgery to remove Tischio's larynx and one lung. The realization of the loss was almost too much for him to bear: "Suddenly, you realize 'I'm alive,' so big deal. But, you have to find a way to get through this." He began using an electro-larynx and had visits from speech therapists. But he disliked the mechanical sound and felt he was making little headway in improving his skills.

Tischio remembers vividly the defining moment that led him to the JFK Johnson Rehabilitation Institute (JRI) and speech pathologist Lynn Acton. "I was outside our house in Manasquan when my electrolarynx dropped into the street and was crushed by an oncoming steamroller. I started to cry like a baby." The experience strengthened Tischio's resolve. He became determined to find a better way to speak: "I decided I would do anything to become independent again."

At a laryngectomy conference in Toms River, Tischio met JRI speech pathologist Lynn Acton. Acton encouraged him to attend the laryngectomy support group that JRI makes available as a community service the third Wednesday of every month. Acton remembers their first encounter well: "Joe was starving for knowledge. He very obviously needed and wanted to improve his situation." Tischio entered esophageal speech therapy with Acton but decided it wasn't for him. The next and most natural choice for communication required a Tracheo-esophageal Puncture (TEP) that would allow Tischio to use a voice prosthesis. Acton explains: "A small tube is inserted in the puncture from the trachea to the esophagus. Air from the lungs is shunted through the prosthesis to create sound." After reviewing Tischio's surgical records, Acton felt he would be an excellent candidate for the procedure. Tischio's surgeon had performed a crico pharyngeal myotomy—a cutting of the muscle in the esophagus that relaxes it and permits good vibration with a prosthesis.

On August 25, Tischio went into the hospital for the TEP procedure and returned to Acton for the prosthesis. Tischio remembers his delight at hearing his own voice: "I said, 'I'm talking!' And I haven't stopped since."

Since Tischio also suffers from macular degeneration, his wife Ginger was deeply involved in the following weeks of instruction on the cleaning and care of the prosthesis, as Tischio continued therapy and learned how to become more proficient at using his newfound voice.

The expression of Tischio's profound gratitude for Acton's efforts on his behalf came in the form of two crystal snowmen Christmas ornaments. One held the word "Believe"—Tischio said it was symbolic of Acton helping him believe in himself again. The other ornament displayed the word "Joy"—symbolizing the joy Tischio believes Acton brought into his life by convincing him to get the TEP so he could communicate in a natural voice.

Tischio has found more than a new voice. As an active participant in the group session for laryngectomy patients at JRI, he is once again using his gift for communication, this time to help people who are going through what he did. "We discuss things and learn from each other. We talk about ways to help ourselves." He is a strong proponent of getting the word out about the procedure and of more training in general to help laryngectomy patients adjust emotionally and physically to the change in their lives.

In a philosophical moment, Tischio reflects, "When all the clouds clear, it's really up to you to make the most of your life." With JRI and Acton's help, Tischio's life is looking more positive than ever.

THOUGHT TO PONDER:
Has there been a giver in your own life whom you can thank in a special way? Every time Lynn Acton saw those precious ornaments, she was reminded of Joe Tischio and his gratitude.

Gratitude
By Mary Lou Johns
Breckenridge, Colorado

We Give To ...

At first, we give to receive.
Later, we give because giving feels good.
Eventually, we give because, well, that's just what we do.
At that time, the giver and the gift become one.

John-Roger and Peter McWilliams

MY TWO GRANDDAUGHTERS were coming up to the farm for the first time. Amanda had been there when she was barely two, but now, at five years old, she didn't remember it. Heather had just turned eleven and was beginning to show interest in teenage things like hair-dos, clothes and rock groups.

I hoped to show the girls a simple, farm life-style where we were entertained by nature instead of TV. I wanted them to experience a working farm and know that milk comes from cows by actually seeing the dairy barn and tasting the warm milk just when it comes from the cow's udder.

So John and I planned a full weekend of outdoor activities. We would give the girls rides in the old Army jeep and on the old John Deere tractor, walk in the woods to find mushrooms and wild strawberries, and build a campfire to roast marshmallows. Hopefully, they'd catch glimpses of deer, wild turkey, and perhaps a fox or raccoon. John even "planted" a watermelon in the cold, hillside spring so that we could find it on a picnic. I was excited about the girls' visit.

And what a wonderful weekend it was! The weather was perfect with sunny days and cooler evenings. We spent our days outdoors and went to bed early after reading aloud around the wood-burning stove. The most fun for the kids was the old barn. There was a rope hanging from the rafters, and they delighted in swinging from it and dropping into the hay, just as John had done as a boy! Their shrieks of laughter echoed across the cornfields.

On the last night, we packed up the ingredients for some'ors and walked out to the point overlooking the valley. We had previously gathered twigs and kindling, just as I'd learned in Girl Scouts. So the fire was ready to be lit. While it was starting and before it was just right for toasting marshmallows, Amanda and I walked to the bluff to look at the sunset. She took my hand, and said, "Amah, thank you for all the plans you made so we could have such a good time!"

I was so touched. A big lump formed in my throat. Imagine this little five year old so clearly expressing her thanks! And to me! It truly made my heart soar. She recognized that I had gone to considerable effort. She was grateful for what I had done. Her sincere thanks validated my efforts. This unexpected expression of gratitude was so joyous for me that I immediately wanted to begin planning another farm trip so I could continue to please her. My love for her grew into a huge ball of glowing light that filled the entire clearing. Hearing those words from Amanda made me realize that the expression of gratitude is an amazing and powerful force.

So often we take for granted those around us. We rarely stop to appreciate their presence, let alone their contributions and talents. Sometimes we think that if everything isn't perfect, we can't acknowledge anything. Yet, when we acknowledge and appreciate another person, we are validating who they are. We give them the gift of noticing who they are. To express your gratitude for another person is the greatest gift of all.

"The expression of gratitude is a powerful force that generates even more of what we have already received."—Deepak Chopra, M.D.

These are Mary Lou's ideas to help us each become a more grateful person:

1. Start a Gratitude Journal. Set a day of the week and on that day, write about your blessings.
2. Find a Gratitude Partner. My partner and I have agreed to email each other Monday with a list of things for which we are grateful.
3. Write a letter to an old friend with whom you are no longer in contact. Express your appreciation for the friendship even though it is past. Send it (or not).
4. Make one social call every day for a month to people or relatives you don't see regularly.
5. Upon waking in the morning, bless your body and thank God for its functioning. This is based on a Hebrew prayer practice, and it is a beautiful and grounding way to start your day.

THOUGHT TO PONDER:

How would you like to be acknowledged? During the next week, be aware of how you are thanked by others. Notice your feelings. Then become an even more appreciative person.

Thinking of the Giver

By John Blumberg
Naperville, Illinois

The momentary thrill of getting rarely equals the lasting joy of giving.
William Arthur Ward

CHRISTMAS CAN BE such a hectic time ... especially for children. It is easy to lose focus on the true purpose of the celebration. As a family we started a tradition five years ago that has evolved into one of our most meaningful and memorable parts of the holiday season.

It began as a gathering around a simple advent wreath for nightly prayer, in preparation for Christmas day. As the tradition has evolved, at the beginning of Advent we now create a beautiful advent wreath full of lights with large candles in the center. It has gone from a simple wreath to a focal point of our family room holiday decorations. We have continued to share a prayer around the beautiful wreath each night of the advent season.

Two years ago we heard a song by Ray Boltz entitled "I believe in Bethlehem". We learned the words and created sign language motions for the song and began to use it as the closing to our nightly gathering. By the arrival of the final lighting of the Advent Candles on Christmas Eve, everyone has once again mastered the words and all the sign language. It makes for a spirited finale to our Advent preparation for Christmas. We think of it as our gift back to the Giver of Life!

THOUGHT TO PONDER:
Do you believe in a Giver of Life? What are you giving back to Him?

My Hero (Straight Talk)

By Bomani Moyenda
Yellow Springs, Ohio

The value of a man should be in what he gives and not in what he is able to receive.

Albert Einstein

MY STEPFATHER IS a strong-willed, no-nonsense man. He came into my life when I was three or four years old, so I have always thought of him as my true father. He began right away preparing me to be my best and to do my best. As I grew into my teens, I would have been fair game to fall victim to peer pressure without his guidance. He taught me to think independently. Kids around me who traveled in their cliques finally gave up trying to include me in their popularity contests. I didn't need that. Oddly enough, I grew to be respected by them because I was not easily influenced.

This is not to say I did not falter at times. But whenever he sensed that I had played the role of blindly following the crowd, he would scold me. My chest would tighten with fear at the intensity of his voice, which, it seemed, could fell mountains. But afterwards, my fear would melt away at the soundness of his reasoning.

He never stayed angry at me. As a matter of fact, shortly after verbally chastising me, he would look either guilty or as if nothing had happened at all! This let me know that I was being "put in check" with love. It also let me know that he did not enjoy getting angry with me, that this was something that he had to actually force himself to do.

In his book *The Road Less Traveled,* Dr. Scott Peck describes love as the willingness to go out of your way to help someone grow spiritually. That's what my big, tough dad did for me. The gift of love doesn't always come dressed in fancy colorful gift wrapping. His gift to me was always straight to the point and timely. And, after all, I was a fast-growing, tough kid and big for my age, so I don't think I would have responded well to soft-spoken psychological parental gaming or "timeouts." I <u>needed</u> his straight talk.

We have never exchanged our love for one another in words. It has always been through our actions. We all know which speaks louder!

He was loud when he supported me, too. His volume was not only reserved for times he was trying to turn me from trouble, but it was there when he wanted to push me forward. It was energetic! At my sporting events I could hear his voice above all the others, piercing through and electrifying me with confidence.

Recently I resumed writing poetry, one of my true loves. During that time, I captured one of my favorite memories of my dad in a poem. For a long time I have wanted to show my dad my appreciation for his support through the years, and I have always enjoyed the element of surprise, so with the encouragement of friends, I planned a poetry reading. I invited my dad and asked him to videotape the presentation for me. No one present knew of my plan to read the special poem I had written for him.

Here's to my dad:

My First Little League All Star Game

(For my one and only hero, Oscar Lee Stewart)
by Bomani Moyenda

I remember that day like it was yesterday
On the little league baseball diamond
Hot, humid, good day for little black boys to hone their skills
We tend to play better in the absence of chill

There I was standing at home plate readying myself to face
The baddest pitcher in the league
Chuck Monroe was his name, 2 or maybe 3 three years older than me
Leaned over, peering in with one hand on his knee

Snarling and snorting, trying to stare me down
But he couldn't compete with my "Oscar Lee" frown
Oscar Lee, the man who had taken the task to raise me up
To walk proud like a man instead of a pup

I could hear his voice slicing air from behind the backstop
"Keep your eye on the ball like I told you, boy!
Knock that ball over the fence like I told you!
Pick out a good pitch and just ride it on up outta there!"

And Chuckie's Daddy hollered for him to bear down and strike me out
What'd he say that for?
Big O really started to shout
"Aint gonna be no strike out here, man!
The ball's going over the fence—you just shut up and watch!"

He was rolling now, when his voice had that pop
I knew there wasn't a man alive gonna make him stop

I signaled the ump for time out, backed out of the batter's box
Leaned down real pro-like to adjust my sox

And take a moment to reflect ...

It was quite common knowledge in our little town
That this kid Chuck was king of the mound
Most of the batters he faced he just mowed 'em right down

But I had to let him know that I didn't care
So when I straightened back up
I resumed my stare

I flashed a big Willie Mays grin
And twirled my bat around
Big O was still spoutin' off
It was time to get down

Now my hands were steady

And I knew I was ready
'Cause whatever confidence I may have lacked
The Big O was right there takin' up the slack

I knew I had Chuck going
'Cause his shirt was all wet
Wipin' sweat off his brow
And he hadn't thrown a single pitch yet

His first two pitches were ball one and ball two
Way off the mark
But I was watchin' like Big O told me
For one to hit clean out of the park

So I hollered
"Hey, man, how long you gonna make me wait?
Throw me my home run ball over this here plate"

Then folks in the crowd started to snarl and jeer
You see, no one had homered off Chuck all year
The next pitch shot down the middle hard and fast
I *smacked* it over the center field fence like a *cannon blast*

"There it is! That's the swing, that's right!"
The Big O bellowed with his monstrous might
I laid my bat down easy and rounded the bases
And noticed surprised looks and astonished faces

But it wasn't at all a surprise to me
I was full of the spirit of Oscar Lee
And didn't mind at all that he was my only fan

No one can give a Black boy confidence
Like a strong Black man can.

To his surprise and joy, I read it to him in the presence of family, friends,
and a few people I didn't even know. It was a heartfelt experience for the
two of us and has drawn us even closer.

It was a gift I gave to the one who had given so much to me!

THOUGHT TO PONDER:
Have you ever let your father know how much he has given you?

A Father's Day Card
By Ralph Geppert
Darien, Illinois

Sometimes we don't give generously because we don't see the generous Giver to whom it all belongs anyway!

Kent R. Hunter

I CAME ACROSS a Father's Day card from my grandson, Frank LaGrassa, which reflects how much a person can affect another's life without really having that in mind. I married his grandmother, Connie, after both of us found ourselves alone after ended first marriages.

Frank, Connie's son, was left with six sons to care for after his wife died at age 38. Frankie was 12 years old at the time. They lived in a very depressed neighborhood and had limited resources. As an example of the influences surrounding them, one of their friends shot and killed a policeman, father of four, during a daytime break-in. Their home was broken into three times, and their coin collection, personal items, and appliances were all stolen. Things were bleak.

Their grandmother, Connie, was working a fulltime job, but she took it upon herself to help those boys as best she could, picking them up after work Friday afternoon and caring for them over the weekend. She scrubbed them from top to bottom and did their clothes every weekend. Going to church with us was an absolute must.

With this devoted grandmother and God's help, Frankie made it through high school and college, the first one in his family to do so. He now has a Master's degree, is a high school teacher, and is very active in his church.

The card that he sent me on Father's day 1994 made it all worthwhile. I only regret that his grandmother has passed away and can't share his gratitude in person.

Father's Day '94

Ralph,

You have truly been a "Father" for each of us in this entire family. I cannot imagine what life would be like if the Lord had not brought you into our lives. We could not have asked for a better role model and a true "giver of one's self." It is very special to witness someone who not only speaks the truth of Christianity but knows how to live it. I would not be who I am today without your guidance and influence. I aspire to be more and more like you in ways I will never really understand or appreciate. Have a Happy Father's day!

Love,
Frank

THOUGHT TO PONDER:
Send a heartfelt card to someone you love today and thank them for what they have given to you. They will never forget it.

Old Turtle

By Cathy Norman
Western Springs, Illinois

The art of acceptance is the art of making someone who has just done you a small favor wish that he might have done you a greater one.

Russell Lynes

I GAVE MY friend, Cathy Norman, a copy of the children's book *Old Turtle* for her birthday. This is the thank you letter she wrote to me:

Dear Barbara,

Not only are you a very special friend, but I am amazed at your gift of discernment which I feel must be divinely inspired! I cannot tell you how thrilled and delighted I was to receive the special book with those fantastic illustrations. A few months ago we attended a church in Indiana and the minister and the drama team read that book and acted it out. The story is so meaningful.

Recently Sue (my daughter) left Declan (her infant son) in a childcare group while she attended her exercise class. When she picked him up, he had a gold star on his shirt because he had said the word "turtle." The teacher had been working with the group with flash cards. She felt that perhaps it was a stretch of the imagination to think he said "turtle" since his only word prior to that day was "dog!" However, since that day, she and Joe have been drilling him faithfully each day, and he now says "turtle" on command, but of course, hasn't had the faintest idea what it means!

*I had even looked for a picture book with turtles but hadn't found one and
then your beautiful book arrived with the absolutely magnificent illustrations
of turtles. I couldn't wait to share it with Declan and Sue yesterday, and they
were also excited. See what a rippling effect your special gift has had!*

Cathy's note was truly a "gift to the giver," and it added even more joy to
the fun I had had in picking out a special gift for her. Little did I know the
far-reaching consequences my gift would have for her whole family!

THOUGHT TO PONDER:
Do you take time to gift the givers in your life?

The Gift of Sharing

By Rosemary Aikens
Lansing, Michigan

I know what I have given you. I do not know what you have received.
                                                        Antonio Porchia

A WEEK AGO this past Saturday, I completed a training session at Meijer,
a local grocery store. As I shopped, I noticed a woman whom I thought I
knew. Surely enough, she and I had ridden the rural transportation system
together when I worked in Retirement Systems. I had a chance to meet her
husband that day for the first time. They offered to give me a ride home.

After we walked out of the store, Janice handed me some money. She reminded me of when I had invited her into my home to warm up and have a
cup of hot tea. I did not realize how much that had meant to her. I was
astounded because I only did what I would have wanted someone to do for

me. Janice went on to tell of the wonderful blessings God has brought into their lives. She and her husband are back together, they have bought a new home and a nice car, and are now debt free. They simply wanted to share some of their blessings with me.

THOUGHT TO PONDER:
Are you sharing the blessings you have received?

A Shared Holiday

God does not work in all hearts alike, but according to the preparation and sensitivity He finds in each.

Meister Eckhart

ANNA EVANS SHARED this precious story with me:

A couple of years ago, my husband and I spent Thanksgiving in Marathon Key, Florida. We made reservations at a lovely ocean side restaurant on Marathon Key Colony for Thanksgiving Dinner. We were seated at an ocean side table and ordered cocktails before dinner. As we looked around the dining room, I noticed a woman seated at a table by herself, alone. My husband and I looked at each other and then my husband got up and approached the lady's table. At first she appeared startled to see my husband approach, but when he graciously asked her to dine with us and share Thanksgiving, reinforced by me nodding for her to please join us, she reluctantly joined our table.

Words cannot express the happiness this lady brought into our lives that evening. Our guest was a single mother whose daughter happened to work at the restaurant and this was their way of "spending Thanksgiving" together. Her daughter was a hostess at the restaurant and continuously came by the table along with several servers that were all

*friends of our guest. We immediately became immersed in hospitality that was very unex-
pected. To this day, my husband and I truly believe that it was our guest who gave us an
act of kindness by sharing her Thanksgiving!*

THOUGHT TO PONDER:
Have you ever invited someone to share your holiday? I guarantee that you
will receive as great or greater a gift than you give them.

Honoring Those Who Serve

By Barbara A. Glanz
Sarasota, Florida

The first great gift we can bestow on others is a good example.

Morrell

MY PASTOR TOLD a story on a recent Sunday that really touched my
heart. He said he was traveling on Delta from Atlanta to Sarasota, and
although usually he is in the very back of the plane, this time his Boarding
Pass said "Zone One." Being one of the first people on the plane, he got to
do some wonderful people watching as others were coming on board.

He was in the third row of Coach, when soon a young man in uniform
came in, stowed his pack in the overhead bin, and sat in the row ahead of
him. Another young lady was seated in that row, and he was able to hear a
bit of their conversation. The young man told her that he had just finished a
tour in Iraq, was coming home on leave, and then would go back in several
weeks.

As they were talking, a woman who had been seated in First Class, came back to the young man's row, introduced herself, and asked him for his Boarding Pass. A bit puzzled, he handed it to her, at which point she, in turn, handed hers to him. She said, "I would like to trade seats with you."

The young man immediately responded, "Oh, no, Ma'am, I couldn't do that."

She smiled a huge smile and said, "Oh, yes, you can, Soldier. **It's an order!**"

So, as everyone around wiped teary eyes, the young man reached up for his backpack and went up to sit in First Class.

Just a few moments later, he said another woman came out of First Class, went down the row to another young soldier and said, "I just want to thank you for serving our country. Would you please trade seats with me?"

And the end of the story is … that by the time that plane took off, **EVERY SINGLE PERSON IN UNIFORM was sitting in First Class!**

What a testimony this is to the difference each of us can make every single day in every single situation when we are in touch with our hearts! That one act started a chain of kindness that touched every single life on that plane that day.

THOUGHT TO PONDER:
How can YOU reach out to someone today to thank them for the difference they are making?

Chapter Nineteen:

"Real Life CARE® Packages"

One of the most amazing things ever said on this earth is Jesus's statement: "He that is greatest among you shall be your servant." Nobody has one chance in a billion of being thought really great after a century has passed except those who have been the servants of all. That strange realist from Bethlehem knew that.

Harry Emerson Fosdick

IN THE PROCESS of researching for my books, I learned about the wonderful history of the first CARE® Package, which originated with CARE, the international relief and development agency:

On a sunny afternoon in May 1946, a small crowd formed on the docks of LeHavre, a French city still in ruins from the war. A local resistance hero, Marcel Fernez, stepped through the gathering of friends and neighbors to sign for a food parcel sent to him by an American he had never met. As he hoisted the parcel up onto his shoulder, Fernez became the recipient of the very first CARE® Package. This plain brown package of food was the creation of a new American charity—CARE (which then stood for the Cooperative for American Remittances to Europe)—founded to help survivors of World War II. In the years that followed Americans sent some 100 million CARE Packages to people in need all over the world; and CARE continues to help the world's poor today.

CARE® (which today stands for "Cooperative for Assistance and Relief Everywhere") still provides people with the ability to touch lives and make a difference. Several of CARE's current donors are people who have become self-sufficient through CARE pro-

grams and want to give others the same opportunity. This spirit has helped make CARE one of the world's largest relief and development agencies in existence today, and it literally thrives on the unconditional caring felt by Americans that transcends politics, race, nationality, and all other barriers separating people.

CARE continues its mission of working with the world's poor and giving them the tools to achieve economic and social well-being. CARE now works with millions of people in more than 60 developing and emerging nations in Africa, Asia, Europe, and Latin America. Its programs encompass health, nutrition, family planning, emergency relief, education, small business support, agriculture, and environmental protection.

In its more than 50 year history, CARE has brought its message of hope to nearly two billion people in 127 countries. You will read some of these stories in the chapter that follows. For more information about CARE, please see the organization's website at www.care.org. Or contact: CARE, 151 Ellis Street, Atlanta, GA 30303; 800-521-CARE ; info@care.org. (CARE and CARE Packages are registered service marks of the Cooperative for Assistance and Relief Everywhere, Inc. and have been used with permission.)

A Bit of CARE

By Klaus Putter
Formerly a German soldier in Hitler's army
Now from Atlanta, Georgia

THIS IS THE story of a real CARE Package received during World War II. Klaus Putter was a young German soldier whose life was changed because of someone in America who cared. We first heard his story at the 50th anniversary of the CARE organization in Washington, D.C., when the first CARE Package, sent in 1946 to LeHavre, France, was inducted into the

Smithsonian in an exhibit memorializing those acts of love. Here is Klaus'
story:

*As a teenage German soldier, I was in French captivity from 1945-1947. We searched
for and removed land mines in the south of France. One day in 1946 while removing a
mine, it exploded, and I ended up in the hospital for Prisoners of War. It was there that
we received CARE Packages from America.*

*That really was a very big surprise because the treatment in those days was not the most
cordial. Hunger and desperation were rampant. When the CARE Packages arrived, our
first reaction was, "What is the catch? What do they do to us now?"*

*We were highly suspicious in those days. No one kept any promises. We had been told
that we would be repatriated after we had removed 1000 mines. We considered that a
"fair deal." German soldiers had planted the mines and German prisoners of war had to
remove them. To find 25 mines a day seemed manageable, meaning that after 40 days,
we would get released. I got blown up with the 2684th mine! Nobody kept promises in
those days.*

*Then, all of a sudden some people were treating us kindly—sending CARE Packages,
We just could not believe it. We debated the issue at great length and finally one comrade
drew the right conclusion: These Americans are different! And thus, we finally realized
that common American people were doing this, just to help, just to support. They sent
gifts to the POW's of a defeated army—WHY????? Would we have done that, sending
gifts to Russian prisoners of war in our captivity? Hardly!*

*We realized that these Americans must be very special, very different people. Receiving
that CARE Package told us that there was someone in the world who wanted to help us.*

*That fact alone made an everlasting impression on me! I do not think I would have joined
an American company, or accepted the move to the United States, or decided to stay here
after retirement without this particular "CARE Package experience."*

*In those days we were very prejudiced. German soldiers were trained and indoctrinated
against all those we were at war with, and receiving that CARE Package of food and
clothing was something that made us think. It shattered all our previously held concep-
tions. It was much more than just food ... it gave us food for thought!*

So I am proud to be here today; proud that the CARE Package meant such a dramatic shift in my beliefs; proud that what meant life and hope to me and so many others will be displayed for all Americans and visitors from other countries to see, and to learn about, to contemplate and to remember. My hope is that this exhibit will inspire people to rededicate themselves to the ideas embodied in the CARE Package, to shatter biases about groups of people, and to get us to see that we are not isolated groups but one global community.

The CARE Package was a signal that people really cared about one another and that life would get better. The war had ended, but that only meant that the fighting had stopped. We lived in the devastation. We were prisoners of war, still dealing with the destruction the war had left behind. Although World War Ii had ended, out personal war to survive in that environment of destruction had not. We were still struggling to find enough food to eat, a dry place to sleep, warm clothes to wear. The arrival of the CARE Packages signaled the beginning of the process of rebuilding. It always has and always will.

I ask that we always remember the CARE Package. It has helped us arrive at this moment from dark times, and it can carry us forward into a brighter future.

THOUGHT TO PONDER:

Klaus Putter went on to become a senior vice president of the Coca-Cola Company. He continues to live in the United States, a long time supporter of the CARE organization. Have you ever thought about the far-reaching impact your small acts of kindness may have as you send your CARE Packages to others in our world?

CARE Package Restores Luftwaffe Pilot's Faith in Humanity
By Dr. Alfred P. Wehner
Richland, Washington (Formerly from Wiesbaden, Germany)

IN THE DARK days following Germany's capitulation, Dr. Alfred P. Wehner, then a young Luftwaffe pilot, received a CARE package that renewed his spirit.

Born in west Germany, he was six years old when Hitler came to power and twelve years old when World War II broke out. Dr. Wehner earned his wings as a fighter pilot in the Hitler Youth Flying Corps at age 15. He was drafted into the Luftwaffe (German Air Force) at age seventeen. Due to a lack of fuel for their planes, he was sent to the Eastern Front during the last months of the war where he became an infantryman in the Wehrmacht (German Armed Forces).

Dr. Wehner was 200 kilometers behind Soviet lines and 500 km from his hometown of Weisbaden when the war ended on May 9, 1945. In two weeks he broke through Russian and American lines to return to his family, sick and emaciated, knowing that if he failed, he'd become a prisoner of war.

He arrived home to total destruction and utter physical and moral devastation. "It looked hopeless indeed. A life of misery in a ravished country, at the mercy of the conquerors, our cities destroyed, and everything that we were taught by our leaders to cherish torn down and gone," Dr. Wehner said. "Hunger was my most faithful companion in those days."

Yet much more devastating than defeat, hunger, and ruins were the shocking revelations that millions of innocent civilians had been slaughtered by his Nazi leaders in concentration camps. "Up until that time I was still holding up my head because I thought that we had fought a good fight for a noble and worthy cause against sinister enemies who finally overwhelmed us on account of their tremendous superiority in material and resources," Dr. Wehner said.

"However, I learned that these monstrous crimes were committed under the flag I had fought for. The shocking truth began to sink in, slowly but devastatingly, that we had fought on the wrong side, not materially, but morally!"

In his starvation and despair, Dr. Wehner received a CARE package from an unknown American.

"It was in those desperate days of 1946 that I received a CARE package. Even more important for me than the urgently needed and most welcome basic food items was the symbolic significance of that package: the fact that a stranger in a far-away country cared rekindled hope in my heart and mind," he said.

"The lasting impact was that someone I didn't know had spent his or her hard-earned money to send a package to a former enemy; that we were not forgotten and outcast, that there were humans that cared for us as fellow human beings. I never forgot that, and I am very grateful for that new hope."

In the following years he studied medicine and dentistry at the Gutenberg University in Mainz before immigrating to the United States and becoming a citizen in 1958. Dr. Wehner now consults in biomedical and environmental research.

Dr. Wehner says, "Given my personal experience, it is not surprising that CARE is my favorite charity. Having been blessed with good health, a wonderful wife and family, and a productive career in biomedical research, I consider it a debt of gratitude to help through CARE and other charities in a very modest way less fortunate human beings somewhere in the world just as someone helped me 50 years ago."

THOUGHT TO PONDER:

Do you have a favorite charity where you can show that you care?

Guideposts for Kids Comfort Kits

I AM BLESSED to be on the National Advisory Cabinet for Guideposts, the ministry started by Dr. Norman Vincent Peale, the author of *The Power of Positive Thinking*. One of my favorite aspects of the ministry is known as "Comfort Kits." These are distributed free to any hospitals that request them. This is their story:

In 2005, The National Center for Health Statistics reported that children under the age of 18 accounted for over 2,000,000 inpatient visits. More than anyone, sick children need to be loved and touched by comfort. That's why Guideposts has created the Comfort Kit for Kids—a small box with a huge impact.

Distributed to children by the hospital chaplains, nurses, child life personnel, or volunteers, the Comfort Kit is filled with special items to turn a child's hospital experience into a meaningful time; and to fill it, to whatever extent possible, with joy. Inside, the child finds a cuddly stuffed star named "Sparkle", an "I'm Special" bracelet, stickers, a stress ball, crayons, a parent feedback card, a stand up prayer card and a personalized name tag to mount on the wall (so that doctors and nurses can call the child by their first name)—and best of all, a special journal that kids use to help them process their feelings and help them find the strength that lies within.

Over the last six years Guideposts Outreach has distributed over 95,000 Comfort Kits to children in over 400 hospitals across 46 states. With your help, we can reach children in their greatest moments of need. We can let them know that someone loves them—and that God in heaven loves them most of all.

Guideposts Outreach makes these kits available FREE to hospitals across the country. For more information please go to www.comfortkits.org. or email us at ComfortKits@guideposts.org.

THOUGHT TO PONDER:

Are you willing to get involved in comforting children in hospitals? You would be touching many hurting children's lives in a special way.

Conclusion

Do all the good you can,
By all the means you can,
In all the ways you can,
In all the places you can,
At all the times you can,
To all the people you can,
As long as you ever can.

John Wesley

IN THE BOOK, *We Give to Live,* Roger and McWilliams write about the extraordinary benefits of giving: "New studies tell us that assisting others, through acts of charity or devotion to causes, improves our physical well-being. Giving is not just a minor influence on good health but the key to bodily and mental well-being. The studies show that for all ages, one way to escape premature physical and emotional deterioration is by staying active in the service of others."

They define the following benefits of giving:

Physical Benefits

* Greater longevity
* Significant reduction in toxic stress chemicals in the body (and so less stress)

* Enhanced functioning of the immune system
* Decreased metabolic rate
* Improved cardiovascular circulation
* Healthier sleep
* Help in maintaining good health

Emotional Benefits

* Increased self-acceptance
* Reduced self-absorption and sense of isolation
* Increased endorphin release (which provides a natural emotional "high")
* Expanded sense of control over one's life and circumstances
* Increased ability to cope with crises
* Stronger feelings of personal satisfaction
* Improved concentration and enjoyment of experiences
* Enhanced compassion, empathy, sensitivity to others
* Reduced inner stress and conflict

Spiritual Benefits

* Greater connectedness to God
* More receptivity to spiritual guidance
* Added involvement in charitable activity
* Heightened sense of appreciation and acceptance of others
* Sustained peace of mind
* Greater clarity about the meaning and purpose of life
* Enhanced quality of life

They go on to say, "Considering how many people in our stress-ridden society are looking for physical well-being, emotional health and buoyancy, and spiritual harmony, there is every reason to believe they will become more involved in helping others if they are given the good news. There seem to be virtually no negative effects to giving and volunteering."

This is good news for all of us.

All religions have a common thread of giving, service, and charity:

CHRISTIANITY—It is more blessed to give then to receive.
JUDAISM—Blessed is he that considereth the poor. The Lord will deliver him in time of trouble.
BUDDHISM—The real treasure is that laid up by a man or a woman through charity and piety, temperance and self-control. The treasure thus is secure and does not pass away.
HINDUISM—Bounteous is he who gives to the beggar who comes to him in want of food and feeble.
ISLAM—The poor, the orphan, the captive—feed them for the love of god alone, desiring no reward nor even thanks.
TAOISM—Extend your help without seeking reward. Give to others and do not regret or begrudge your liberality. Those who are thus are good.
SIKHISM—In the minds of the generous, contentment is produced.

Jeremy Langford in his article "Accepting the Gift of Peace" says, "Cardinal Joseph Bernardin taught me that to share God's love we must first know that we are loved and that we all have special gifts. Finally, and most importantly, we must recognize that our gifts are not our own—they belong to God and are ours to share. The last stage is crucial, for in acknowledging where our gifts come from, we get out of the way and allow God to truly work through us."

In this book we are celebrating gift-giving. Always remember that the most priceless gifts do not cost money, but come from the heart:

The gift of listening—One of the greatest things we can do for another person is to just listen without interrupting, daydreaming or thinking about our next leap into the conversation.

The gift of a compliment—A simple and sincere, "You look wonderful in blue," "That was such a beautiful note," "What a fantastic meal!" or "You always brighten my day whenever I see your smile," can make someone's day.

The gift of showing affection—Demonstrate how much you care for others with hugs, kisses, a gentle squeeze of the hand, a pat on the back, smiles.

The gift of laughter—Everyone loves to laugh. Try to see the humor in day-to-day living and share it with others. Also develop the ability to laugh at yourself.

The gift of cheerfulness—This means no complaining, no feeling sorry for ourselves, no nasty comments. no gossip. Our gift of cheerfulness will be precious for everyone including ourselves.

The gift of doing a favor—Help with the dishes, type a letter, run an errand, babysit so a busy mother can have a break. Every day go out of your way to do something kind for someone.

The gift of contact—Write notes as simple as "thinking of you today". Make phone calls, send emails, reach out with support.

The gift of solitude—There are times when we want nothing more than to be left alone. Be sensitive to those times and give the gift of solitude to others.

The gift of acceptance—Accept with fortitude the things we can't change. This gift makes a difference in the lives of your friends and family.

The gift of prayer—The hidden gift. Let your friends and loved ones know you pray for them—and then do it!

I celebrate all of you who are making a difference in this world by truly giving of yourselves. Sometimes we give out of necessity, social custom, or habit. But at other times our giving is out of pure generosity and love, and the feeling that comes from this kind of giving fills the heart and soul with the utmost joy.

In Genesis 12:3, God tells Abram, "And I will bless you and make your name great; and so you shall be a blessing; And I will bless those who bless you." So, as we use the gifts God has given us to bless others, gifts will come back to us manifold.

I wish for you, my readers, the gifts of strength, health, a giving spirit, and all the love your heart can hold.

With love and blessings,

Remember that when you leave this earth, you can take with you nothing that you have received—only what you have given: a full heart enriched by honest service, love, sacrifice and courage.

St. Francis of Assisi

Bibliography

Autry, James A. *Love and Profit.* New York, NY: William Morrow & Co., 1991.

Blanchard, Ken and Barrett, Colleen. *Lead with LUV.* Upper Saddle River, NJ: FT Press, 2011.

Brucker, Virginia. *Gifts from the Heart: Simple Ways to Make Your Family's Christmas More Meaningful.* Toronto, Canada: Insomniac Press, 2006.

Coey, Nancy. *Finding Gifts in Everyday Life.* Raleigh, NC: Sweetwater Press, 1995.

Frankl, Victor, *Man's Search for Meaning.* New York, NY: Washington Square, 1963.

Glanz, Barbara, *The Simple Truths of Appreciation—How Each of Us Can Choose to Make a Difference,* Naperville, IL: Simple Truths, 2007.

Glanz, Barbara, *CARE Packages for the Workplace—Dozens of Little Things You Can Do to Regenerate Spirit at Work,* New York, NY: McGraw-Hill, 2006.

Glanz, Barbara, *CARE Packages for the Home—Dozens of Little Things You Can Do to Regenerate Spirit Where You Live,* New York, NY: 2010.

Glanz, Barbara, *CARE Packages for your Customers—An Idea a Week for Customer Service,* New York, NY: McGraw-Hill, 2007.

Glanz, Barbara, *Handle with CARE—Motivating & Retaining Employees,* New York, NY: McGraw-Hill, 2002.

Glanz, Barbara, *What Can I Do? Ideas to Help Those Who Have Experienced Loss,* Minneapolis, MN: Augsburg Books, 2007.

Gostick, Adrian, and Elton, Chester. *The Carrot Principle.* New York, NY: Free Press, 2009.

Halberstam, Yitta and Leventhal, Judith. *Small Miracles—Extraordinary Coincidences from Everyday Life.* Holbrook, MA: Adams Media Corporation, 1997.

Halberstam, Yitta and Leventhal, Judith. *Small Miracles II—Heartwarming Gifts of Extraordinary Coincidences.* Holbrook, MA: Adams Media Corporation, 1998.

Hsieh, Tony. *Delivering Happiness,* New York NY: Business Plus, 2010.

Jamal, Azim and Harvey McKinnon. *How Giving Back Enriches Us All,* New York: Penguin Group, 2008.

Kouzes, James M. and Posner, Barry Z. *Encouraging the Heart,* San Francisco, CA: Jossey-Bass, 2003.

Lawson, Douglas M. *Give to Live—How Giving Can Change Your Life.* La Jolla, California: ALTI Publishing, 1991.

Murray, Milton. *Words of Wisdom for Writers, Speaker, & Leaders.* Silver Spring, MD: Philanthropic Service for Institutions, 1993.

Nowak, Kate. *May You Be Blessed.* Naperville, IL: Simple Truths, 2007.

Ornish, Dean. *A Program for Reversing Heart Disease.* New York: Random House, 1990.

"The Healing Power of Love," *Prevention Magazine,* February 1991, pp.60f.

Rath, Tom and Clifton, Ph.D., Donald O. *How FULL Is your Bucket?* New York, NY: Free Press, 2004.

Roger, John and McWilliams, Peter. *We Give to Live.* Prelude Press, Inc., 1993.

Rogers, Carl. *On Becoming a Person.* Boston: Houghton-Mifflin Company, 1961

Ryan, M.J. *Giving Thanks: The Gifts of Gratitude.* San Francisco, CA: Conari Press, 20007.

Sanders, Tim. *Today We Are Rich,* Carol Stream, IL: Tyndale House Publishers, 2011.

Schuller, Robert. *The Be-Happy Attitudes.* Waco, TX: Word Books, 1985.

Selye, Hans. *The Stress of Life.* New York: McGraw-Hill, 1976.

Stress Without Distress. Philadelphia; Lippincott, 1974.

Siegel, Bernie S. *Love, Medicine and Miracles.* New York: Harper & Row, 1986

Walker, Cami. *29 Gifts: How a Month of Giving Can Change Your Life.* Philadelphia: First Da Capo Press, 2009.

Youngs, Bettie B. Ph.D., Ed. D. *Gifts of the Heart: Stories that Celebrate Life's Defining Moments.* Deerfield Beach: Health Communications, Inc., 1996.

Some very special children's books about Giving:

Bartone/Lewin. *Peppe The Lamplighter.* New York: Lothrop, 1993.

Brumbeau/de Marcken. *The Quilt Maker's Gift.* Duluth, Minnesota: Pfeifer-Hamilton, 2000.

Fleming/Cooper. *Be Good to Eddie Lee.* New York: Philomel, 1993.

McCloud, Carol. *Have You Filled a bucket Today? A Guide to Daily Happiness for Kids.* New York: Nelson Publishing & Marketing, 2006.

Pfister. *The Rainbow Fish.* New York: North-South Books, 1992.

Rylant/Catalanotto. *An Angel for Solomon Singer.* New York: Orchard Books, 1992.

Sabin, Ellen. *The Giving Book: Open the Door to a Lifetime of Giving.* Water Can Press, 2004.

Spinelli/Yalowitz. *Somebody Loves You, Mr. Hatch.* New York: Bradbury Press, 1991

Author Biography

Internationally known speaker, consultant, author, and a **member of the prestigious Speaker Hall of Fame**, Barbara A. Glanz, CSP, CPAE, works with organizations that want to improve morale, retention, and service and with people who want to rediscover the joy in their work and in their lives. Barbara was voted "best keynote presenter you have heard or used" by Meetings & Conventions Magazine, July 2010, and that same year she was selected as a "Legend of the Speaking Profession" by the Veteran Speakers. Her signature story of "Johnny the Bagger®" has been viewed by millions of people worldwide.

She is the author of twelve best-selling books:

* *The Simple Truths of Service Inspired by Johnny the Bagger (Co-authored with Ken Blanchard)*

* *The Simple Truths of Appreciation—How Each of Us Can Choose to Make a Difference*

* *180 Ways to Spread Contagious Enthusiasm™*

* *What Can I Do? Ideas to Help Those Who Have Experienced Loss*

* *CARE Packages for the Workplace—Dozens of Little Things You Can Do to Regenerate Spirit at Work*

* *Handle with CARE—Motivating and Retaining Employees*

* *CARE Packages for Your Customers—An Idea a Week for Customer Service*

* *CARE Packages for the Home—Dozens of Ways to Regenerate Spirit Where You Live*

* *Balancing Acts—More Than 250 Guiltfree, Creative Ideas to Blend your Work and your Life*

* *Building Customer Loyalty—How YOU Can Help Keep Customers Returning*

* *The Creative Communicator—399 Tools to Communicate Commitment Without Boring People to Death!*

Using her Master's degree in Adult Education, Barbara lives and breathes her personal motto: "Spreading Contagious Enthusiasm™." She is the first speaker on record to have presented on **all seven continents and in all 50 states**. Barbara lives on the beach in Sarasota, Florida, and adores her four grandchildren, Gavin, Kinsey, Owen and Simon.

For more information, she can be reached directly at 941-312-9169; www.barbaraglanz.com; bglanz@barbaraglanz.com. She is available for keynote speeches and workshops worldwide.

Send Us Your Stories of Priceless Gifts

We would love to include YOUR stories in a second edition of this book. Your stories may be stories either of what you have given or what you have received. Do not worry about your writing skill as we can edit the stories for you. We just want to share more creative ideas and goodness with the world.

Please email or send them to:

stories@barbaraglanz.com

OR

Barbara A. Glanz
Giving Stories
Barbara Glanz Communications, Inc
6140 Midnight Pass Road #802
Sarasota, FL 34242

CPSIA information can be obtained at www.ICGtesting.com
Printed in the USA
LVOW13s0850181113

361703LV00005B/5/P